The Once and Future Film

Future Film

British Cinema
in the Seventies and Eighties

JOHN WALKER

The Once and Future Film

British Cinema in the Seventies and Eighties

Methuen.London

First published in Great Britain in 1985
in simultaneous hardback and paperback editions
by Methuen London Ltd,
11 New Fetter Lane, London EC4 4EE

Copyright © 1985 by John Walker

Typeset by Wyvern Typesetting Limited, Bristol
Printed and bound in Great Britain

British Library Cataloguing in Publication Data
Walker, John
    The once and future film : British cinema in
    the seventies and eighties.
    1. Moving-pictures——Great Britain——History
    I. Title
    791.43'0941   PN1993.5.G7

ISBN 0-413-53540-1
ISBN 0-413-53550-9 Pbk

For
BARBARA
and the new generation of cineastes
JESSICA and BARNABY

Contents

viii   *Contents*

Introduction

A search for British cinema

Here during a quarter of a century many films were made projecting Britain and the British character.

Plaque outside Ealing Studios

The wind stirred the greasy chip papers, rustled the crumpled crisp packets on the dusty steps and rattled at the building's dingy doors, the glass encrusted with dirt. I pushed one open and went through to a dingier interior. The red carpet was stained and worn. In one corner a video game machine whizzed and banged, flashing with manic colours. A stale smell of frying hung in the air, the only evidence, apart from a boy feeding coins into the machine, that life continued.

It took an effort to remember that I had come to this place, a backwater forgotten by most people, in search of entertainment. After a wait, someone finally came and silently sold me a ticket; someone else grimly tore it in half and even spoke – 'Non-smoking on the left!' – as I was left to stumble my way across an even dirtier and older carpet and settle in a dusty seat.

I had arrived at the cinema five minutes before the programme began. Six minutes later, four elderly figures shuffled in and sat as far away from each other as possible. After another five minutes, a gauze curtain twitched, the lights dimmed and there followed a quarter of an hour of advertisements, some with certificates from the Board of Censors as if they were real films, and trailers. Then the lights went up with an announcement on screen that ices, drinks and refreshments were available in the foyer.

When the film began, there was a hair caught in the gate of the projector; its shadow quivered over the action. I went to complain, but I could find no one. The sound was closer in quality to an old wind-up gramophone with a worn needle than modern hi-fi. After an hour, the sound went. The audience had dwindled to three, resignedly twiddling their hearing aids.

I had made a journey of four miles to the cinema. I live in Clapham, an area not far from central London. There are no cinemas in

Clapham, although there used to be several. Seventeen years ago, when London was swinging and British cinema was undergoing a renaissance, I had even attended a world premiere in Clapham, of *Up The Junction*, directed by Peter Collinson from Nell Dunn's best-selling book of genteel slumming in South London. It had been, I remembered, a dreadful movie. Shortly after, British cinema underwent a collapse, though presumably the two events were not directly connected. All there is, up the junction now, is bingo halls and even some of them have closed in the last year.

It was hardly surprising, I reflected, that fewer and fewer people were going to cinemas, even if they could still find them. The buildings seem redundant, relics of another age, as condemned to oblivion as bowling alleys. I love watching films. So do my children. So do my friends. I even enjoy watching them in cinemas, although I see far more at home, on television or video recorder. I have to travel to the cinema, but I can stroll down the road for a ten minute walk and be in reach of half-a-dozen video hire shops, some of them open until 10.00 pm seven nights a week, should I have a sudden craving for a movie. Some will even deliver the film to my door. On a weekday, I can hire a film for 50p, a quarter of the price of one cinema seat.

It is only in Britain, of all the countries in the West, where cinema audiences are still dwindling in numbers. Everywhere else, the decline that began with the coming of television has been reversed. In America, films flourish. Steven Spielberg's *ET* grossed more at the US box office in four months than all the films showing in all the cinemas in Britain took in 1983.

Could it be that British cinemas *and* British movies have deserved each other and their incredible shrinking audiences?

I've always thought of films in terms of an aesthetic experience, a view compounded by the many critics I read in weekly and daily newspapers or magazines. It is an outsider's attitude. The cinema is a business like any other, full of people who would rather make money than films. From inside the industry, critics are an unreliable part of the merchandising process. To read a special issue of the show-business newspaper *Variety* or the British weekly *Screen International*, where film makers are trying to sell their products to each other, is to realise that it resembles a fairground full of hucksters making extravagant promises.

Dogging the heels of every successful film are a dozen cheap copies, trying to cash in on its appeal. In recent years, the wares being touted are a combination in varying degrees of sex, violence and fantasy. At the moment the cycle of mad killers knifing nubile young girls (which had its beginnings in *Psycho*) continues, together with prurient comedies about adolescent sexual voyeurism – *Porky's* was the hit responsible – and rip-offs of *Star Wars* and *Conan The Barbarian*. Most of these films never make the circuits, earning money in obscure cinemas and from sales to video publishers and cable television stations.

But amid all the advertisements in a recent *Screen International* featuring psychotic knifemen, machine-gun blasting mercenaries, naked girls and smirking teenagers was a series of understated advertisements for films from the British production company Goldcrest, who backed *Gandhi, Chariots of Fire* and *Local Hero*. It was a reminder that art does flourish in films and that recent British successes have not pandered to sensational tastes, but have included some films of enduring worth and others, even if more ephemeral, of value.

The British cinema has always been in a state of crisis. Occasionally, though, it has been a centre of excellence, the place where the best, the most exciting work is being done. Or, at least, where the films touched a social nerve, reflected the society in which we lived, even if obliquely, as in the great days of Ealing comedies. The last time that happened was in the early 1960s. It seems now, more than 20 years later and against all the odds, to be happening again.

I set out to try to discover why, and, by talking to a representative sample of those involved, to find out how things went awry and whether there is a chance that the British could emulate the rest of the West and sustain an indigenous industry.

I talked to individuals rather than institutions, the many special interest and pressure groups and trade associations that exist. The responses of such groups are predictable, knee-jerk reactions that have been set forth in many (mainly unread and certainly unacted upon) reports.

As well as being the year made famous so long in advance by George Orwell's minatory prophecies (of two-way television, among other horrors of Big Brother), and despite the British Film Institute, with typical perversity, calling it The Year of Television, 1984 was to have been designated the Year of British Cinema; on second thoughts the Year was changed to 1985.

Appeals on its behalf are planned during this Year – probably along the lines of Save A Whale – to preserve this endangered species.

But what, these days, exactly is British cinema. Does it still really exist? And, if it does, is it worth celebrating? I went in search of it, although to understand the present it is also necessary to examine the past, particularly the recent past when the British film industry was plunged into a crisis. What follows is an outsider's view of a complex and ever-changing business over the last decade or so.

I hoped to find reassurance that a new generation could discover, and an older one recapture, the excitements and pleasures of a night out at the movies, seeing films that, as the memorial to Ealing Studios put it, projected a nation and a national character.

John Walker
November 1984

I Winners and Losers

Michael Winner at home

'There's nothing I can do to save the British film industry and there's nothing I intend to do.'

Michael Winner

The year of 1982 was a marvellous one for British cinema. In Los Angeles on 29 March, a somewhat surprised David Puttnam and Hugh Hudson, producer and director of *Chariots of Fire*, received the Oscar for the best picture of the year. Colin Welland, accepting his Oscar for scripting the film, bellowed, 'The British are coming!' (in what he now says was a private joke) to an audience containing many ambitious young English directors and some older actors and actresses who had already gone west in search of big bucks.

But 1982 was also the year that admissions at British cinemas reached their lowest-ever level, below 60 million. In the peak year of 1945, when cinema was almost the only entertainment, admissions numbered 1,585 million. Even in the last decade, people have declined to go to the cinema in ever greater numbers. In 1970, the number of attendances was 193 million. Five years later, it had shrunk to 116 million. If the slide continues, there'll be hardly a cinema left by the end of the 1980s.

In 1983, there was a very slight upturn. It was again a good year for British film making. Once more, a British director went bounding up the steps at Hollywood's Oscar ceremonies to accept the award for best picture. On that occasion, Sir Richard Attenborough had been the favourite to win with his stirring *Gandhi*. He had spent 20 years trying to raise the finance for it, but had been turned down by British and American producers because they were convinced it was uncommercial. And there was little surprise when Ben Kingsley won an Oscar for his brilliant performance in the title role, which other actors – Alec Guinness, Albert Finney, Tom Courtenay – had considered in earlier times. The British had not gone away.

Gandhi was one of the movies that brought British audiences back to the cinemas. Others were the succession of expensively made, heavily promoted films – 'blockbusters' to the trade – which included *Octopussy*, the latest James Bond, and the third Star Wars film, *The Return of the Jedi*.

At the same time, though, cinemas continued to close. In the peak year of 1945, there had been 4,703 cinemas in Britain. By 1960 there were 3,034. In 1970, there were 1,529. By 1980 there were 1,652 screens, which seems an increase. But the figure is distorted by having two or three small cinemas in one building. In 1980, the seating capacity was 688,000 whereas in 1970 it had been more than double that number, 1,466,000.

Sadly symbolic was the closure of the Biograph, near Victoria Station in London. The Biograph, originally called the Bioscope, was one of London's oldest and once the finest cinema in Westminster. It was the first to be registered under the Cinematograph Act in 1910. Since that time it had gone through many changes, all of them for the worse, including a period when it was a favourite haunt of cruising homosexuals. An office block will replace it.

The habit of changing large cinemas into two or three smaller auditoriums, a process that had begun in the 1970s, has stopped. It would, exhibitors said at the time, give people a wider choice of films. Art movies and foreign-language masterpieces would reach wider audiences. But in the summer of 1983, every triple cinema seemed to be showing the same three films: *The Return of the Jedi, Octopussy* and *Flashdance*, a romantic teenage fantasy of a young girl who turns from welding to ballet dancing and falls in love with a rich man, filmed in the appropriate style of a commercial for underarm deodorant.

Pundits decided that the growth of video had made small cinemas unacceptable to the public, who wanted an experience they could not have in their homes: wide screen excitement and stereo sound. They considered reconverting triple cinemas back to one large auditorium.

There was a palpable air of excitement about British movies that had not been present since the beginnings of what came to be known as the New Wave in the early 1960s. Then talented new directors emerged: Karel Reisz, John Schlesinger, Tony Richardson, Lindsay Anderson. And a succession of films – *Saturday Night and Sunday Morning, A Kind of Loving, Look Back In Anger, Tom Jones* – that brought a new spirit, iconoclastic and exuberant, into movie-making. The New Wave soon ebbed, though, and the film industry resumed its constant state of crisis and subservience to Hollywood.

But, for a moment, there had been a mood of optimism, matched by a period of high creative endeavour. But not even in the 1960s had British movies won Oscars for the Best Picture two years in succession. Two successes don't make an industry, of course. The winners in 1984 were all-American, although Lewis Gilbert's *Educating Rita* in which Julie Walters established herself as a star, and Peter Yates' *The Dresser*, with splendid performances from Albert Finney and Tom Courtenay, were strong contenders for awards. At another time they might have been among the winners, but the Americans, anxious for the health of their own cinema, could hardly be expected to vote British again. So was there hope for the future, a justifiable feeling that British cinema is at least alive again, if not entirely well?

The problem facing the local industry is an old one. It was put into words 40 years ago:

'Everyone is agreed that we need a truly national film industry, and need equally a share in the world's screen time. The methods of achieving this, however, are a source of conflict. The danger of domination by United States interests is clear enough. But on the other hand you have big interests associated especially with the names of Rank and Korda, who claim that we must make films costing from a quarter to half a million and break into world markets on production values comparable to those of Hollywood.

'On the other hand there are the smaller independent groups at Ealing and Elstree, who would limit expenditure from fifty to a hundred thousand, in the expectation of gearing their economies to home cinemas, breaking into world market on merit, as specifically British products but not depending – at any rate for some time – for receipts from overseas.'

Delete Ealing and Elstree, both dead as independent forces, substitute EMI and Lord Grade for Korda and multiply the figures by 20, and the divergent attitudes remain today.

But the argument continues with a difference. The audience for cinema has declined far faster in Britain than elsewhere in the world. Even as late as the 1970s it was still possible, provided a producer trimmed his budget to the absolute essentials and spent his money on what appeared on the screen, for a British film to cover its costs in Britain.

That can no longer be done. 'You take other countries in the world and attendances are going up, revenues are going up,' said Denis O'Brien of HandMade Films, currently one of the most successful independent production companies. 'In Britain, it's dramatically down. We should be getting a minimum of 10 per cent back on a film here. But we're not. It's close to there being no market at all.'

I sought the opinions of Michael Winner, who has been Britain's busiest independent producer and director for the last decade or more. His career has spanned good times and bad and he has survived and prospered.

Had the British film industry a future? I asked him. 'It's more likely to be dead than alive,' he said.

Winner has many opinions – as listeners to BBC radio's *Any Questions?* will know. But his views on films are backed by knowledge gained the hard way. He understands the strategies needed to survive. There are few British producer-directors with his breadth of experience, and none who have worked so hard or so consistently during the last 20 years. He has never been a favourite of critics, possibly because of his habit of reminding them of his own time as a journalist – 'I've been closely associated with the British film industry since the age of 10, when I used to write about it on the school noticeboard. At 13, I had a column in 60 papers,' he said.

Criticism, he seems to suggest, is, like masturbation, a childish activity. But whatever the critical reaction to them, his films have usually found a large enough audience. His *Death Wish* in 1974 not only made Charles Bronson into a star in America as well as Europe but began a still continuing cycle of films about solving urban violence by violence. Winner has worked in England and Hollywood for British and American companies.

He began his directing career during the heady days of the early 1960s. Since his first feature film *Play It Cool* in 1962 he has made 20 movies, ranging from his early British comedies, such as *The Jokers* (1966) to two of the best of latter-day westerns (*Lawman* (1971) and *Chato's Land* (1972)), horror (*The Sentinel* (1977)), gangster (*The Big Sleep* (1978)) and costume melodrama with *The Wicked Lady* (1983), a remake of a British success of the 1940s.

Winner lives in an opulent Victorian mansion stuffed with art and antiques of the period. In one corner of his hall was propped the whip from *The Wicked Lady,* used in a scene of a fight between two women that caused a public row with the British film censor, which he won. He also gained invaluable publicity for the film.

No doubt Winner was well aware of *Idol of Paris,* a film made in 1948 by Leslie Arliss, who directed the first version of *The Wicked Lady.* Arliss's film gained great notoriety at the time because its two leading ladies also fought a duel with whips.

Winner has battled with the censor before, and usually won. He fought against cuts being made in *Chato's Land* and *Scorpio* (1972). It's these triumphs that have led him to be appointed chief censorship officer of the recently formed pressure group, the Society of Independent Producers.

'When I first started cinema was the only popular art form,' he said. 'In recent years, there has at least been an increase in markets for films through video and – in America – cable. Very important new markets that have brought in quite substantial sums of money. But the theatrical side has diminished and continues to diminish in this country.

'The tragedy of the British film industry is that people equate our periods of great film making with periods of success. Of course, they are a success because they are great films. But invariably, they've gone hand in hand with bankruptcy for the people who made them.

'Korda went into liquidation. Ealing Films under Michael Balcon – probably our greatest single period of film – went into liquidation.

The studios are now used by BBC television. Rank in the 1940s and early 50s lost £7 million making quite good films and nearly went down. Had they not been part of a conglomerate they would have gone down.

'Then you have Michael Balcon again at Bryanston in the 1960s, providing the next most memorable period in British films. I did the last film for Bryanston. I was there when they couldn't pay the bills. The British public have unfailingly refused to support British product enough to make the home market pay for that product.

'And although quality English product has always had a cachet abroad, and has always played to the intelligentsia in what I would call stage-show situations – one theatre in New York, one theatre in San Francisco – it has never captured either a local audience or an international audience, sufficient even to break even, never mind to show profit.

'And the occasional sighting of *Gandhi* or *Chariots of Fire*, of profitable pictures, doesn't mean that there is a herd of like animals running behind them or around them. There is not.'

Was he suggesting that the audience was to blame?

'I would never blame an audience for not turning up. An audience is looking for light relief, and if they don't consider the Ealing comedies as light relief (because they were too sophisticated for them), it's just a fact of life. In a way I blame the film makers. And primarily, the producers.

'What this country has always lacked is great management. The Americans have managed their major film companies so that they are cushioned against the failure of the films, because they have diversified – into television, etc. But they sit on a 200 million home audience. Here, it's a 60 million home audience. It's a hell of a difference.

'It's easier to get finance from America. You've only to look at the number of films financed each year compared with here – probably a hundred to one.

'What happened in the 60s was quite unique. Instead of having one successful film, like *Gandhi*, we had three successes, all of which the Americans believed were repeatable: *Tom Jones*, The Beatles and *James Bond*. The Americans said, My God, there is money to be made in English films. And they literally put executives on aeroplanes, opened up an office in London and financed a lot of films. By the end of the 60s they had lost a great deal of money doing that. They shuttered the offices and brought the executives back in disgrace.

'That was the last time the Americans full bloodedly believed that we were capable of making a programme of internationally successful pictures. It's never been believed since, and it has never happened since. And never happened then. Because it was an illusion.

'The Americans failed, as we had done. There is no solution. There are many factors that make it bad – our management has failed to produce a series of on-going films, and something in the British nature has compounded this.

'In the early 60s, *Tom Jones* and *James Bond* produced international stars in Albert Finney and Sean Connery. Films are often made because people want to use an actor. The actor often banks the film more than the script or the producer or the director. In fact, usually does. What happened to those actors? Albert Finney went into shock and stopped making films. Sean Connery did not make many films.

'In a strange way, all of us failed to get in there and exploit the moment when we were hot. The Americans don't do that. When an American becomes a star he tends to jolly well work. The English get nervous and don't work, because they are afraid. Finney admits this today.

'I would say historically that, forgetting the times when cinema was a big industry here because it was the only mass entertainment – and, you know, a half-trained gorilla could have succeeded – forgetting that period, there is no evidence that England has ever managed to uphold a flash of light and turn it into an ongoing lit situation.

'And there's no evidence, because we had *Chariots of Fire* last year and *Gandhi* this. You can't make *Son of Gandhi* and *Daughter of Chariots of Fire*. Unrepeatable films, you see. The interesting thing is that America and Hollywood have always run on repeatable films. They make one gangster film with James Cagney, they make ten more. They make one comedy with Richard Pryor, they make ten more; one Neil Simon comedy, they make ten more. That sort of operation gives you an industry. *Chariots of Fire* and *Gandhi* give you an exposition of talent but not an industry.'

Winner's own transformation from a director of English social comedies, deriving from the Ealing tradition, to a maker of action films was accidental. It happened because an agent introduced him to Gerald Wilson, a Canadian-born writer who was trying to break into movies.

'He had never written a film and he said to me, I want to write a western. He seemed to be enthusiastic, so I took a chance as I often did, and gave this fellow some money.

'I said, I've bought it. Go and write it. So he wrote this western, which was *Lawman*. Now I received this western about 1968–9 when the English situation was dying. This was more luck than judgement. If he'd have said he wanted to write something else, I'd have probably said yes.

'So I took the western to the company I was with at the time – United Artists – and they liked it very much and I was employed to make a western. I've never been further west than Fulham and now suddenly I was in Mexico with a part-American, part-British crew but an entirely American picture. Burt Lancaster, Robert Ryan, Lee J. Cobb. So as a result of that, the same writer wrote another western and a number of American pictures and it was a kind of short hop from people shooting each other in the nineteenth century to my doing pictures where people shot each other in the twentieth century.

'So I had slipped into a totally new type of film for me, namely the action film, and I had also slipped into America at a time when the English industry was collapsing. Probably the worst time for the English industry was 1970 to 73 – it's got worse since, but that was a very bad time. And as it happened I was doing terribly well in those years.

'There is no question that the entire American operation is more professional than here. No question! From the bottom to the top. They are harder working. You don't have, as I've had, carpenters walking out because they want more money. They don't talk about the catering every two minutes. They are much harder working.

'Now we have wonderful people. But we do have a tendency to cut our nose to spite our face. This is not the unions; this is the individual members saying, we don't want to do overtime, we don't want to eat that lunch, we want a better lunch. As a pro-British person, this saddens me. But it's not enough to prevent anyone making a film here.

'If people were making money out of making films here, they'd all want to make films here. But you have to have a type of film that can be repeated. A *genre*. *Gandhi* is not a genre film. *The Wicked Lady* is a genre film. If *The Wicked Lady* is a big hit, you will then have a number of British costume melodramas, or comedy melodramas.

'I did two films with Lew Grade. Lew Grade raised a lot of finance for British films. People put him down all the time. But Lew Grade only did what everybody else did before him, which was to lose money on British films. People may not have liked the films he made. But he went out and slogged away and got money for hundreds and thousands of British actors, directors, technicians to work. I think the man should be applauded for that. Naturally, I wish he'd made a great hit of it.

'You know, the British love to pull down their own people who do anything, love to be jealous. They really turn on people who create employment. Since 1956 there has not been a single day when a British actor, writer or technician was not at work paid for by me. Not one day since 1956. Now, in any other country that would be applauded. But the English love to knock success. They love to knock effort. When I see a lot of people leave this country, I don't blame them. I happen to love the country in spite of that. It's considered vulgar to do too well here, or to work too hard.'

Did he try to finance his films in Britain?

'Where can you go in England if you want finance for a film? Rank does not finance films any more. EMI finance films a little bit, Goldcrest finance films a very little bit. That's it! I can't think of anyone else. The number of films those two companies finance is very insubstantial compared to the American majors. It's quite possible one would call in on those people, concurrent with calling in on the majors.

'Very occasionally people – often I think the wrong sort of people – manage to raise money in the City. Goldcrest raise money in the City, so I congratulate them for that. The trouble with the City is that they very seldom come up with the money. People always say, the Arabs will put money in. The City will put money in. Richard Attenborough tried 20 years or so to get money off the City.

'I've occasionally met people in the City. But it's a big bore. There have been a few occasions where the City put money in – Dimitri de Grunwald got money from the City for a few films, but they didn't do well. People who tend to get money from the City are out-of-work people who've got time to wine and dine the City, go to their houses and pursue them. I don't have time to do all that. And I don't want to do that. I'm not a social entertainer. I'm not a Butlin's Redcoat for the City. I'm a film maker.

'They say to me in the City, films are a bad risk. I always say, how many film companies have gone broke in the last few years? Very few. I can tell you a lot of property companies went broke. *The Nightcomers* was financed by one of the biggest property companies in England. The property division went broke and *The Nightcomers* made a profit.

'People say, there is no British industry. There *is* a British industry. There always has been. And I think there always will be. It depends upon your definition of the word industry. I would say, if five films are made a year, that's certainly an industry. In the last year or so, Channel 4 has made a lot of films.

'I'm not sure whether they are films or not. They play in art houses for half an hour, some of them, and then go on television. But I guess they're something to do with it. They've been a great employer of British technicians and actors. They've had no popular success, nor are they going to. Or they are very unlikely to.

'It is said in Hollywood, by the very top management, that if any one year we made all the films we rejected and rejected all the films we made, the result would be much the same. It'll be most interesting to see what happens to Goldcrest after their one hit. Maybe they will, uniquely, in the history of British cinema, maintain a programme of films and make money. Maybe. I hope they do. There is no factual evidence to suggest they will.

'America has a home market that represents in film terms 50 per cent of the world gross of a film. We represent four per cent of the world gross of a film. The world is interested in America because

America is the driving force in the west. They are more interested in America than in what goes on in London. If we'd had a film industry in Victorian times, the world would have been more interested in England.

'The European countries have done what we have not done. The Italians have succeeded with their spaghetti westerns and action films and comedy films – the Terence Hill, Bud Spencer type. The Italians have succeeded in getting films together which, while they don't play successfully in America, and they don't play successfully in England, they play Germany, France, Japan, the Far East, South America. They've made a little niche for a group of their films and it's big enough to show profit.

'The French have done the same. The English films have never even found a market sufficient to cover their costs, on an on-going basis, outside America. English films are considered worthy, but dull by the general world audience, with rare exceptions. But, you know, cinema is a young person's medium. It is a lively, thrusting medium. The audience gets younger and younger. The British are not known for virility. Energy is not a national attribute.'

Did he aim his films at a young audience?

'You don't aim films anywhere. You develop such material as interests you from what you can find. You obviously don't develop material which has no chance of being made. And you're conscious of what is likely to be accepted. It takes a long time to develop a script and work on it. And then you hope that there will be an audience for it.

'But you can only direct it and produce it through your own eyes. You can't say, what will the audience think? What audience? A French farmer? A black factory worker in Detroit? A Chinaman? An Australian businessman in Sydney? What is the audience? I can't think for all those people. I can't think for any of them, because I don't know what they like.

'When I made *Death Wish*, which was turned down for six years by everybody, I just thought it would appeal everywhere. I couldn't actually say why, it's just what I thought. And I was proven right. Equally, I've made films where I was proven wrong.

'I'm really very unlikely casting for the sort of films that I've become famous for. I'm a very meek and mild person. As you can see, I live in this Victorian house, surrounded by the most conservative antiques and art. There I was making *The Jokers* and I have become, through fate, the director of street mugging and violence. But that's where life took me. I've tried to fight against it. I waited some time after *Death Wish* and deliberately did a comedy: *Won Ton Ton, The Dog Who Saved Hollywood*. Unfortunately, it was not a success. Because it was not a success, people did not then say he's a comedy director.

When I made *Lawman,* people said how can Winner make a western, he's a comedy director? Then they said, he's not a comedy director, he's an action director.

'So that film did not help me get back into another field. *The Wicked Lady* is not a hard, violent picture. If that's a success, it may lead to other areas. But people employ you because they want to see a profit on your labour. And if they see your labour in a particular field has spun off profit in the past, that is the field they are most likely to seek you out for. I don't blame them. That's a very human situation. So you can only fight against it so much unless you wish to stay out of work for ever.'

Had he ever wished to become a producer on a larger scale? 'I'm not interested in running a big operation. I'm not interested in producing a lot of films with other people directing them. I enjoy directing. Directing is what I always set out to do. From time to time, if I like somebody very much, I have occasionally dickered with producing a film for him. I was going to produce a film for Lindsay Anderson.

'But the script we did together did not come off. I consider myself a film director for hire. Like all film directors who've got any brains, we don't wait to be hired we also seek out and develop our own material and often produce it ourselves. I've produced virtually every film I've made, whether or not I get the credit. With *The Wicked Lady*, I found the subject, bought the subject, got the star and signed every cheque on the picture and every contract on the picture. I did produce the picture. But the chaps who financed it wanted the credit and good luck to them – I don't mind. I don't have to prove anything in that area.

'The thing about the film industry is that if there were a more entertaining way to make a living we would go to it. But there isn't one. So we have to stay here. The problem with being a film director is that you're fired after each job. So every six months or so you are fired, you are out of work. And then you have to find some more work. And that's not the easiest way to earn a living. I'd have liked to have worked in the old days, when a director was under contract to a studio for five years and you just went and did it. Rather pleasant.'

But a studio director had no choice about the films he made. Would he have liked that? 'You don't have much choice today. Because there are so few films made, they all want to play safe. So if I want to make a wonderful comedy, they say, Mr Winner, you haven't done very well with comedy. But here is a film where six people get shot in the street And slashed! You can make this. So you don't have that much choice anyway.'

Did he think his reputation as a maker of violent films was justified?

'*The Wicked Lady* was a film where you could have had a high level of sadism, but it didn't call for that. It was an adventure, a comedy-melodrama. And it didn't call for that excessive violence. If you make a film about street mugging, it must call for violence – that's what it's about. Violent people. It's about the most violent people in society. I'm dictated to totally by the nature of the screenplay. You don't say, let's have a nice rape, it will sell tickets. If that were true, you'd say, why don't we have ten rapes and we'll sell ten times as many tickets. But that doesn't follow.

'The level of violence in films goes up because the public will not accept any more cutting away to the curtains blowing or the trees waving in the wind. Because they see on their televisions or their newsreels the truth, they want to see more of the truth. Young people have always liked excess. The audience gets younger. Young people are brought up on horror comics, which are some of the most violent things ever, fairy stories, which are incredibly violent: people are being murdered, Humpty Dumpty is breaking into a million pieces. *The Wicked Lady* is doing very well. But *Death Wish 2* did better.'

And will there be a *Death Wish 3?* 'Probably. I have a very unusual story line for it. I wouldn't mind doing *Death Wish 10*. After all, how many films go to three? Not many.'

Despite Winner's fights over censorship, he has yet to protest when television companies slash chunks out of his films for their screenings.

'I know they cut *Death Wish*,' he said. 'But we signed a contract that gives them the right to cut it. I'm a great believer in keeping your word.'

But did he mind? 'I don't like a film being cut for television, particularly in America, where they cut it to ribbons. Sometimes it's not understandable. But if you sign a contract going in, that permits the film to be cut, then you've got no right to complain. I ask them to put in a line, "Edited for Television", which they very rarely do. We know things are permitted in cinema, with certificated films in places people go to selectively. One doesn't want to lose that by having the same thing shown on television. There are different community standards for television. We usually make a television version of our films – I made one of *Death Wish 2* and *The Wicked Lady* – but they are often further cut.

'The TV version is not just cut by me, it's restructured. So, for example, in *Death Wish 2* we have put back five or six little scenes which were cut out of the cinema version. It is another Michael Winner version of the film. Not the one Michael Winner wanted to make, but the one at least he made because he knew he had to.

'Television sales, world wide, are very, very important. And cable in America these days will pay $5 million or $6 million a picture. Video can pay a lot today. World-wide you can get at least $5 million for the video rights to a good film. It's a lot of money. And that's up-front. But it depends upon the success of a film, you see. There are times when the cable and video money up-front is the hinge as to whether the film is made or not. But you still need some backing to finish off the pot, no question.'

Was he in favour of official subsidy to help the film industry?

'It's rather ironic in England that films do not come under the Minister for Arts. They come under the Ministry of Trade. British films are always asking for subsidies. Personally, I'm split on that. I'm hesitant, as a human being, to say that films should have more government money, taxpayers' money, when people are homeless, without medical treatment and other things. I find that a difficult thing.

'Then I say to myself, well, film is part of the fibre of the nation – let us have something. Where I am absolutely at odds with everybody else in the industry is that I do not think it should be given to the National Film Finance Corporation, which has always been a disaster. The NFFC is the biggest single disaster in the British film industry. It has been mismanaged throughout its term of life and what could have been a glowing leadership situation has been a mess. They've lost every penny and pretty quickly, too. And they ain't done too much for the industry in losing it.

'The Government is now talking about abolishing the Eady Levy which I think is right. Why should cinemas, which are doing badly, have to pay a levy to British films? They are talking about replacing it with a levy on films for television, which I think is correct. The duopoly of television has kept prices falsely low for years. They're talking about a levy on video-tape, which I think is reasonable. And they're talking about the government physically adding money to those two levies.

'I think that is right, but I think the money should be given out in the way that Eady money is given out: so much percentage of the UK box office is added to by this fund. Then the people who have a commercial interest in making films people want to see will have an added reward if it's British film. I think that, as I believe they do in France, they shouldn't give the company any Eady money – their share of the pot – until they make their next British film. They should put it in an interest-bearing account and hand it to them when they make their next British film. So it encourages on-going production. Then every production company that has made a British film always has, sitting in the background, some money he can't get his hands on until he makes another British film. That to me is the only intelligent way to do it. Not to give it to some moron at the National Film Finance Corporation to waste.'

Winner lit another cigar and leant back in his chair. 'That's what they should do,' he said. 'I may write to *The Times* about it.'

2 Decline and Fall

The end of the National Film Finance Corporation

'The American cinema has, of course, always won; and never more decisively than now when it holds us more firmly captive than ever.'

Lindsay Anderson, 1983

Mamoun Hassan, managing director of the National Film Finance Corporation, resigned from the post in June 1984 in order, according to an official statement, to return to independent film making. The real reason was that he knew by then that his position was a hopeless one. For two years he had waited for a government report on the film industry which would decide the future of the NFFC. It had been postponed first by a general election and a change of Minister and then by an extraordinary series of delays. Publication was announced and then that announcement was withdrawn on half a dozen occasions.

It finally appeared in July 1984 as a slim 18-page White Paper recommending the abolition of the Eady Levy (named after Sir Wilfred Eady, a Treasury official) which had been established by Harold Wilson when he was President of the Board of Trade in 1950. It amounted in its final version to a tax on exhibitors, based on the box office returns of British-made movies. It had brought in £2.7 million in 1983, some of which had gone to the NFFC, the British Film Institute and to the National Film and Television School.

The report also recommended the privatisation of the NFFC, with Rank, Thorn-EMI and others – what the report called 'certain organisations in the film, television and video sectors' – putting up £1.1 million a year to finance it and the government establishing a fund of £1.5 million a year for five years.

Hassan regarded privatisation as an absurd move. 'Really, what point is there in having a corporation whose brief is such that it would be no different from the brief of a private company? When people talk airily about the privatisation of the NFFC, it's meaningless,' he said while the government was still making up its mind what to do. 'If we were in a monopoly position I could understand that things might be different if we were privatised. We are badly underfunded; the funds we have are nothing to the funds that Goldcrest has or EMI or Virgin or HandMade. What is the point in the Corporation becoming yet another underfunded film company? If you feel it's not doing a job, you do away with it.'

Hassan, born in Saudi Arabia, had been managing director of the NFFC – on a salary last reported as £22,785 plus £9,000 or so expenses – since 1979, during the most threatened time in its existence. The Labour government were preparing film legislation when he arrived, but four months later they were out of office before any changes were made. The next year, the Tories wrote off the NFFC's old debts and provided an income from the Eady Levy which amounts to around £1.5m a year.

The NFFC's status has always been a little odd. According to the statutes, it has to act as a commercial organisation. From such a standpoint, it could be accounted a failure. It has nearly always lost money. The number of profitable films it has invested in can still be counted on the fingers of two hands. It has never had the money to invest in large-scale movies that might have made it big profits. Instead, it has had to stay in the area of highest risk, of low and medium budget film making. 'The industry expects us to be more than commercial. There is an unwritten brief to take a chance,' said Hassan. 'In the early days, a producer usually provided 70 per cent of the finance and the NFFC put in 30 per cent. Then the Corporation was backing 60 films a year and you don't make qualitative judgements on those numbers of films. Commercial return meant something quite concrete: that one of the major distributors was going to handle the picture.

'What does that mean now, when one film out of ten makes a profit? The qualitative judgement becomes paramount, because the distributor does not put up 70 per cent of the finance. The Corporation now puts up much more than 30 per cent quite a lot of the time – 50 or sometimes 60 or 70 per cent. It is becoming harder to abide by the rules. But there is the mythology within the industry. The industry looks to us to comfort the private sector and to take the hard risks with the difficult subjects, if the producer and director have a track record, or to take a chance with new talent.'

Decisions at the NFFC were made not by Hassan alone, but with a board of seven directors which at the time of writing included two journalists, Felicity Green and Barry Norman, an exhibitor, Romaine Hart, a producer, David Puttnam and the head of the National Film and Television School, Colin Young. Recently, they voted against his recommendations that the NFFC should invest in three films: Merchant-Ivory's production of *Heat and Dust*, about past and present British attitudes to India, Nagisa Oshima's *Merry Christmas Mr Lawrence*, produced by Jeremy Thomas and based on Laurens van der Post's novel set in a Japanese prisoner-of-war camp, and *Moonlighting*, Jerzy Skolimowski's film of three Polish builders stranded in Britain during the military takeover in their country, which was produced by Mark Shivas. All three have been among the better films of recent years. Hassan argued that you shouldn't look at the passport of the people involved, but at the subject. If it illuminated British life and society and attitudes then the NFFC should invest. The board disagreed.

He feels that the argument would not have arisen if there had been more money available. One film involving a foreign-born director would pass without comment among nine productions. When it was one of two or three, then disagreement was inevitable. 'We need more money to be able to take more chances to have more failures so that we can have successes,' he said. 'But that will not solve the problem; it's also one of distribution and exhibition. There is the problem of the artist. And there is the problem of the audience as well. We can't let them off the hook. If they want to see rubbish, if they don't want to see anything which has imagination or feeling in it, then obviously we're going to have a dead industry. It might make money, but that isn't what I consider an industry. There's a limit to the amount of excitement and sensation that you can create. There's no limit to the amount of feeling you can create.'

Hassan had come to the NFFC after heading the BFI's production board and had no wish to take over his former employer's functions, for the BFI enjoys special privileges with the unions that keep the costs down of the productions it backs. '*The Draughtsman's Contract* cost the BFI £350,000. Had we made it it would have cost a minimum of £1 million. It would have been totally noncommercial.' Nor does he feel that a wealthier NFFC would threaten anyone. It would be possible to prevent an individual gaining control by insisting that the job of managing director should be held for four years only. That is the length of time Hassan has run the NFFC. He said on taking over the job ('it was an accident, really. It was put to me that someone had to do it') that he would stay for no longer than five years. He had intended to leave by 1986 after overseeing the Corporation's current investments, the first time for many years that it had backed a number of films at once. In his first four years, the NFFC put money into five feature films: *Memoirs of a Survivor*, Lindsay Anderson's disappointing *Britannia Hospital*, Chris Petit's enigmatic thriller *An Unsuitable Job for a Woman*, Bill Forsyth's delightful and successful *Gregory's Girl*, and Francis Rossi's *Babylon*, an attempt to portray the lives and problems of young West Indians living in London. 'Out of the five films, two I like very much, one I respect, one I dislike and one is a great sadness to me because it could have been very good but wasn't,' he said.

In 1983, for the first time, he had an investment of £4.5m in 'a portfolio of nine films', providing him with the opportunity of demonstrating how he would like to see the NFFC function. 'What I've said is that the minimum is quadruple our present money or nothing. The way we've been investing recently is in one film at a time. Each film then becomes a NFFC-type film, which immediately influences people to come back to us with that kind of film. Whereas we don't have a kind of film; we're waiting to be persuaded. I think that less than £10 million makes it very difficult. We should be in a position that if we really think a project is worth doing, we put up 75 per cent of the budget. Instead of just waiting around for the producer to find the rest of the money in a very, very cautious private sector we should put up as much as allows the film to get made.

'And we should make at least eight or nine a year. We should be in a position to get into any picture we want to – up to a budget of £5 million, anyway. We never put up less than 25 per cent because it's pointless. If the producer can get 80 per cent of the money, he can get 100 per cent. If you put up only 20 per cent you can have no influence whatever on the production. You can't keep costs down, because you're a small shareholder and you're told to shut up. But we should have more to put into a particular film if we so chose. And we should be in more pictures and different kinds of pictures. As a really serious, commercial organisation.

'When we try to sell our films abroad, in Europe we find the governments there are tilting the market in favour of their own producers and their own films. They provide huge subsidies. In Germany there is help from various bodies that amounts to £40m altogether. In France, Holland, Sweden, Norway, Denmark it's the same; they all realise that the local industry has to be supported. The support here is ludicrously small.'

It was a happy accident that the NFFC had so much money to invest in 1983. What happened was that other projects had failed because the producers had been offered work which had taken priority. 'When we invest in a picture we try to keep the costs down,' said Hassan. 'One of the things we do is to insist on the producer getting very small sums of money himself. So we find ourselves in competition with the major studios, who offer more.'

During 1982, the NFFC invested in three films. Only one, Chris Petit's *An Unsuitable Job for a Woman*, produced by Peter McKay and Michael Relph, went into production. Jeremy Thomas had been going to produce *The Hole in the Middle*, which was to have been the first feature film, unless you count *The Great Rock 'n' Roll Swindle*, to have been directed by Julien Temple. Instead Thomas had produced *Eureka* for Nicholas Roeg, and Oshima's *Merry Christmas Mr Lawrence*. Timothy Burrill, a producer whose credits include *Tess*, had planned to produce *The Wheel,* directed by Mike Radford, for which the NFFC had advanced money for writing the script in 1981. But he was busy producing the American-financed *Pirates of Penzance,* which was made in Britain, and *Superman III* and *Supergirl I* for Alexander Salkind. ('His remuneration from them was probably in excess of the budget we were talking about,' said Hassan.)

The portfolio Hassan had arranged included *Loose Connections,* Richard Eyre's second film following his brilliant debut with *The Ploughman's Lunch; Another Country,* the first feature film directed by Marek Kanievska, based on Julian Mitchell's successful West End play exploring the public school and homosexual aura that produced such spies as Guy Burgess; *Secret Places,* from Janet Elliot's novel of a Jewish refugee schoolgirl in an English public school during the Second World War; *The Company of Wolves,* scripted by Angela Carter and directed by Neil Jordan, a young Irish novelist and director; *Dance with a Stranger* based on the story of Ruth Ellis, the last woman to be hanged in Britain, directed by Alan Clarke from a script by Shelagh Delaney, who had been part of Joan Littlewood's extraordinary Theatre Workshop, the vitality of which spilled over into movies in the 1960s; *Defence of the Realm,* written by the Martin Stellman who scripted *Quadrophenia,* and produced by David Puttnam; *Nanou,* written and directed by Conny Templeman, a graduate of the National Film School, and produced by Simon Perry, and *Where The Wind Blows,* Jimmy Murakami's animated version of Raymond Briggs' cautionary cartoon of an ignorant, well meaning elderly couple caught in a nuclear holocaust and trustingly following government instructions on survival until they die from radiation sickness. In the event, *The Company of Wolves* was wholly backed by Palace Video, a young company that had moved from marketing video cassettes to distributing films and on to production, and ITC, cautiously re-entering film production for the first time since the departure of Lord Grade.

By the time the last of those films was released in 1985, they were no more than an epitaph for the NFFC. 'We hope all will make it on the big circuits,' said Hassan. 'It is problematic when you are making films that are off-centre and dealing with distributors whose main experience is with major pictures. It's difficult sometimes for them to know how to nurture a picture, how to start small and get bigger. Their expertise is in starting big – and ending big. Their technique of wave or general release implies, I think, that the audience already has an idea of what category the film is. So you spend your money in focusing on the little difference between that film and what the audience might expect.

'When you are backing pictures which are one-off basically, you need a very different kind of approach; you have to create the image of the film itself. That means a different kind of distribution and a different kind of expertise, and I don't know that the majors have that. I wish we had the kind of classics division that the majors have in the States. Because then you get the care for a one-off picture and you also know that, if the pictures can go big, there are the financial resources there to allow it to do so. There is the EMI Classics, which has just been announced but we don't know how that's going to go.'

I asked Hassan whether he favoured the establishment of a British Film Authority. 'I dislike centralisation, particularly the way it occurs in British society,' he said. 'The moment you have centralisation you have nothing but the most second-rate activity; everyone plays safe. You mustn't create an authorised version of film or thought.' Other countries have produced such decentralised authorities. In Sweden, the Film Institute contained several different committees, each with slightly different briefs and different amounts of money to hand out to film makers.

Apart from financing films, the NFFC through its development fund advances money for the writing of scripts on the basis of treatments and then even subsidises producers who want to set up a 'package' of writer, director and stars. It has only £200,000 a year to spend. Three of the scripts of the NFFC's current nine investments – *Loose Connections, Defence of the Realm, Another Country* – have been written with money from the fund. The development fund uses consultants from the industry, including Jack Rosenthal, who acts as a script consultant to Goldcrest, Sandy Lieberson, who ran the European end of the American The Ladd Company until he joined Goldcrest in 1983, and Alan Parker, the director. 'They're not only considering treatments for the Corporation to develop, but treatments that, once they become scripts, the industry might back,' said Hassan. 'Not very often is a script taken up. Our strike rate recently has gone up to about one in five.'

There were times before he quit when Hassan seemed very anxious to return to film producing or directing. 'It is a very frustrating job,' he said. 'You've very little money and you've an indusry that doesn't want to change. You've got exhibitors with serious problems. You've distributors who are really concerned with American product. You've film makers who don't have a clear idea of the target audience because they've been so divorced from the audience for so long. They don't even have a clear idea of their target audience for art movies. There isn't the machinery that allows them to have any feedback. You have a government that doesn't care very much about the film industry. It's not just the present government, but all of them since about 1949. I don't think we can change things on our own. We could have a lot of money and still do very little. But I know that if we weren't around, things would not change.

'A lot has to be done to cinemas, to make them places you go to because it's fun to be there. If you want to see a film very badly, you'd go to a gent's lavatory to see it. But that isn't what an industry is based on; it depends on people going to the cinema as a matter of habit. At the same time, it's worth trying to break the mould a little. I didn't think I'd change things very much, but as long as I disturbed it a little, it would have been worthwhile. I don't know whether I've done that. Probably not.'

The White Paper made no recommendations for funds to replace those supplied from the Eady Levy to the British Film Institute's production board which finances experimental films and has had two art house successes in recent years with *The Draughtsman's Contract* and *Ascendancy*. It is as if the government wished to create a return to the situation that existed for most of the 1970s. There was then, with only slight exaggeration, no money to make films, no cinemas to show them in, no audiences to pay to see them. Even if there had been money and films had been made and many of them had been good, it is unlikely that audiences would have returned to the surviving cinemas, any more than dried-out alcoholics are tempted back on the bottle by a new cocktail.

Where was the initiative to come from when much of the talent had been attracted, naturally enough, to Hollywood? Hooray for Hollywood, but who was for Britain? The British film industry has, over the years, organised itself into a mess. Various attempts have been made to regulate and regularise its activities, but to little effect.

There had been commissions and select committees and various pressure groups all making endless reports until one President of the Board of Trade complained that the film industry occupied a disproportionate amount of time. None of the reports have ever changed anything; like cans of bad movies, they moulder, forgotten, on dusty shelves.

Harold Wilson, one of the few politicians to take an intelligent interest in cinema, set up an Interim Action Committee – 'interim' rightly suggesting that no action would be taken – and floated the suggestion of establishing a British Film Authority, which horrified many film makers.

The Tory attitude has been one of non-involvement or the dismantling of any official involvement. At the moment there are two ministries – the Board of Trade, which has overseen film since 1925, and Education and Science – involved in its affairs, while the overlapping business of television is supervised by the Home Office.

Since the 1920s film producers have been seeking financial help from the government, in the form of subsidies or loans. Attitudes to official intervention are mixed, ranging from Winner's disdain to Sir Richard Attenborough's plea, during the 50th anniversary celebrations of the British Film Institute in October 1983, for more government funds for experimental productions.

The BFI has played a critical rather than crucial part in the industry. Its National Film Theatre and regional film theatres keep the classics alive and encourage a cult following for many potboiling American movies. The admirable London Film Festival gives audiences a rare chance to see the best of foreign cinema and also screens as many decent British films as it can find, even though in recent years many of them have been films made for television. It is true that few other of the world's festivals share the London Festival's admiration for British movies en masse. The New York Film Festival in 1983, for instance, showed a majority of French films and no British ones at all.

Some film makers have feared that semi-official bodies, given the slightest encouragement, could control the industry, although without them films that reflect British society are not likely to be made. 'It's almost impossible for a country of our size to maintain a genuinely indigenous character for their film industry unless they do have some subsidy,' said Michael Relph, a producer whose experience goes back to the small glories of Ealing Studios. 'We need something – tax concessions or a levy – which in effect boosts the home market. Some subsidy is needed to preserve the British cultural element in movies.'

Relph can recall when the Eady Levy used to increase by 30 or 40 per cent the takings of most British films, making the difference between profit and loss. 'A levy is no longer significant if it only comes from the cinemas, that's for sure,' he said. Most of the Eady Money went to American-financed megabuck movies. In February 1980 the Department of Trade imposed a cut off figure of £500,000 as the most any film could receive from the fund. Previously, when *Superman* – about as British as the Stars and Stripes – earned more than £3.5m during the first six months of 1979, it had taken more than a million pounds in Eady money. The five most successful films of 1980 (*Watership Down, Death on the Nile, Midnight Express, The Wild Geese* and *The Thirty-Nine Steps*) raked in 70 per cent of the Eady pay-out between them. A limit of £50,000 was also imposed on short films, defined as less than 33.3 minutes long. Understandably. One short, *Hot Wheels*, had taken £249,925 in Eady Money, more that year than such top earners as EMI's glossy *Death On The Nile* (£246,875) or Rank's *The Thirty-Nine Steps* (£138,485). The reason was a simple one: it had gone on release with *Grease*.

Relph, though, approved of the way the Eady fund worked, with the greater share of the money going to the most popular films. 'It was levied on the exhibitors who obviously wanted to encourage popular films,' he said. 'If it is, as some demand, applied to films on television as well, then it should have the same effect, of rewarding popular films, which is what television wants.'

In March 1983, the Association of Independent Producers asked the government to abandon the Eady Levy and replace it with an Industry Subscription Fund that, they estimated, would bring in £35 million a year to produce British films.

The money would be raised in three ways: by a levy of 1/4p per person per film broadcast on television, including cable stations, which would bring in £10m, a levy of £1 on every blank video tape, which would contribute a further £20m, and a 5p levy on cinema seats which would bring the rest.

This money would then be split between the National Film Finance Corporation (£17.5m), film producers (£12.25m distributed according to box office returns), cinemas (£3.5m as improvement funds) and the National Film and Television School, which would receive £1.75m.

The authors of the report, who included David Puttnam, pointed out that when *Chariots of Fire* is shown on television it will be seen by many more than the three-and-a-half million who watched it in the cinemas. But its cinema audience paid more than £7m for the privilege, whereas the most that it would earn from TV would be £250,000.

'For more than 20 years, film has been evolving from a medium whose principal form of exhibition was the local cinema into one which reaches the vast majority of people in their own homes,' the AIP wrote.

Relph was among those who feared that the NFFC could become too powerful, although he no longer has any need to worry. 'If the levy is increased it would be a terrible mistake to give it all to the NFFC. It would make whatever little group is making decisions there virtually dictate the whole trend of British cinema,' he said. 'Also the BFI has become a rival to the NFFC. There's a conflict there, particularly as one is getting it from the Arts Ministry and the other from the Department of Trade. It all adds to the muddle.'

Relph, a former governor of the BFI, would like to see the BFI abandon its productions, with the NFFC being given some extra funds to support avant garde film makers. 'If it had £5 million a year it would be very adequately funded,' he said.

Fears that the NFFC could have ever dominated British film seem exaggerated. It was set up in 1948 with a working capital of £5m and began with the disadvantage of making a large loan to the extravagant, impulsive but often admirable Sir Alexander Korda. Unlike Korda, it had to be careful with its money, backing small budget movies rather than the big blockbusters that, when successful, turn the biggest profits.

In its earliest days, it was headed by Lord Reith as chairman and James Lawrie, a former banker, as managing director. Neither had practical experience of film. Its function broadened into what it described as a specialised bank. For a long time now it has been a bank without many funds to call on. From 1950 to 1965, the NFFC put money into 658 films. In the following 15 years, the number fell to 94 films.

Even so, the NFFC remained confident about long term prospects for the film industry, providing no one wanted to get rich quick. In its annual report for 1971, Sir John Terry, its managing director, wrote, 'It is the Corporation's conviction that film production in Britain will expand, and opportunities for employment increase, in direct proportion to the lowering of costs.

'Here the major contribution must be made by top talent, which has for too long been forced to seek the maximum cash fees obtainable owing to the remoteness of "profits". But this tendency can be reversed if top talent is remunerated through a share of the distributor's gross receipts, or by an investment of fees in accordance with the Corporation's new lending policy.

'When the astronomical fees disappear there will be every reason for other fees to descend to a saner level and for outdated crewing and other practices to be modified.'

Most of those hopes remain unfulfilled, although smaller independent producers are now using such methods to persuade costly actors and actresses to appear in their low-budget films.

By the annual report for 1982, the tone had grown more cautious. There was even a hint of desperation behind its pleas. After 70 years, film should hardly need to justify itself in such a defensive manner:

'With all its problems the film industry bestows social, cultural and commercial benefits. It can be of service to other media by providing product; it can offer entertainment of a kind, and in a context, that is distinctive; it can be commercially highly successful.

'A strategy is required which, taking account of the multifarious ways in which film is used, will help keep cinemas open and provide broad and realistic support for the production of films reflecting British life and manners.'

The purpose was to increase the pressure on the Tory government, whose interest in supporting film has never been more than tepid, to extend the Eady Levy to include films on television and blank video cassettes, so supporting the Independent Producers' pleas. 'There is, indeed, little logic in taxing films shown in the cinemas and not those transmitted on television where the larger audience sees them,' it stated.

The NFFC has always suffered from a problem that afflicts official bodies; its mistakes are rarely forgotten. At the Cannes Film Festival in 1982, Thorn-EMI showed their movie, *Memoirs of a Survivor*, directed by David Gladwell, in which the NFFC had invested.

The film, based on a novel by Doris Lessing, starred Julie Christie, making a return to the cinema after a long absence. Even so, EMI's executives were gloomy about its prospects.

'We're going to have to pay people to come to see it,' said one. They were wrong at that particular moment. The Cannes' audience fought to get into the cinema. But they were right in the longer term. In Britain, audiences rushed for the exits and it quickly disappeared from view. That disaster is in EMI's past. But it is still remembered as one of the NFFC's failures.

'We didn't make the films, we financed them,' said Hassan. 'We were the midwives, not the parents. We could only choose from that which is presented. On paper *Memoirs of a Survivor* was much less risky than a lot of others we have done. It was based on a book that had been a best-seller in the States, Germany and Norway. It was Julie Christie's return to the scene and it was a very tiny budget indeed.

'We had a director who had made a film about a minefield of a subject – *Requiem for a Village* – and done it with tact so that it was very accessible. And EMI wanted to invest in it.

'We all thought that, given a break, we'd get our money back. We didn't. But, looking at the upside, it was certainly much less than a million pounds and given a very small piece of luck, we could have got it back.

'When it opened here (and it was very badly distributed by EMI) in the first three weeks at the Shaftesbury, it was in the Top 10 films in London. It was just that people saw it and the word of mouth was bad and it died.' It cannot surely be long before the NFFC suffers the same fate.

3 Monopoly Money

Thorn-EMI and Rank

> 'Rank Film Productions are looking forward to the challenge of the 80's with confidence. Here is where film makers of the future will find co-operation and fulfilment.'
>
> Anthony Williams, Executive Director Rank Film Productions, 1980

History has an uncomfortable way of repeating itself in the film industry. Whatever its executives learn from, it is not the past. The attempts by Lord Rank and Alexander Korda to break into the American market in the 1940s with expensively made films featuring international stars was repeated a generation later, with similar disastrous results, by Barry Spikings, head of production at EMI, and Lord Grade.

There was a curious sense of *déjà vu* at a press conference in November 1983 at which Verity Lambert, the newly-installed head of production at Thorn-EMI, announced her future plans. Around £100 million would be spent over three years on making up to 15 films, she said, adding, 'I believe all have international appeal.'

Mike Hodges was to direct a comedy, *Illegal Aliens*, written by Mel Smith and Griff Rhys-Jones, best known for their performances as part of the BBC-TV series *Not The Nine O'Clock News*, a programme that had done something to fill the gap left by Monty Python. Bill Forsyth was directing *Comfort and Joy*, another of his wry looks at Scottish life. Dennis Potter, who had gained an international reputation following the Hollywood version of his BBC-TV series *Pennies From Heaven*, was re-examining the story of *Alice in Wonderland* in *Dream Child*, to be directed by Gavin Millar, also known as a television director. The fourth was a thriller, *Slayground*, starring the same Mel Smith, together with Billie Whitelaw and Peter Coyote.

Bryan Forbes had made a virtually identical speech fourteen years earlier, in August 1969, four months after he had become head of production at EMI's Elstree Studios, following EMI's takeover of Association British Picture Corporation in February of that year. At *his* press conference he announced that EMI would be spending around £100 million in making 15 films, at a cost of between £5 and £10 million each.

They included Peter Sellers starring in *Hoffman*, Joseph Losey directing *The Go-Between*, Kevin Brownlow and Andrew Mollo making *The Breaking of Bumbo* from Adrian Sinclair's script, Richard Attenborough's *The Feathers of Death*, Lionel Jeffries's *The Railway Children*, Paul Watson's *A Fine and Private Place* and Frank Nesbitt's *Dulcima*. Forbes himself would direct *The Raging Moon* and there was still a director to be found for *Forbush And The Penguins*.

Forbes described it as 'the most serious and ambitious attempt to revitalise the British film industry in 20 years'. EMI would need to sell their medium budget pictures to the Americans, he added, but they would be sold individually, after they were made.

It is hoped that Verity Lambert, in echoing Forbes's words and budget, escapes his fate. 'We have attempted to present talent at all levels and we are prepared to be judged on the ultimate results,' was Forbes's slogan to the world.

Perhaps inevitably in a difficult situation, he produced some duds. *Hoffman* was one of Sellers's dreariest films. *The Breaking of Bumbo*, eventually directed by its author, has never been released. Forbes cancelled *A Fine and Private Place* while it was being shot on location in Cornwall because of 'adverse weather conditions' (although I spent three days on the film set in glorious sunshine). *Forbush and the Penguins*, which eventually involved the work of three different directors, was the sort of film *only* penguins would enjoy.

There were good films produced under Forbes's regime, notably *The Go-Between* and two family films of unusual quality: *The Railway Children* and *The Tales of Beatrix Potter*. Forbes's own *The Raging Moon* (1971) was a touching love story between Malcolm McDowell, as a bitter paraplegic in a wheelchair, and Nanette Newman as a dying cripple.

Forbes, who had already proved himself to be a talented writer and director and a good actor, had little time to reveal his capabilities as a production chief since he resigned in March 1971, thirteen months before his contract was up for renewal.

By the mid-1970s, Elstree studios was existing on a staff of under 50. Since then it has survived and prospered as a studio for hire, with independent producers moving in for long or short stays.

It was not until the arrival in 1976 of Barry Spikings and Michael Deeley as joint managing directors of EMI Films that EMI appeared to have any particular production policy. Spikings, a former journalist, and Deeley, an experienced producer, had acquired the production company British Lion in 1973.

EMI had been looking for new management and took over British Lion in order to secure their services. On their arrival they put into effect a policy that they had inaugurated at British Lion. It was to make American films for the Americans. At British Lion, they had backed Nicholas Roeg's *The Man Who Fell To Earth,* which was the first British film to be made in America without financial backing from that country.

There was a moment when it had seemed as though the policy was going to pay dividends. They financed Michael Cimino's *The Deer Hunter* (1978), a muddled allegory about the Vietnamese war which was nonetheless a commercial and critical success, winning five Oscars, including one as the best film of the year. Their first profitable productions also included Sam Peckinpah's *Convoy* (1978) and Walter Hill's *The Driver* (1978).

Deeley moved to America to oversee production there and, after some office in-fighting, soon left the company. In May 1979, when Lord Delfont became chief executive of EMI, Spikings took over as chairman and chief executive of EMI Films.

Unlike his predecessor or his successors, Spikings showed little interest in wanting to revitalise or even keep alive the local industry. He even moved EMI's main production office to Los Angeles.

Spikings's apparent belief was that if he could break into the American market with big budget, basically American movies, then he would have the power to create a market for smaller British movies. The blockbusters would batter down the walls that kept British films out and they would rush through the gap. It was an attractive theory, unless you were a British producer seeking finance for your film.

Spikings and his fellow executives rejected virtually every British film they were offered, including *Gandhi* and *Chariots of Fire.* Hostility to EMI's policies seethed throughout the industry and finally surfaced when Spikings rejected *Local Hero.* The film's producer David Puttnam, fresh from winning an Oscar for *Chariots Of Fire,* erupted.

'I was very bitter,' said Puttnam. 'I became absolutely hysterical with EMI. Following Barry Spikings's turndown I sent a letter the like of which I've never sent in my life. It was the most vicious letter I've ever written. I told them they should get rid of Spikings promptly.

'I felt it was a betrayal. It was a double betrayal, because Barry had actually encouraged me to believe that it was just what he wanted.

'But more important than that, I thought it showed complete ineptitude on their part and a complete betrayal of their published policy. That had happened once before. I was able to force *Bugsy Malone* on Rank, absolutely force it, because of a series of public pronouncements on the sort of films they wanted to make. And if they happened to be writing about *Bugsy* with foreknowledge they couldn't have done better. So I made such an issue of it, that I really made it difficult for them not to have the film.

'EMI thought *Local Hero* was overpriced at £4 million. You had to believe in Bill Forsyth. His success with *Gregory's Girl* wasn't seen to be synonymous with the expenditure of £4 million.'

EMI was in financial difficulties, its profits having dropped to £11 million in 1979 compared to £65 million two years earlier. In March 1980 Thorn took over EMI at a cost of £169 million to create Britain's biggest showbusiness conglomerate. Thorn, who had the largest share of British production of television sets, hi-fi and record players, was involved with video-disc systems and communications satellites.

EMI's difficulties had resulted from a slump in the record business and the costs of its medical electronics division, which ate up the profits. But it still owned 250 cinemas, a third share in the Columbia–EMI–Warner distribution company and a successful film studio at Elstree, as well as a controlling stake in Thames Television.

Thorn's approach to the glitter of showbusiness was a more austere one. Its management is said to have been horrified by the salaries paid to the executives of EMI's film division. It was at this moment that Spikings produced a succession of expensive flops.

There was *The Jazz Singer* (1980), a second remake of the original talkie which this time substituted a modern singing star, Neil Diamond, for Al Jolson but failed to update the story of a cantor's son or to prevent Laurence Olivier giving a period performance of remarkable staginess as the cantor.

There was *Can't Stop The Music* (1980), packaged by a flamboyant Hollywood producer, Allan Carr and a fictionalised account of the formation of the Village People, a group of male singers who dressed as homosexual stereotypes. The film was given a big publicity build-up. A preview of some of the big musical numbers was given to the British press by Carr himself. (I recall being berated by one of Spikings's executives for not responding enthusiastically enough to Carr's speech telling us what a wonderful film it was. 'Don't you realise who this man is?' he kept asking me.) But the result was a tiresome, sniggering mess that lacked any narrative interest and failed to attract any kind of audience.

And there was John Schlesinger's *Honky Tonk Freeway*, a comedy that cost more than £25 million to make and lost it all. 'For all his faults Barry Spikings tried to do something that was on the right lines,' said Don Boyd, the producer and originator of the film, which was made on location in America. 'His big mistake was not supporting the British industry as well. If he'd done that, he'd have been a hero. He ignored the British side and concentrated entirely on big-budget American films. It's a big crap game there, hit or miss, and I think he had his numbers come up too early with *The Deer Hunter*. The American majors are also fiercely possessive of their market. EMI were always regarded as the last people you took a project to, instead of possibly being the first. It wasn't as easy for them to get their product to the market.

'*Honky Tonk Freeway* is talked of as causing his downfall. People forget that after *Honky Tonk Freeway* Spikings made seven large budget American movies, which involved £50 million worth of investment. If he had spent £10 million here, everybody would have been ecstatic. But what did he do? Made *Britannia Hospital* in partnership with the NFFC! Turning down *Local Hero* was the final nail in his coffin. It was his major political mistake. His policy of trying to compete with the American majors and getting to a point where the whole system took him seriously was worked out, intelligent and brave.'

The trouble was that Spikings's policy did *not* work out. The films he chose to make attracted few audiences either in America or in Britain. Almost the only EMI films of the period that had any British connection were the series of period films scripted by Anthony Shaffer from the works of Agatha Christie and produced by John Brabourne and Richard Goodwin. The first, *Murder on the Orient Express* (1974), directed by the American Sidney Lumet, set the style with its starry cast – Sean Connery, Albert Finney, John Gielgud, Anthony Perkins, Lauren Bacall, Ingrid Bergman and Vanessa Redgrave – and its sumptuously shot, old-fashioned style.

Its successors – *Death on the Nile* (1978), *Evil under the Sun* (1982) – with their frequent flashbacks to the crime and long-winded explanation of the solution at the climax, and glamorous actors and actresses passing through on their way to better films, have declined into a deadening formula for boredom.

Spikings, with a sudden change of policy, announced that production would be divided between Britain and the States and would include some low-budget productions. But then Verity Lambert, who had made her reputation as head of Euston Films, a subsidiary of Thames Television making films for the small screen, was appointed director of production at EMI. Two months later, in January 1983, Spikings quit.

The new management reorganised the company, creating Thorn EMI Screen Entertainment under a new chief executive, Gary Dartnell, bringing together all their film and video interests. It claimed to be the largest movie conglomerate in the world. In terms of film production, though, it ranks much lower. So far, a greater emphasis has been put on the company's distribution and marketing of video cassettes.

Rank, EMI's great rivals, were even less active in the 1970s and 1980s. There seemed little coherent policy in their film production, with the company shunning expensive movies and making little attempt to break into the American market, preferring to back a mixed bag of films.

But at the beginning of the 1980s, Rank appeared to be in a much more positive moood. They had two productions about to be released, Nicholas Roeg's *Bad Timing*, starring Art Garfunkel and Theresa Russell, and David Wickes' *Silver Dream Racer*, starring David Essex, a British pop-singer and actor, and, for a wider appeal, the American actors Beau Bridges and Cristina Raines. The film did reasonably well, taking more than £400,000 at the British box-office, which was around three times as much as *Bad Timing*.

At the beginning of 1980 Rank's head of production, Anthony Williams, in an advertisement for the company in the trade press, made the optimistic announcement that Rank was where future film makers would find co-operation and fulfilment.

In May, at the Cannes Film Festival, Rank said that they were going to spend £12 million on making films in the near future, with four times as much being committed in the next few years.

A month later, in a move for which no explanation has been forthcoming, Rank announced that they were stopping production altogether. Since then, the company has done little more than invest some money, providing distribution guarantees, in such films as *Educating Rita* and *The Boys in Blue* (1983), a small scale comedy starring the double act (Tommy) Cannon and (Bobby) Ball who had made their names in television.

Although neither Rank nor EMI had been doing much for local film making, both still exerted an enormous influence on British cinema, for between them they had a virtual monopoly of the exhibition of films and so could control, to a great extent, what movies the public saw.

At a conference of the Cinema Exhibitors Association, an independent cinema owner asked the then managing director of Rank Film Distributors when he and other independents would be allowed to show *The Empire Strikes Back*, bearing in mind that three years after release it was likely to be seen on television.

'You'll get it when I decide you can have it,' came the reply. Rank's man added that by then he would have 'booked it into the cinemas in the key runs and played it into the ground'.

It was 'a speech of brutal candour', remarked John and Roy Boulting, the brothers whose activities as producers, writers and directors added much to British cinema of the 1950s and 1960s.

Rank's power came from their distribution of films made by such major American companies as Walt Disney, Twentieth Century Fox, United Artists and Universal. The other American majors, Paramount, Columbia and Warner, have a similar arrangement with Thorn-EMI, as it now is. The Americans thus gained access to one of the two major cinema circuits. The two British companies, in turn, were guaranteed a supply of the profitable films for their cinemas without having to enter into lengthy negotiations or to bid for them against other cinema owners. 'They do not compete. They divide. And what they divide is the spoils,' as the Boulting brothers put it.

Apart from avoiding competition, the two circuits also indulged in 'barring', which prevented independent cinemas from showing the big films until every possible profit had been wrung out of them. Barring is a straight monopoly practice. It gives exclusive rights to show a film to the major cinemas in Britain's big towns. It operates over distance and time to prevent other cinemas from showing the film.

In 1966, these practices led the Monopolies Commission to investigate film distribution in Britain and deplore the dominance of the Associated British Picture Corporation (as it then was before being swallowed up by EMI and then Thorn) and Rank.

The Commission came to the conclusion that bars were not in principle against the public interest. But it added that the practice of barring was detrimental to the service which the industry gives the public and pointed out that the two companies effectively determined production and so gave the public little choice over what films they could see.

The lack of competition between Rank and ABPC 'operated and might be expected to operate against the public interest', the Commission reported. It also objected to the preference which Rank gave to its own documentary films (which were mainly the dire and bland *Look at Life*) in its own cinemas.

At that time the two companies, together with other interested parties, signed a Statement of Intent. In it, Rank and ABPC undertook to extend the practice of giving trial runs to films of possibly limited appeal and of giving selective bookings to art films. Rank also promised to stop giving preferential treatment to its own films. Nevertheless *Look at Life* ran for three years before it ceased to be profitable, even with its advantages of guaranteed distribution.

One might describe the attitude as that of any salesmen with a stranglehold on the market: you can see any movie you want, providing it's showing at one of our cinemas.

Consumers have only one possible response in such circumstances. And, indeed, they stopped going to the cinemas, while the distributors bewailed the falling audiences, but did little to change things, least of all to take notice of the Commission. That body made loud noises in its report, but its actual recommendations were mild and not calculated to alter much. It was as if the fact of the investigation was enough in itself, making any action unnecessary.

The Commission was able to pinpoint the problem (not that it required much skill to do so) but did not know what to do to solve it.

Over the years, the two companies have wound their strictures so tightly around the industry, like ivy propping up an ancient building, that, if they were removed, the whole structure might collapse.

The fear is that if Rank and Thorn-EMI had to give up their dominant position, it would bring about the end of British cinema, since cinemas doing no more than break even would be shut down once they lost the protection of being part of a larger group. But even within a large group, cinemas are not safe. Rank shut down more than 20 in 1981. The situation now is so dire, that any action, however radical, might be an improvement.

Britain has suffered since the 1930s from the disproportionate power of a distribution duopoly. As the first fly-by-night flea-pit owners began to go out of business or were taken over, two companies grew to control the industry. Their names have changed over the years; but the cinemas have stayed the same.

Over the years, too, various government bodies have examined the situation and declared it unhealthy. But nothing has changed. Indeed, no industry can have had its various aspects investigated by so many official bodies and select committees, with so few changes being made in the way it is regulated.

The Monopolies Commission tried again in 1983. Rank, naturally one of the two exhibitors under scrutiny, spent some £700,000 in legal fees in their submissions to the Commission – a bigger budget than a movie such as *The Draughtsman's Contract*.

What always surprises those ignorant of the ways of Wardour Street is not the frequent investigations of how the business is run in Britain. It is the fact that, having all the aces up their sleeves, the companies have still failed to make their fortunes from film.

In its heyday, Rank had what seemed to be the perfect set-up: not only did it make movies in its own studios, but the film was developed in its own laboratories and distributed by its own distribution company to its own cinemas. At every point in the chain, the money came rolling back to Rank. And yet, in its heyday, it lost £7 million.

In America, after an independent cinema owner sued when he was prevented from booking the film he wanted, studios were given the choice of either making films or owning cinemas, but not both. Here, there have been no such restrictions. Nor are there likely to be now.

Rank hardly makes films any more, but is content to hire out its studios to independent producers. The rest of the links in the chain still remain. But cinema is now among the company's minor interests; they have diversified into more profitable fields, although the company has gone through a bad period in recent years which has led to new management being brought in.

As the number of cinemas has shrunk, so the proportion of those owned by Rank and Thorn-EMI has grown. Today, the two control 39 per cent of the country's screens in just over a third of Britain's cinemas (many, of course, have two or three screens). Nearly half the cinema audience (48 per cent of seating capacity) goes to their cinemas. They take £6 out of every £10 at the box office. In the 1950s, they controlled one in five of British cinemas and in the 1960s, one in four.

That percentage is far from a monopoly, as Rank and Thorn-EMI's lawyers are keen to point out. But the two control the important cinemas, the 'first run' houses, and their deals with the major American studios provide them with the pick of the films and the incentive to show them rather than British movies.

In 1983, the Monopolies Commission again concluded that a monopoly situation existed in favour of EMI and Rank. They once again condemned the practice of barring. 'Competition between distributors is restricted because they do not generally offer to license films to exhibitors except in the sequences determined by the bars. Competition between exhibitors is restricted because they do not generally attempt to obtain licences except in accordance with the bars,' it reported.

During the period of 17 years between the two reports, the number of cinemas had declined by more than a half and the audience had fallen by nearly a third. In real terms, too, the cost of going to the pictures had increased by more than a third between 1970 and 1981.

The Commission added, 'It appears to us that the record of the cinema industry in the United States has been better than that of the British industry, both in attracting the public into its cinemas, and in holding down the rate of increase in admission prices in real terms. Similarly, the record of the cinema industries in Western Europe appears to have been better, in that the rate of decline in admission has not been so rapid as it has in Great Britain.'

Even so, the Commission came down in favour of the status quo. The lawyers' fees were not wasted. For Rank and EMI had convinced the Commissioners that any change would be for the worse.

They wrote: 'We concluded that an effective remedy would necessitate substantial reductions in the market shares of both EMI and Rank as exhibitors, in ways which would not lead to the re-creation of the degree of concentration in exhibition which exists at present.

'Such a remedy would be likely to require the divestment of substantial numbers of EMI's and Rank's cinemas. Taking into account the decline in cinema audiences, the continuing need to close cinemas, and the fact that some surviving cinemas are making losses, we concluded that such a remedy is not practicable and cannot be recommended.'

Rank and EMI both advanced persuasive arguments for the public benefits of large cinema circuits. EMI claimed that it could thus discover the best way of introducing technical innovations, such as multi-screen cinemas, and that it could take risks in the exhibition of films that would be unacceptable to a smaller operator.

It could afford to keep unprofitable cinemas open if there was a chance of profit in the future and its size enabled it to negotiate 'keen prices' for ice cream and sweets, which made a crucial contribution to the cinema's continuance.

Rank made much the same points, adding that a large chain could afford to train staff properly, cut expenses by having a centralised operation and experiment in a way that smaller cinemas could not do. The arguments have a great deal of force. The problem is that they do not have much connection with reality.

Neither Rank or EMI cinemas have gained a notable reputation for adventurous programming. Indeed, independent cinemas have been enjoying a revival precisely because they show intelligent films intended to appeal to wider audiences than sensation-hungry teenagers.

Rank informed the Commission that 'the decline in cinema audiences that has occurred has not been brought about in any way by the structure and practices of the industry. The industry has been and continues to be under the greatest competitive pressure to adapt to changed circumstances. Rank considers that it has done everything in its power to respond to that competition and to maximise the audience available.'

The Commission did not share this complacency. Its views were mild compared to those of Roy and John Boulting in their analysis of the barring system and tied suppliers.

'A challenge at law is, perhaps, long overdue,' they wrote in a combative pamphlet, *Whatever happened to the British Film?* subtitled *Or could there be Life after Death?* which they had printed and distributed to MPs and film makers.

'The industry has for too long tolerated the intolerable – a concentration of power irreconcilable with the healthy functioning of a free society,' they wrote.

The Boulting brothers, twins born in 1913, were no longer particularly active in British movies when they wrote their report. But their achievements more than gave their views the force of experience. They formed their first film company in 1938 and in the late 1950s began to turn out a series of comedies that managed to enrage and amuse people of every class and political persuasion.

Those who applauded *Private's Progress* (1958), with its satire on the officer class, abhorred *I'm All Right, Jack* (1959) notable for Peter Sellers' performance as a pedantic, petty-minded shop steward.

The Boultings had no doubt that film, television and video were of immense importance. 'Here are the most potent media of communication the world has ever known, instilling ideas, conditioning behaviour and, at all times, shaping the form and character of society for future generations here and throughout the world,' they wrote. 'We have responsibilities then, that cannot be ignored, even though facing them brings us into conflict with long entrenched and powerful interests.'

The Boultings' revolutionary solution to the problem was that film renters and distributors should be obliged to invest in the production of British films 20 per cent of their annual gross earnings from all outlets in the United Kingdom showing films until such time as the British film industry could stand on its own feet.

The television networks would also contribute a proportion of their earnings to a production fund. The scheme would exclude pornographic films.

They also wanted an end to the barring system and the exclusive deals between the major American studios and the cinema circuits. The Eady Levy would be retained, but the NFFC could be safely made redundant.

'It is perhaps inevitable that those who have dominated the past should wish to control the future,' they said. 'It will be for legislators and laymen alike to decide whether the concentration of so much power in so few hands is desirable.'

Both Rank, now down to 88 cinemas, most of them with three screens, and Thorn-EMI are trying hard to improve their distribution systems. Rank co-operate with the British Film Institute in screening, on one evening a week in some of their cinemas, films that the BFI has chosen, which are often foreign-language classics or recent releases that would not otherwise be seen, at least a gesture in the right direction.

In December 1983, Thorn-EMI established a Classics Division to distribute films that needed careful treatment, something other than the mass marketing slam-bang approach. The films it will handle range from specialised English-language movies to foreign ones.

This marketing approach has been developed to good effect in America, where films such as Bill Forsyth's *Gregory's Girl* had been turned into successes. Thorn-EMI's Classics was not tied to using the company's cinema circuit for its release, but was free to place its films wherever suitable. Its first release was *Ziggy Stardust and the Spiders from Mars*, a film of a concert given by David Bowie in his early flash and glitter days.

At the same time, the company formulated new policies to spread releases throughout the year rather than concentrating on school holidays, keeping the price of seats at 1983 levels (except when showing a blockbuster) and setting regular performance times at the company's ABC cinemas.

Philip Nugus, Thorn-EMI Screen Entertainments's new director of marketing, who had previously worked in the company's video division, commissioned some market research into the nation's cinema-going. According to the report, the public went to the cinema to see a particular film and were not deterred by the condition of the building or enticed by its amenities. But few, no more than 17 out of every 100 of the 15- to 24-year-olds who make up at least half of the audiences, knew what films were showing. If they were unable to see the film they wanted, very few considered going to see some other film. Instead, they preferred to visit a pub. As a result of the survey, Nugus decided that more should be spent on advertising films, particularly on television. As a comparison, breweries spent £27.5 million in 1983 on advertising whereas the film industry spent £5.4 million or £1.5 million *less* than it spent six years ago.

It is too early to know what effect Thorn-EMI's more vigorous approach will have. Certainly these days, it is no longer difficult for a film of commercial potential to find its way into one of the two major cinema chains. There are so few films around that neither can afford to pick and choose as they did in the past. They fall with joy on any film that promises to make money.

But the problem remains that, of the two most influential companies in the British film industry, only one, Thorn-EMI, is showing any confidence in actually making films and even their attitude is tempered with caution.

4 The Sinking of Lord Grade

Lew Grade's ITC

> 'The film industry is here to stay and a good film
> will always attract an audience into the cinema.'
>
> Lord Grade, Cannes 1974

Spikings's efforts to raise EMI to the level of a major American studio
pale into insignificance against Lord Grade's attempt to storm Hollywood. His progress had the tragic inevitability of a slow motion rerun
of the Charge of The Light Brigade. It was magnificent, but it was not
film making. The classic trajectory of a tragic hero was to be his,
beginning with overweening pride and a challenge to the gods and
ending in humiliation and total disaster.

Lord Grade – Lew to his friends, Low Greed to readers of the
magazine *Private Eye* – looks like a child's drawing of a film mogul: a
short, heavily built man, light on his feet, who is usually preceded by a
foot-long cigar. His rise from Charleston dancer to one of the most
powerful men in British showbusiness is a story that has often been
told, many times by himself. It is possible that he always nurtured
ambitions to be a film producer for all his involvement in television as
one of the showbusiness triumvirate – the others were Prince Littler
and Val Parnell – who controlled Associated Television (ATV), one of
the first commercial television stations, broadcasting to the Midlands
during the week and to London at weekends.

Grade's particular sphere of activity was ITC, an ATV subsidiary
concerned with the production of television series. In 1959, Val
Parnell described ITC in grandiose terms that anticipated Grade's
aspirations. ITC would provide, said Parnell, 'opportunities for co-
operation in the production and distribution of television film which
will be of direct benefit to Britain and the United States, and through
world-wide distribution will foster the growth and maturity of international television. London can become a second and perhaps more
lasting Hollywood.'

Over the years Grade became the favourite target of those who
objected to commercial television. They disliked the transatlantic
flavour of the television series he made. His most successful local
programme, the soap opera *Crossroads*, became the main target of

obloquy, the symbol of all that was wrong with a broadcasting system based on appealing to the greatest possible audience. There is a story that one ATV producer, in charge of a successful and serious programme, asked for an opportunity to work in light entertainment. 'Let me do a leg show,' he said. 'I can do other things besides culture.' 'Culture?' came the reply. 'Look at the ratings. You haven't got culture. You've got *success*.'

Success was what Grade sought, and he was not finding it in television. In 1967, ATV lost its London outlet at the weekends. In the reorganisation of franchises in 1982, it became no more than a partner in a new company, Central Television, serving the Midlands.

As his position in television was eroded, so Grade turned more to films as an outlet for his immense energy and his exceptionally shrewd commercial instincts, not least of which was his seemingly infallible knowledge of what the public wanted. In this he resembled the first Hollywood film moguls: he identified with the mass audience; he liked what they liked. He was also approaching 70, an age he reached in December, 1976, when, according to the rules of the Independent Broadcasting Authority, he would have to give up his chairmanship of ATV.

Grade had always made his television series with one eye on transatlantic sales. ATV's *The Avengers*, a slick and amusing action series featuring an imperturbable bowler-hatted private eye and his leatherclad female assistant, still enjoys a cult following on American television. *The Saint* was the first British-made series to be shown on an American network, providing Roger Moore with the basis of his image as a suave secret agent that he was to perfect in the *James Bond* films. But it was becoming harder to sell television series around the world. On the other hand, television retained its insatiable appetite for films. What could have been more natural for Grade than to transfer his expertise from the small to the larger screen?

From the beginning, he was determined to conquer the American market. Like Rank and Korda before him, he wanted success on a grand scale. His company, which was to incorporate several subsidiary production outfits, changed its name from Associated Television Corporation to Associated Communication Corporation in 1978. Grade admitted to wanting to become the biggest film producer in the world. And for a while, in terms of quantity, he was.

His instincts cannot be faulted. Other foreign entrepreneurs have managed to establish themselves in America. Alexander Salkind and his son, Ilya, have succeeded triumphantly in overcoming many difficulties, and using British studios and technicians to do so. Alexander, a Russian-born financial genius, was a less than popular figure for many years. Indeed, whereas most films finish with a party for everyone involved, his still seem to end in a flurry of law-suits. The Salkinds became successful producers with *The Three Musketeers* in 1973, directed with wit and gusto by Richard Lester. Their formula was the same as that tried by Grade later and others before: a familiar subject that allowed scope for glamorous settings and costumes and plenty of stars, some in small roles to keep the costs down (although they were to pay Marlon Brando £3 million for a brief appearance in one movie).

The Salkind's cleverest ploy was to get another full-length film, *The Four Musketeers*, out of the material Lester shot so that they had two features almost for the price of one. Almost, because some of the actors sued for breach of contract, arguing that they had been paid to appear in only one film.

Both films were successful, although the technique did not always work. *The Prince and the Pauper* (1977), directed by Richard Fleischer in Hungary, where costs were even lower than in Britain, was a flop. But by then the Salkinds had bought the rights to the all-American hero Superman and had begun work on a series of glossy adventure films that still continues to draw large audiences and swell their bank balance.

In a different way, the two Israeli film makers Menahem Golan and Yoram Globus have prospered by making low-budget films that mixed sex and comedy or sex and violence, the lowest common denominators of the teenage audiences who are the most enthusiastic cinema-goers. Their *Lemon Popsicle*, *Hot Bubblegum* and *Private Popsicle* are among the crassest films ever made. They have brought no prestige to their makers, but plenty of profits.

There seemed no reason why Grade should not have been able to emulate one or other of these producers. He had the money and the ambition and was not inhibited by notions of good taste.

In 1974 he began what became, for a few years, an annual ritual at the Cannes Film Festival: the announcement of an enormous expenditure on feature films. The first year, he said that he would make at least six films in the coming year. The next year, he announced he would be making ten features. In 1976, he announced plans to produce thirty films by 1980.

In 1977, he was talking of spending $125 million; in 1978 the figure was $120 million. In 1980, a year before the end, he announced that he would be making 18 films, again at a cost of $120 million. Nor was this the usual fantasy that passes for production plans at Cannes. He did in fact make more than 80 films in six years, an achievement that would have been greater had the total included a reasonable number of successes.

Grade's pre-eminent ability was as a salesman. His method of selling his movies was the same as he had used for selling television series: they were pre-sold around the world and the money garnered in this way was used to make the film.

Success depended in the first instance on his salesmanship, which was virtually irresistible. As Shirley MacLaine was to write, with some bitterness about her disastrous television series *Shirley's World*, which she had made at Grade's persuasion, 'Give him a captive audience and he can sell anything.' But continuing success also depended on Grade's ability to deliver the goods. It is one thing to talk up a product, it is another to make sure it matches the enthusiastic description. And it was here that Grade failed.

His approach was that of the Hollywood tycoons: one big hit a year is all you need to more than cover your losses on your less successful movies. He had little to lose anyway, since the costs of the failures had been covered by selling them in advance. With a production schedule of a dozen or more films a year, it seemed impossible that he could fail to make at least one hit. But he achieved the impossible with ease.

He depended upon stars and grandiose projects, since you cannot interest a distributor in giving you money for a cheap film with unfamiliar actors. Grade's first production pre-dated his grander plans, for in 1971 he backed *Desperate Characters* starring Shirley Maclaine, one of the few films with claims to seriousness that he ever made.

'It's such a big hit you wouldn't believe it,' he told Hunter Davies, biographer of the Grade Family, after the film's first American preview. 'Every distribution company wants it. I was going to distribute it myself . . . Doing it myself, we could gross two million dollars. I've just been offered a deal which guarantees four to six million.' The film was not a commercial success.

What, in retrospect, is astonishing is this failure to come up with a hit. He played safe by filming best-selling books, such as Jack Higgins's thriller of a Nazi spy, *The Eagle Has Landed* (1976), and Ira Levin's thriller of Nazi survivors *The Boys from Brazil* (1978). Or he remade past classics, such as *All Quiet on the Western Front* (1979), *Les Misérables* (1978), *The Man in the Iron Mask* (1974), *Great Expectations* (1974) and *A Tale of Two Cities* (1980). The latter were made as co-productions intended for showing on television in America and in cinemas elsewhere and must have covered their costs.

He hired good directors and star actors and still he failed to stir audiences. *The Medusa Touch* (1978) is a typical example of Grade's style. It was a co-production to cut down on risk. It had a script by John Briley, the writer who did the final screenplay for *Gandhi*; it was directed by Jack Gold and the cast was headed by Richard Burton, Lee Remick and Lino Ventura, a durable Italian star; in support were some of Britain's best character actors: Harry Andrews, Alan Badel, Jeremy Brett, Michael Hordern and Gordon Jackson. *The Medusa*

Touch was a psychological horror story about a writer who discovers that he can destroy things by thinking about them. As a subject, it recalled Brian de Palma's *Carrie* of two years earlier, about a young girl who takes revenge on those who humiliate her.

But *Carrie* was a success because it built up a tension before releasing it in a sensational and bloody climax of destruction. It was an exceptionally efficient shocker and those entertained by such films flocked to it. *The Medusa Touch* was more inhibited, less prepared to transgress good taste and it allowed Burton to wallow in an exceptionally windy and melodramatic performance as the writer at first tortured by his powers and then revelling in them. Both films depended for their impact on special effects. But the climax of *The Medusa Touch* was no more than a few bishops being crushed beneath falling masonry in Westminster Abbey, a scene unlikely to cause much of a frisson unless you happened to be an ecclesiastic.

The film's structure, too, dulled the suspense, since much of it was flashback – Burton confessing his destructive past to a psychologist – with the result that his experiences, unlike those of Carrie, lacked immediacy.

There was a similar ending to both films, with the return to life of the dead. In *Carrie*, an arm suddenly emerges from a newly-dug grave. In *The Medusa Touch*, a machine registering Burton's brain waves suddenly resumes a regular pattern after his life-support system is switched off. There is no escaping the power of the first image and the dullness of the second. Grade's films rarely rose above mediocrity.

Grade made films in every popular style. He revived the gallant masked cowboy in *The Legend of the Lone Ranger* (1981), no doubt hoping to duplicate the success of *Superman*. But the director made the fatal mistake of concentrating for much of the film's length on the cowboy's youth, before he got to galloping about on a white horse to the William Tell overture, shouting 'Hi ho, Silver!', which was what audiences wanted to see.

Grade tried Foreign Legion films: *March and Die* (1976); horror: *The Monster Club* (1981); fantasy: *Hawk The Slayer* (1980); and spin-offs from television: *Rising Damp* (1979). Some films, such as *Hard Country* (1980), which was set in Texas, were bad enough never to be released in Britain except on video cassette.

Grade's ability to anticipate public taste seemed to have deserted him. In 1980 a row over a thriller *The Long Good Friday* did little to enhance his reputation. Grade had set up a subsidiary company, Black Lion, to make low-budget features and films for television. Its first venture had been a movie of *Porridge*, a situation comedy set in prison and starring Ronnie Barker which had been originated by the BBC, whose charter prevents it from making cinema films. It had cost £650,000 and took around $2.5 million at the box office.

Barry Hanson, the producer of *The Long Good Friday* had made two previous films for Black Lion, *Very Like A Whale* (1980) and *Bloody Kids* (1979), which had both been screened by ATV. In this case, Hanson and the film's director, John Mackenzie, thought they were making a film for cinema release. But when it was delivered to Grade, he decided to cut some of the violence and screen it on television. From his point of view, a television showing had financial advantages over a cinema release for a film that, at a cost of more than £1.2 million, had gone over its original budget. A television showing would mean that two thirds of its costs could be written off against the advertising revenue levy paid by the commercial television companies. Showing a movie in a cinema would involve a greater outlay, in providing prints of the film and in advertising, which can cost as much as the film itself, and a much slower return on the original investment.

Hanson and Mackenzie fought to prevent the mutilation of their film and finally won. HandMade Films, created to make *Monty Python's Life of Brian*, bought the rights to it and put it out on release. Ironically, *The Long Good Friday* is probably the best film that Grade made, a tense and exciting thriller notable for the aggressive acting of Bob Hoskins as an East End gang boss who finds himself out of his depth dealing with the IRA.

It showed up Grade's other films for what they were, rootless productions of no relevance to any nation, lacking purpose or passion.

Grade's ambitions went beyond making films, for he realised that a film producer's success is dependent upon distributors and exhibitors. A film has to be seen as well as made. In 1975, he made a co-production deal with an American cinema circuit, General Cinema Corporation, that would guarantee an American release for the films they made together, an arrangement that lasted for two years until Grade acquired a production base in Los Angeles and also, with EMI, which was headed by Grade's brother Lord Delfont, set up an American distribution company, Associated Film Distribution. The partnership was necessary because Grade on his own was not making sufficient films to supply a distributor.

In Britain, Grade set up his own distribution company and, in 1979, paid £12 million for the Classic Cinema circuit, which was the third largest in the country although for the most part consisting of small, somewhat run down buildings away from the city centres and with a reputation for showing semi-pornographic and horror movies. But the purchase gave him a guaranteed outlet for his films and was a step to challenging the duopoly of EMI and Rank. Like them, he had achieved an integration of production, distribution and exhibition of his movies.

Grade once warned that if he found it difficult to get a proper release for his films in North America, he would buy cinemas there, too. The extra expenditure, though, began to drain his resources, since the sheer size of America makes distribution there a massive undertaking, involving heavy advertising costs. The only way such an operation could possibly pay was by a succession of hit movies. But neither he nor EMI was able to deliver the sort of film that had crowds rushing the box office.

Grade's last spectacular disaster was *Raise The Titanic* (1981), a film to which he had committed himself wholeheartedly, despite the reluctance of other production companies to become involved. He had decided to put up the considerable finance himself. The film, based on a successful novel, was the story of a group of Americans who manage to bring the wreck of the Titanic to the surface, despite the efforts of the dastardly Russians to prevent them.

The film soon ran into problems involving underwater photography and attempts to re-create, in a convincing manner, the huge, sunken liner and its raising. The film's cost rose alarmingly until it reached more than $35 million.

On its release, it was a resounding flop. *Raise The Titanic* isn't actually a bad film, but it is a very boring one. As with many of Grade's films, there is no narrative thrust. Characters' love affairs are sketched in briefly at the beginning of the film and then ignored. The Russians never provide much of a threat so the suspense is limited to whether the group will succeed in raising the liner and that is limited to a great many murky underwater shots. There is little evidence of the vast expenditure on the screen and the raising of the liner looks what it is, the filming of models. Grade possibly damaged the movie's prospects before it opened by posing next to a small-scale model of the Titanic. While audiences may suspend their disbelief in the cinemas, they rarely like to be reminded of the trickery involved in filming.

But Grade himself had the final word on the film. 'Raise the Titanic?' he said. 'It would have been cheaper to have lowered the Atlantic.' By this point, he was in deep trouble. It was not merely the cost of the film that was pulling him under, but the expenses of maintaining his distribution set-up. In 1980, ACC admitted that it had made substantial losses on its films and its record division. A year later, it announced losses of £13 million. Its music publishing division and the Classic cinema chain were put up for sale.

The company was not only losing money, it was in debt. Grade's immediate answer to his problems was to sell off some assets to raise cash. He sold three feature films to Universal. Two of them, *On Golden Pond* and *The Dark Crystal* (the third was *Sophie's Choice* starring Meryl Streep) turned out to be by far the most critically and commercially successful of all the films that Grade had produced. It is conceivable that had the pair been available for release earlier, they might have saved Grade from the loss of his company and his position that swiftly followed.

On Golden Pond made the most of its conjunction of fiction and reality, casting Henry Fonda and Katharine Hepburn as two old codgers facing the prospect of death and Jane Fonda as a rebellious daughter who makes a final peace with her father. Its mix of nostalgia and sentimentality was an enormous hit, gaining for Fonda an Oscar just before his death.

The Dark Crystal was the third film for Grade made by Jim Henson, the talented American puppeteer of the Muppets. It was Grade who had seen the potential of the Muppets, who appeared on the children's television show, *Sesame Street*. He had brought Henson and his colleagues to Britain and created *The Muppet Show*, a fast-moving entertainment, mocking some aspects of variety while indulging in showbusiness sentimentality, that became a favourite with viewers around the world and created a profitable subsidiary industry in merchandising records, books and toys.

In the circumstances, a feature film was inevitable and *The Muppet Movie* (1979) had some of the hectic pace and fun of the television programmes, although it did not sustain it so well. A sequel, *The Great Muppet Caper* (1980) was far less successful in mixing puppets and actors.

Henson's *The Dark Crystal* (1982) was, with a budget of $25 million, a much more expensive and ambitious work, an attempt to create a coherent fantasy world, an alien universe peopled by odd and often grotesque creatures. Brian Froud, an English artist with a taste for drawing goblins, was brought in as 'conceptual designer' and Alan Garner, one of the finest British writers for children, was hired to help with the script.

The result was a compelling fantasy, full of fascinating detail, of tiny and strange creatures moving on the periphery of one's vision. The film was at its most successful in suggesting horror: the decaying master-race the Skeksis, huge upright lizards, and their stag-beetle like soldiers, the Garthim, were especially effective. But it was handicapped by its story, which followed the usual fairytale formula of a boy and girl journeying from innocence to experience, from ordinary life to heroic behaviour. While the girl was allowed to display her heroism, the boy remained far more feeble. And the final struggle between good and evil was resolved by its representatives – the saintly Urru and the vile Skeksis – combining into one creature, which seemed, in its context, a metaphysical cop-out.

Not even the saintly Urru could have saved Lord Grade from shareholders angry at the company's large expenditure and small returns from films. Some put the total loss ACC had made as high as

$100 million. The failure of *Raise The Titanic* gave his critics the opportunity they needed.

To appease them, Grade said that he would close down his American distribution company and revert to making films only for which all the finance had been raised in advance. After a fierce boardroom battle, ACC was taken over by an Australian businessman, Robert Holmes a'Court, and Grade left the company.

Grade has continued to work, becoming chairman and chief executive of Embassy Communications International, the London end of an American company with interests in film and television, which plans to make four or five films a year in Britain.

He was to be seen in Cannes in May 1983 as ebullient as ever, announcing a $100 million programme of productions which included a $20 million film, *The Chinese Bandit*, to be produced by EMI Films's former chief executive, Barry Spikings.

Grade's attempt to establish a film production company to rival the major American studios is unlikely ever to be repeated in Britain. The risks are too high. Even if there were a producer ambitious enough to want to try, the money is not available. Grade had behind him the resources of a rich television company (ATV had made profits of more than £6 million in 1979). Nor are there British producers who want to make $30 million movies; they prefer smaller, indigenous films that reflect the social circumstances around them. To them, Lord Grade is an anachronism rather than an exemplar, a figure from the past and not a part of the future.

The Classic cinema chain was bought by The Cannon Group, run by the Israeli film makers Golan and Globus, who immediately began working enthusiastically to raise the morale of their staff and improve the amenities of the cinemas. They have since set up a new company Cannon-Gala – by acquiring Rive Gala, a long-established distributor and exhibitor – to distribute and show in a few art-house cinemas some of the best foreign films by such directors as Claude Lelouch, Jacques Rivette and Federico Fellini.

Britain is merely a small part of a world-wide expansion by Golan and Globus who are film producers with a bias to low-budget sex and sensation. But they are, at least, improving the conditions of the cinemas they own. At their annual convention in November 1983, the managing director of the Cannon Classics, Barry Jenkins, said that in the previous twelve months there had been a 16 per cent increase in business.

'It is not enough to show good films,' he said. 'We must also make the cinemas attractive, clean and inviting, with bars and good food, beautiful lavatories and rest rooms, a friendly and welcoming staff and an atmosphere which is warm and inviting.'

He was also planning to introduce late night shows, starting around

9 pm, to attract a young audience and to instal better equipment in the theatres. If the group can combine all that with showing good films, then possibly they will attain their aim of 'bringing back the missing millions who have lost the habit of going to the cinema each week'.

5 Carry On Hammering

Hammer Horrors and 'Carry On' Films

'To me, the natural development, if we hadn't had this sudden unhealthy interest in sex, would have been to make films more and more horrifying.'

Michael Carreras, 1970

There always have been a few British producers and directors who have worked successfully within strictly defined genres. Film making at this level becomes a production-line process, with one movie hardly distinguishable from the next. The process usually begins with a film that is a hit, often an unexpected one. Then all that the producer or director need do is to try to repeat the process, mixing the same ingredients, adding a slight variation so that the audience can imagine that they are experiencing something different, but not too different.

From MGM musicals to *Lassie* to *James Bond* to *Jaws* to *Star Wars* to *Halloween*, Hollywood has perfected the process, relying on it now to a greater extent than ever, since independent producers, who need to succeed to survive, have a greater desire to play safe than the studios they replaced, whose old mass-production methods ironically allowed more room for individual endeavour, limited though it still was.

In postwar Britain one studio, Hammer Films, and one producer, Peter Rogers, provided a regular trickle of similar films that gave the country an international reputation for two distinct kinds of movie: cheap and cheerful, in the case of Rogers's *Carry On* films; gaudy and gruesome (and hardly more expensive) from Hammer.

Neither Hammer's horrors, nor Rogers's romps attained the heights of film making. They were closer to the older tradition of 'quota quickies', when British film makers shot cheap movies as fast as possible (no doubt to put them out of their misery) in order to meet the regulations that cinemas should show a certain percentage of British films. But both demonstrated that a low-budget movie need not necessarily be bad. And both, in their ways, celebrated a particular British tradition.

Both ventures faltered in the 1970s, which, ironically, was precisely when horror films and corny, smutty comedies from other sources came to enjoy an unprecedented popularity that continues to this day.

Young audiences around the world paid a great deal of money to watch madmen with knives slice up teenage girls, usually just after the girls had indulged in some sexual activity. Crass and prurient comedies centering around adolescents discovering sex were surprisingly successful.

None of these recent films were quite what Hammer or Rogers had been doing; but they were near enough in style and content for the British failure to exploit a market that they had helped create seem inexplicable.

Hammer, run by Sir James Carreras and, later, by his son Michael, had been set up in 1947 and, after its first year, maintained an average of six films a year, a steady procession of low-budget movies, including several series based on popular figures from long-running BBC radio programmes: *Dick Barton – Special Agent*, *P.C. 49* and *The Man in Black*.

Then, in 1955, came *The Quatermass Experiment*, their first film to appeal to audiences outside Britain. Nigel Kneale adapted the script of his television serial about a scientist who deliquesces into a throbbing blob of alien matter. It was one of the first scientist-into-blob movies that became popular during the late 1950s.

Audiences then hated extra-terrestrials and preferred being horrified by aliens rather than by chainsaw-wielding humans.

Hammer made a sequel, *Quatermass II*, and *X the Unknown*, an unofficial sequel featuring a slurping, semi-liquid monster which fed on radiation. (Behind most of the horror films of the time lay the fear of nuclear holocaust.)

With their reliance on secondhand inspiration, and their realisation that horror was suddenly profitable, Hammer naturally turned to reviving those earlier examples of English Gothic, *Frankenstein* and *Dracula*. The success of their two remakes, in 1957 and 1958, surprised them. One result was that two actors, Christopher Lee and Peter Cushing, were both provided with a career that was to last almost a lifetime of typecasting.

Both movies were directed by Terence Fisher (born 1904), a journeyman director whose film career had begun more than 20 years earlier. Fisher, a modest craftsman, was astonished in later years when Hammer's horrors, originally derided by critics, achieved a cult status among younger cineastes.

Five more Frankenstein films, five more Draculas as well as another Quatermass and revivals of vampires, wolfmen, mummies, zombies and Dr Jekyll and Mr Hyde had given Hammer continuing profits so that as the 1960s ended and the 1970s began, it seemed they were to become a greater power in British films.

In 1970, Hammer signed a production deal with EMI to produce three films a year. The contract was renewable at the end of each year. Sir James, who was occasionally known as 'The Knight of Horror' in Wardour Street, felt it need never run out. They also had a co-production deal with AIP, an American company employing the genius of producer-director Roger Corman and specialising in horror and motorcycle films for the teenage market. It provided an opportunity to break into the lucrative US market, something that Hammer had failed to achieve.

Hammer had nine films in production, their highest-ever total. 'In America, they are all determined that it is going to be the summer of the double horror picture,' said Sir James at the time. 'They're sure the kids are going to go berserk for this type of film.'

Not all Hammer's films were intended for the international market. They also had a line in British comedies, usually based on television series such as *The Army Game* and *On The Buses*. But Sir James was less enthusiastic about them. 'You can't sell a British comedy anywhere except in England,' he said. 'We make pictures to sell all over the world and if they don't measure up to that, we throw the script in the wastepaper basket. You spend just as much money on a British comedy as you do on the type of adventure-horror picture that we do. What market have you got when you've completed it? This one, and a little bit of Australia and New Zealand. If it doesn't really hit, you're on to a big, big loss. With our films, 80 per cent of our revenue comes from overseas. We can't compete with Peter Rogers.'

Hammer films were tightly budgeted. The 20 per cent of the film's revenue that came from Britain – if the film did the expected business – was enough to cover the production costs when the Eady Levy was added to it. It could take some time to recover these costs, but the films continued to play for years in various double bills. 'You can do every possible permutation,' said Sir James. 'A Dracula with a Frankenstein, a Frankenstein with a Mummy, then a Dracula with a Dracula. Towns like Barrow have played Draculas 13 times. I don't know why.'

Sir James, a toothy, enthusiastic man whose brilliance was in selling, had developed an unusual approach to making movies. He had created a valuable brand image. The words 'A Hammer Production' on a film poster were almost enough on their own to draw an audience, who knew what it could expect: lush colour, thrills tinged with sex, sudden shocks in old-fashioned settings.

'We keep very much in touch with our exhibitors. When a Hammer picture comes out, they don't ask what it's about; they just book it,' said Sir James.

In order not to disappoint exhibitors, the advertising campaign for a Hammer movie was considered first, sometimes before the script was written. If the theme of the film did not result in a striking poster, if it could not provide an enticing slogan – 'Drink A Pint Of Blood A Day' was the message for *Taste The Blood of Dracula* – then the project was scrapped. It was, literally, back to the drawing board.

America was the one market Hammer failed to penetrate. Their biggest overseas successes came from Roman Catholic countries such as Italy and Spain. 'In our pictures, the cross wins every time,' said Sir James. 'When the monster is defeated by the cross, in Catholic countries the audience stand up and cheer. All Roman Catholic countries are wonderful for business.'

Michael Carreras, less outgoing than his father, thought that Americans – 'they're such an insular people' – would only watch films about America. 'American horror films are very much tongue in cheek. I've never seen anything remotely real in an AIP picture. Our Gothic horrors have the quality of realism. All we can do is make the Hammer-type of horror, with all the blood and guts you need.'

Hammer had discovered by trial and error what type of horror appealed to their audiences. Dracula was the most popular figure, followed by Frankenstein and his monster and The Mummy. Their attempt to revive the werewolf in *The Curse of the Werewolf* (1960), starring Oliver Reed in the title role, had been one of their few outright failures. 'The trouble is, what do you do with a werewolf?' said Michael Carreras. 'He either looks like Dracula with much more hair or you put him on all fours and he turns into a yapping dog, which has its own problems.'

When Hammer began making horror films, they used to shoot differing sequences for different markets. The Japanese version would have more blood and gore than the British. For Europe, there would be an occasional naked girl. But by the 1970s, the situation had changed. The same version, with the occasional naked girl and more explicit horror than their earlier movies, was shown all around the world.

The Vampire Lovers (1970), directed by Roy Ward Baker, added humour as well as a lesbian eroticism to the usual mixture. 'Boobs all over the place', said Michael Carreras, not quite approving of the trend. A similar approach informed *Lust of the Vampire* (1971), directed by Jimmy Sangster, which also featured female vampires caressing young girls before sinking their fangs in their necks.

'One thing we have learned is that Dracula, Frankenstein or The Mummy is sacred and the audience don't like it if you interfere with them,' said Carreras. 'We intend to go right back in style to our original films. We made one very big mistake by doing a Jekyll and Hyde film and changing the whole premise. It was a good film and Wolf Mankowitz did a good script. But the public didn't like it because it wasn't what they wanted. We'd interfered with the original. You have to be careful.' In Mankowitz's version, *The Two Faces of Dr*

Jekyll (1960), directed by Terence Fisher, the doctor changed not into an evil monster but into a handsome man-about-town.

Despite Carreras's insistence on a return to tradition, Hammer's last version of Robert Louis Stevenson's story was *Dr. Jekyll and Sister Hyde* (1971), in which the good doctor's drug-taking habits turn him into a woman.

These variations on familiar themes indicate that a certain desperation was beginning to surface. There are, after all, limits to what one can do with a monster. The suggestion of mockery that crept into the later Hammer films was reminiscent of what had happened to the monsters of Universal's original cycle of horror movies in the 1940s when Frankenstein's monster, the Wolf Man, Dracula, Dr Jekyll and Mr Hyde and the rest had ended up as stooges for the comedians Abbot and Costello and the horror tradition had expired in a fit of giggles.

Hammer seemed to be in a similar bind, unable to revitalise the tradition in any other way than by facetiousness. There were other means of frightening audiences, as John Carpenter demonstrated with *Halloween* (1978), a film made with a Hammer-sized budget that went on to take more money at the box office – $40 million at the last count – than any other independently produced film. Carpenter's inspiration was demonstrably Alfred Hitchcock's *Psycho* (1960) and it began a cycle of movies about mad knife-men threatening pretty young girls.

Hammer decided that vampirism offered the best chance of commercial survival. 'There's not much sensual fun, except for very kinky people, in stitching bodies together as Frankenstein does. But vampirism is the number one blood chiller,' said Carreras. 'It's sensual and sexual. We all give our girl friends a good bite on the neck occasionally. In our first *Dracula*, the victim didn't scream and rush round the room; she lay back on the bed and waited for him in anticipation.'

Carreras thought, correctly as it turned out, that horror films would, and should, become more violent and was disturbed by the increasing amount of sexuality in films. 'To me, the natural development – if we hadn't had this sudden unhealthy interest in sex – would have been to make films more and more horrifying, until you really had horrifying horror films,' he said. 'There's always a texture of unreality about horror films, the feeling that they happen in a land of fantasy: the castle on the hill, the little village underneath. In our horror films, the circumstances are unreal. Once you enter that fantasy world, you can go quite far in scenes of violence without frightening people lastingly, beyond the cinema doors. I don't like the motorcycle films or films of teenage violence, because they involve realism – real violence that can be done outside the cinema.'

He wanted a return to the Gothic qualities of Hammer's earlier horror films and anticipated a glorious future. 'We've a lot more new blood around, and I mean that in the nicest way,' he said. Indeed, Peter Sasdy, a director from television making his first feature film, brought a florid conviction to *Taste The Blood of Dracula* (1970), set in Victorian England, and *Hands of the Ripper* (1971).

But Hammer's success had brought rivals. Amicus, a company run by Max J. Rosenberg and Milton Subotsky, an American producer resident in Britain and specialising in low-budget horror, used directors who had worked for Hammer, including Freddie Francis and Roy Ward Baker, to make films usually containing four stories linked together and aimed at an identical audience.

Amicus's *Madhouse* (1974), a co-production with AIP, was an in-bred but amusing movie about a star of horror movies involved in a series of actual and horrific murders, which starred Vincent Price and Peter Cushing playing their public personas with great relish.

Freddie Francis (born 1917), a notable cinematographer, not only worked for Hammer and Amicus but directed a series of low-budget horrors for Tyburn Films, produced by his son Kevin. These also capitalised on Hammer's style and stars. *The Ghoul* (1975) starred Peter Cushing and Veronica Carlson, both Hammer habitues. AIP, too, began to make films in a similar vein, including *Count Yorga, Vampire* (1970) and *The Return of Count Yorga* (1972). Italian and Spanish directors were also satisfying their audiences' love of the triumph of the cross and affecting Hammer's sales in Roman Catholic countries. Audiences were turning to another type of violent, action movie: martial arts adventures, made in Hong Kong, which made Bruce Lee briefly a star.

Carreras tried an amalgam of the two genres, in partnership with Run Run Shaw, the dominant figure in Hong Kong's thriving movie world. *The Legend of the Seven Golden Vampires* (1974) pitted Hammer regulars Peter Cushing, as Dracula's old adversary Professor Van Helsing, and the decorative Julie Ege against a Chinese monk who becomes possessed by the spirit of a vampire. The result was an uneasy mishmash of styles. The second, *Shatter* (1974), was a straight-forward thriller directed by Carreras himself, but no more successful in combining kung-fu with an interesting narrative. But just as Carreras had been the first to make Westerns in Spain, thus starting a minor industry, so others have followed his Easterns in Hong Kong with commercially successful thrillers using the exotic skills of the martial arts.

Carreras tried one further co-production, this time with a West German company, to make *To The Devil A Daughter* (1976), directed by Peter Sykes and based on one of Denis Wheatley's stories of black magic. Christopher Lee starred, together with Richard Widmark and the cast also included Nastassja Kinski.

The result was overblown and obscure. It was to be the last movie in the Hammer style. The company survives, making horror movies for television but with little of its original panache, under two of its former employees, Roy Skeggs and Brian Lawrence.

A similar fate has overtaken Peter Rogers's *Carry On* series, which began in 1958 with *Carry On Sergeant*, based on *The Bully Boys*, a farce by R. F. Delderfield about a sergeant who bets that he can turn his new recruits into a squad of perfectly drilled soldiers. With National Service still in force and the Second World War a not too distant memory, comedies of service life were still enjoying popularity. Among the cast were Kenneth Connor, Charles Hawtrey, Kenneth Williams and Shirley Eaton. It was more serious than its successors, attempting a realism amid the comedy, an expression of genuine emotions, which was not present in the later films. The film, which cost no more than £72,000 to make, easily covered its costs so that Rogers decided to apply the formula to some other institutions and made *Carry On Nurse*, using the same director and some of the same cast. That film was a much greater success, even making money in America. A series had begun. Gerald Thomas directed them all, and when the scriptwriter, Norman Hudis, went to Hollywood after the first six he was replaced by Talbot Rothwell.

The cast, like the jokes, was almost unvarying. Connor, Hawtrey and Williams were joined by Sid James, Joan Sims and Hattie Jacques, with other familiar comic actors joining in from time to time. *That's Carry On* (1978), a compilation film of some of the funnier moments from the series, emphasised how little the films changed over the years – apart from the introduction of colour from 1962 – and how interchangeable the jokes and routines were.

The characters, too, remained unchanging, whether the film was set in ancient Egypt, Tudor England or India. There was no attempt to create a realistic period atmosphere, as Monty Python were to manage in their comedy films. The films' roots, it was clear, were in pantomime, another unvarying entertainment whatever its ostensible setting.

It was this unreality that usually gave the jokes their point and the humour its force. The fun emerged from a group of slightly anarchic comedians at loose in a stuffy world, the same sort of incongruity that had provided the amusement in the Marx Brothers' movies.

The difference was the difference between the American vaudeville tradition and the English music-hall, with its delight in puns, preferably with a sexual innuendo, and bawdy jokes. The humour was blue and the jokes were often familiar.

Carry On Emmanuelle (1978), a send-up of soft-core pornography was the first of the series to receive an 'AA' certificate, although a few frames showing a naked breast had been removed from the earlier *Carry On England* (1976) in order for it to qualify for an 'A' certificate.

The regularity with which the films appeared slowed down in the mid-1970s. Until then, *Carry On* films had been made at the rate of two a year. Two had appeared in 1971, *Carry On At Your Convenience*, set in a factory making lavatories, and *Carry On Henry*, which mocked the television series (and film) on the life of Henry VIII. Its best joke was in the casting of Sid James as Henry, playing his usual fly lecher, a slight variation on the wartime spiv.

Carry On Abroad (1972) made fun of package holidays in Spain, *Carry On Matron* (1972) returned to the hospital that always provided the best setting for the series, *Carry On Girls* (1973) used a beauty contest, *Carry On Dick* (1974) was based on highwayman Dick Turpin, and *Carry On Behind* (1975) was set in a nudist camp.

Rogers seemed to have exhausted institutional humour, which gave the first films a slightly subversive air, and, by the 1970s, was happy to hang a series of routines on any convenient peg. Dick Turpin, for instance, seems to have been chosen as a subject because of the opportunities it provided for a series of jokes on the highwayman's Christian name. It is a film obsessed with genital japes. One central routine consists of Jack Douglas following men into a urinal in an attempt to identity Dick by a tattoo 'on his diddler', to use the film's phrase.

Many of the films' jokes consisted of nothing more than a mention of sexual activity. In *Carry On Henry*, the King discovers a reluctant Cromwell, played by Kenneth Williams at his campest, wrestling on a bed with his over-eager queen (Joan Sims), who promptly faints. There followed a typical exchange:

> James: 'Why did she faint?'
> Williams: 'Lack of fresh air.'
> James: 'Yes. She hasn't been getting any.'
> Williams: 'That, too.'

Rogers made an attempt to break the formula with *Carry On England* (1976), in which Kenneth Connor was the only familiar actor on view, although he was joined by Windsor Davies, popular through appearances in television situation comedy. It was the least successful of the series.

Kenneth Williams and others returned for *Carry On Emmanuelle* but that, too, came adrift in trying to mix two incompatible genres. *Carry On* films depend for their fun on a primness about sex and not the 'if you've got it, flaunt it' approach of semi-pornography. The humour of *Carry On* films needed a buttoned-up approach to sex and so was increasingly at odds with the attitudes of the time.

Rogers was unable, too, to find suitable substitutes for his ageing cast. It was possible to laugh at Sid James as a randy bachelor in the first of the series when he was 45, but harder to accept him in the same role in his 60s. Death began to remove the regulars: James in 1976 and Hattie Jacques and Peter Butterworth not long after.

It was difficult for Rogers to move successfully into sexier comedies because that ground had already been taken by another series which began with *Confessions of a Window Cleaner* (1974), directed by the veteran Val Guest (born 1911). Robin Askwith, a personable young actor, provided a contemporary variation on the Sid James character which was more appealing to the under-30s who were the cinema's most regular patrons.

The Confessions . . . films looked even cheaper than Rogers's *Carry Ons*, even though he was notorious for paring the budget down to the minimum. *Carry On Emmanuelle* cost more than £320,000 to make, however, and although that was still little, even by the standards of local films, it was more than could be recovered from exhibition in Britain. This, possibly more than the advancing age of its participants and changing social attitudes, is the reason that the series has lost what impetus remained.

It is hard to change a series that depends upon stereotypes for its humour, but the success of other films of low-budget, low-humour type, such as the American-made *Porky's* and *Airplane*, showed there was still an audience for such films. Both acknowledged sex in a way that *Carry On* films did not, although what distinguished *Porky's* was that its cast was mainly teenage.

But while a *Carry On* film would be content to display the fluttering effeminacy of Charles Hawtrey or Kenneth Williams muttering, 'I do feel a little queer', *Airplane* had Peter Graves, indulging in self-parody as a butch pilot, placing his hand on the knee of a young boy while making hearty suggestions.

Although Rogers has announced his intention of making further *Carry On* films, none have been forthcoming since 1978. The series survives on television, in shows that further cannibalise the films to provide a half hour's amusement.

It is hard to believe the series will ever return to the cinema, for even the most recent have acquired a period charm as a type of indigenous film making that is no longer commercially viable.

6 The Old Guard . . .

Anderson, Schlesinger, Reisz, Richardson,
Hitchcock, Neame, titillations and TV spin-offs

'If our films lose their sense of reality, they are
lost. Our small industry cannot compete with the
huge Hollywood machine in its own grounds. Nor
would our audiences wish it to try. British
audiences are very jealous of the reputation of
British films.'

C. A. Lejeune, 1948

The New Wave of the British cinema, which gathered momentum in
the early 1960s, had broken by 1970. In many ways, the movies,
splendid and stirring as they were, had been dimmer reflections of the
greater achievements that had informed theatre and literature, which
responded faster to change in social conditions, notably the rise of a
provincial, or regional, consciousness and the weakening of the
metropolitan control of the arts.

The grammar school-educated graduates of red brick universities
had begun to assert their power. The films had bobbed along in the
wake of John Osborne's *Look Back In Anger*, of Joan Littlewood's
uproarious Theatre Workshop productions, of the novels of Kingsley
Amis, Alan Sillitoe, John Braine and the rest.

Most of the best British films of the period – for example, *Saturday
Night and Sunday Morning* (directed by Karel Reisz), *This Sporting
Life* (directed by Lindsay Anderson), *A Taste of Honey* (directed by
Tony Richardson) – were based on best-selling books or successful
plays. They starred actors, such as Albert Finney, Tom Courtenay,
Peter O'Toole and Vanessa Redgrave, who had made their repu-
tations on the stage.

Tony Richardson and John Osborne became the creative forces
behind Woodfall Films – backed by the financial and entrepreneurial
skills of Harry Saltzman – after the two had worked together on *Look
Back In Anger* at the Royal Court Theatre. Lindsay Anderson, too,
was part of the Court's abrasive group which temporarily banished
gentility from the English stage.

In the 1970s, as the Americans withdrew their support from British films, the industry seemed to have collapsed, although, of course, it had not. It was simply that interesting films were made elsewhere. Actors, directors and talented technicians, from cameramen to special effects experts, kept busy, but they were working on American or foreign-made movies.

Those who had been in the vanguard of British cinema in the 1960s were now taking a less active role. Anderson (born 1923), the great polemicist of the local industry, made *O Lucky Man!* (1972), a lively satire starring Malcolm McDowell as an innocent in a corrupt world. But, apart from *In Celebration* (1974), a version of David Storey's play for American cable television, he turned to stage and television, trying to set up a repertory theatre in the West End.

His next film was not until 1982, the rancorous *Britannia Hospital* (1983), once again starring McDowell. As Peter Nichols had done in his play, *The National Health* (filmed by Jack Gold in 1973), Anderson used a hospital, with its combination of officious bureaucracy and its close concern with matters of life and death, as a metaphor for the nation.

In *O Lucky Man!* enlivened by its soundtrack of excellent songs from Alan Price (who wrote some less engaging ones for the later film), Anderson had managed to score hits on establishment targets, particularly the excesses of science and the idiocies of the judiciary. With *Britannia Hospital*, he allowed rant to replace wit, becoming not only increasingly didactic but less in control of his material. Dilys Powell, the most respected of British critics, was one of the few who admired the movie for its undoubted aggression and the savagery of its humour. But the raggedness of its construction, with its many subplots – a royal visit to the hospital, a clash between unions and management, a mad scientist emulating Frankenstein – and the dullness or hysteria of much of its acting, all combined to blunt its point.

After the success of his first American film, *Midnight Cowboy* (1969), John Schlesinger (born 1926), returned to Britain to make one of the finest films of the time, *Sunday, Bloody Sunday* (1971). Penelope Gilliatt, in a perceptive script about articulate people, allowed her characters scope to express their feelings with wit and elegance. The film's concerns – love and loss among the middle-classes – were familiar enough. But there was the twist of bisexuality: a young sculptor (Murray Head) is loved by a woman (Glenda Jackson) and a man (Peter Finch). As a result, its themes of love and possession were rendered fresh. In contrast to the flamboyance and panache of *Midnight Cowboy*, Schlesinger's direction was unostentatious, concentrating on domestic intimacies. A less gaudy film than some of his earlier British movies – *Billy Liar* (1963), *Darling* (1965) – it was more deeply felt and emotionally engaging.

At which point Schlesinger stopped making movies that were specifically British in setting and theme. He had hoped to be able to film Peter Luke's hit play, *Hadrian VII*, and also Evelyn Waugh's *A Handful of Dust*. Such plans collapsed and he returned to Hollywood to make *The Day of the Locust* (1975) from Nathanael West's classic novel of the film colony, with its small-time actors observing the American dream from the outside. It is a powerful film, of mob violence and individual impotence, which Schlesinger followed with another American film, the thriller *The Marathon Man* (1976), a tense and bloody thriller played against the filth and corruption of big cities.

In both, Schlesinger displayed a passion and intelligence that, in better circumstances, might have added some needed energy to the British industry. Yet these qualities were largely missing from his *Yanks* (1979), set in Britain during the Second World War and dealing with relationships between the locals and American soldiers, characters who hardly escaped the stereotyping of the time: over-dressed, over-sexed and over here.

Schlesinger returned to the States to make *Honky Tonk Freeway* (1982), the least enjoyable film he has so far directed. Financed by Thorn-EMI, the British company whose policy then was to make American films, it was a raucous, expensive, over-inflated picaresque comedy whose theme was one that might have appealed to a director such as Preston Sturges: a small town community who, faced with extinction because it has no exit to a new freeway, decides to rectify the situation. The treatment was nearer the bludgeoning humour of Stanley Kramer's over-emphatic *It's a Mad, Mad, Mad, Mad, World*. *Honky Tonk Freeway* was a commercial disaster. That Schlesinger remains a great director was proved by his small-scale film for BBC-TV, *An Englishman Abroad* (1984), Alan Bennett's play based on an anecdote of the life in Moscow of Guy Burgess, the upper middle-class British spy who defected to the Russians. Deftly and with great economy of means, Schlesinger displayed those qualities lacking in *Honky Tonk Freeway*: a sense of fun and compassion.

Schlesinger was not the only British talent to turn to Hollywood. Karel Reisz (born 1926) was another. Reisz, with Anderson and Richardson, was one of the theorists of the Free Cinema movement of the fifties. He had directed *Saturday Night and Sunday Morning* (1960) and produced Anderson's *This Sporting Life* (1963).

In the 1970s he made two films, both American, one of which was *Dog Soldiers* (1978) probably the best treatment so far of the Vietnamese war and its effect on American consciousness.

Reisz's *The French Lieutenant's Woman* (1983), filmed in Britain, was a dogged attempt to translate to the screen a novel that had defeated many previous directors and scriptwriters. The problem was one of capturing the double-edged tone of John Fowles's novel which veered between Victorian pastiche and a modern analysis of social attitudes of the time. Harold Pinter's solution in his screenplay was to set a film within a film, switching between the lives of the modern actors who were making a film of a Victorian love story and scenes from the film they made, with both stories echoing the same obsessional passion.

For all its gloss and the fine acting of Jeremy Irons and Meryl Streep, especially in their Victorian incarnations, the film was jerkily unsatisfactory, with the rhythms of both stories being constantly upset. Nevertheless, in the context of the British films of the last decade or so, it remains a great achievement.

Tony Richardson (born 1928) was attracted enough to America to move there in the 1980s. One result was *The Border* (1982), with Jack Nicholson as a cop patrolling the dividing line between the USA and Mexico. It showed some sign of the director's talents which had been missing from his two British movies of the 1970s, a dull thriller *Dead Cert* (1973) and *Joseph Andrews* (1977), the nadir – it is to be fervently hoped – of his career. Based on Henry Fielding's novel of the adventures of a guileless footman, it was obviously intended as a sequel to Richardson's *Tom Jones* (1963), the exuberantly comic masterpiece of the British New Wave. It lacked the wit, pace and style that had made the earlier film such a surprising delight.

Perhaps the biggest disappointment of the period was the return to London of Alfred Hitchcock (1899–1980), still as apparently English as ever, to make *Frenzy* (1971). Hitchcock, in search of a suitable subject after the expensive failure of his spy film *Topaz*, had turned to Arthur La Bern's novel *Goodbye Piccadilly, Hello Leicester Square* and engaged as screenwriter Anthony Shaffer, author of a theatrical hit, *Sleuth*, which mocked the whole genre of whodunnits while playing dazzling variations on their themes.

London offered Hitchcock a temporary escape from the pressures and the expense of Hollywood. *Frenzy* cost $2 million to make, half the price of *Topaz*. He used some excellent British actors: Barry Foster, Jon Finch, Alec McCowen, Vivien Merchant and Anna Massey. But halfway through shooting, Hitchcock's wife Alma suffered a stroke and had to be taken back to Los Angeles. After that, his interest in the picture seemed to wane. The result was a curiously old-fashioned film, in which Hitchcock was content to revisit the most famous sites in the city he once knew so well. It was a tourist's view: the locations were those already familiar from hundreds of films and travelogues, the Thames Embankment and Covent Garden's fruit markets and narrow streets. The dialogue, too, sounded as if it had been written around the time of his first talkie, *Blackmail*. Hitchcock's approach was dated, so much so that a glimpse of the Hilton Hotel seemed a gross intrusion into the film. All that was in keeping with modern sensibilities was his treatment of the rape and murder, which was filmed in great detail and with apparent relish. It was as shocking as if Robert Donat had put his hand up Madeleine Carroll's skirt when they were handcuffed together in *The Thirty-Nine Steps*.

The old master's technical skills were still in evidence, but only in a few scenes did the film rise above the ordinary. In Britain, where Hitchcock's reputation had always been high, the movie was not liked. In America, where audiences no doubt expected London to appear Dickensian, it was a greater success and earned its costs back several times over.

The greatest British director from an earlier period of vitality, David Lean (born 1908), finished directing *Ryan's Daughter* in 1970, a story that was not equal to his epic treatment. Apart from an abortive attempt to remake *The Mutiny On The Bounty*, he did not direct again for fourteen years, until *A Passage To India* (1985).

The busiest and most polished exponent of the style of British film that was closer to theatre in its subservience to actors was Lean's former associate, Ronald Neame (born 1911). He began his career as a focus puller. By the age of 22 he was a cameraman and went on to become a director of photography and a producer, working with Lean on a succession of notable films during the 1940s, including *In Which We Serve, Blithe Spirit, Great Expectations* and *Oliver Twist*. From the 1950s he began to direct and soon found that he had to look to America for financial backing. 'I personally would rather make a film in this country than anywhere else in the world,' he told me in 1970. 'But I would have been out of business many years ago had it not been for the tremendous American support and finance. I've made a picture almost every year for as far back as I can remember and certainly for the last ten years it's been American money that has financed it.'

In a discussion on the decline in cinema audiences as long ago as 1951, he had said, 'We must be more daring.' He wanted adventurous films, such as *Henry V, Hamlet*, and *Red Shoes*. 'That way, we will attract a new type of audience to the cinemas, who will come with a keen anticipation that the programme they are going to see will be fresh and different,' he had said.

As a director, he often lacked the daring he was demanding. His career has been marked by some splendid films, such as *The Horse's Mouth* (1959) with Alec Guinness, *Tunes of Glory* (1960) with

Guinness and John Mills, and *The Prime of Miss Jean Brodie* (1968) with Maggie Smith. But they were conventional cinema.

'It's playing safe. And I'm the first to admit it,' he said. 'I've never been fortunate enough to lay my hands on an original screenplay that's been sufficiently satisfactory to me to want to make. The moment I want a script written, the kind of writer I want is too expensive for me to hire until I've got finance from a film company. I'm not very bright at getting money out of people; I find that by going to them with a tried and tested piece of material, I can get from them the finance I need. If I go to the actor or an actress with a tested piece of material, I'm more likely to get them to join me.

'I think all film financing companies have always lacked the courage to come out of a completely different hole and to make something quite new and quite different. They will always, I'm afraid, solidly back the previous success. Those of us who would like to break away are in the end dependent upon people to put up the money for us. I might have three or four subjects I want to film, but I will probably be forced towards the one perhaps I'm least excited in because that would be the one the people putting up the money will think, world-wide, will give them the best chance of getting their money back.

'If I make a film for a million dollars or less – which sounds a lot of money, but isn't – I will be allowed to be pretty experimental. But not all subjects lend themselves to be shot in back streets or up in attics with a hand-held camera. There's still got to be the bigger, more expensive type of films to be made – which, I'm afraid, I've rather got used to making.

'If you have become too used to driving a beautiful six or eight cylinder car that sounds as smooth as smooth as can be, and has automatic gears and power steering, it's pretty hard to go back and drive an old secondhand car with grinding gears and a stalling engine. You can do it, but you do get used to the luxury. When I was an operating cameraman, Ossie Morris was my focus puller. When I became a cameraman, he became my operating cameraman. When I became a director, he became my cameraman. There's a whole little group around me that's worked with me over the years. They've all become very successful and highly paid. So when I make another film, I want them. You can say, quite rightly, why don't you drop them if they're too expensive, why don't you train young people. But you do tend to get used to a certain kind of production. If I were young and directing my first film, I'd accept any conditions. I've grown too old and, perhaps, too comfortable.'

Neame began the 1970s with a musical version of Dickens's *A Christmas Carol*, retitled *Scrooge*, with Albert Finney in the lead. It was, inevitably, made with American finance. 'Americans have a higher regard for British film makers than the British,' he said.

'I remember the very early days when David Lean and I and many others had a little organisation called Independent Producers. We worked with Rank, and Rank backed us very solidly. During the period that he backed us, with a great deal of money, we made some landmark pictures.

'Rank really spent money in these days to try to break into the American market and he never could. The door was seen to be firmly locked on the big market outlet which the films were beginning to need because their price was such that they had to have a market beyond the shores of Britain. I think he very nearly broke through. But before he did, the money ran out and the banks closed in. And rightly. We were overspending for a home product. And then, I think what really happened was that American television became dominant – a set in every home, if not three or four – and one of the cheap forms of filling their time was to buy British pictures cheaply.

'The American public first learned to appreciate whatever qualities British films had via their television. They were in a sense educated to appreciate what we had to offer. So suddenly, the door to the American market swung open of its own accord. The bigger American audiences started to go out and see British films in America. But by that time J. Arthur Rank – who, I think, was a wonderful man – had lost heart and also could not afford it.

'It was a long time ago now, but it's still reflected in the thinking of our British film industry today, still reflected in the attitude of the heads of the organisation. They feel much safer if they invest a small amount of money in something that is a safe, sure-fire British product, that will earn its costs back in this country and does not have to rely on an overseas market, certainly not an American one. In that way – and who can blame them? – they've returned to solvency.

'It's an unfortunate truth that film making is a very big gamble. It seems to me that the only way it can pay off is to make enough films each year to reasonably expect – if you're a good gambler – that one or two of them will make a lot of money and that those one or two will carry the loss of the others.

'Almost all the American majors – at some time or another, spread across a year or two – manage to come up with a picture that makes them a fortune. With the earnings of one or two big pictures they pay for the loss of the majority of their product. We in England have never had the resources, never had that amount of money to invest in production.'

Neame's solid craftsmanship added a sturdiness to such popular films as *The Poseidon Adventure* (1972), an absurd melodrama of a sinking liner that helped create a huge market for movies about disasters. He fed that appetite with the less successful *Meteor* (1978). In between, he made *The Odessa File* (1974), based on Frederick

Forsyth's novel. As with his other recent films, it was marked by good acting and a professional gloss indistinguishable from blandness.

But most of the British films on general release could not even rise to that level of professional skill. They were dull and lifeless. The creative energies of the period were to be found in art, popular music, fringe theatre and television.

If one film were to be singled out as the quintessentially British movie of the 1970s, the most typical of its time, it would be *Percy* (1971), produced by Betty E. Box (born 1920) and directed by Ralph Thomas (born 1915). It was the product of a style that had made British films so depressingly insular and predictable for thirty years or more: unambitious in its treatment, unconcerned with any social realities, uninvolved with its characters, content to be well-crafted and to meet the simplest expectations of its audience, mixing a little sex with a lot of farce, simple humour with mildly dirty jokes.

The film's attitude to sex was one of timidity and even fear, to which British audiences have always responded with eager understanding: in pantomimes, seaside postcards and *Carry On* films. Such attitudes are also exemplified by the long-running stage comedy *No Sex Please, We're British,* which was dated in its social assumptions even when it opened in London around the same time as *Percy*. (Oddly, the film version of the farce, directed by Cliff Owen in 1973, was a flop. The play's producer has persuaded television companies not to screen the movie in order to protect the play's future.)

The film's producer, Betty Box, was a member of a family who were a dominant influence in British cinema of the 1940s, 50s and 60s. She was the sister of Sydney Box (born 1907), a prolific producer and writer. Sydney's wife, Muriel (born 1905) often worked with him on films, not only collaborating on scripts and production but also becoming one of the few successful woman directors. The work of all the Boxes was marked by a conservatism, even when addressing itself to matters of Labour politics, in *No Love For Johnnie* (1961), or sex, in *Rattle Of A Simple Man* (1964).

Betty Box had worked with Ralph Thomas many times following his directing *Doctor In The House* (1954), a comedy whose medical humour has a perennial appeal; it became the basis of a long-running television comedy series in the 1970s.

Percy might have undergone a similar transformation, had its subject matter concerned itself with people playing doctors and nurses in hospital wards, or to jokes about bowel movements. But it was slightly more risqué. It concerned a young man (Hywel Bennett) who has a penis transplant and is anxious to discover the original owner of his new organ.

The script was by an elegant and witty writer, Hugh Leonard, who eschewed those qualities to deliver the expected jokes and farcical situations.

The mixture of smut and prurience (the dominant image was a series of sequences of attractive girls lifting bed-sheets, peering underneath and making encouraging noises) was a potent one. *Percy* was successful enough to be followed, in 1974, by a sequel, *Percy's Progress*, in which Percy (now Leigh Lawson), the last sexually active man in the world, is pursued by importunate women.

Sex was something the British found extremely ridiculous, if the movies of the time are any evidence. There was an insatiable audience for such comedies. Not a big audience, but one that seemed always willing to return for more, although it is probable that the same films kept larger audiences at home. As seemingly voracious was the demand for films that promised some sort of sexual excitement, although they usually failed to deliver any.

Movies such as *The Love Pill* (1971), directed by Kenneth Turner, were churned out on the cheap, displaying neither wit nor sensuality. *The Love Pill* concerned a village grocer's sugar balls, which combined the qualities of a contraceptive and an aphrodisiac, turning women into raving nymphomaniacs.

Distributors titillatingly retitled Continental films to attract the desperate. *Addio Alexandra!* (1969) turned up in Soho two years later as *Love Me, Love My Wife*. *El Vampiro de la Autopista* (1970) took six years to reach Britain as *The Horrible Sexy Vampire*, a title almost as inept as the film. From *Danish Dentist on the Job* (1972) to *There's No Sex Like Snow Sex* (1976) and beyond or below, the distributors showed great ingenuity in their innuendos.

The relative success of the British-made *Confessions* inspired some to rename West German pictures as *Confessions of a Male Escort*, *Confessions of a Sexy Photographer* and *Confessions of a Sixth Form Girl*.

British producers usually preferred to give their movies titles containing *double entendres* as subtle as *I'm Not Feeling Myself Tonight* (1976).

A dirty raincoat was almost *de rigueur* wear for a seat in the stalls so that it was hardly surprising that the better-dressed, who did not wish to watch films with newspapers folded over their laps, stayed at home. It was the cinema of J. Arthur Wank. Many distributors and film makers seemed to have decided that the only means of survival, or a quick profit, was through soft-core pornography and sexual farce, genres that could be made cheaply and still attract an undiscriminating audience.

The other great source of inspiration (to use the word loosely), as well as income, was feature versions of television series, usually comedies. These were all marked by showing no improvement, in their longer and more expensive manifestations, over the programmes seen in the comfort of home. Some were noticeably inferior, for although an anecdote could be stretched to fill a half-hour's television entertainment, several such anecdotes strung together did not make a cinema film.

Many seemed to have been directed with less care, and no more expense, than the television originals. Audiences nevertheless turned out in surprising numbers to watch wide screen rehashes of their favourite programmes. *Steptoe and Son* (1972), directed by Cliff Owen took more than £1 million at British cinemas and was followed by *Steptoe and Son Ride Again* (1973). But the ripe acting of Wilfred Brambell and Harry H. Corbett as the querulous scrap-merchants seemed diminished. It was evident that television series, where the comedy depended more upon character than incident, failed to make a successful transition to the cinemas. The small-town soldiers of *Dad's Army* (1971), directed by Norman Cohen, were as lost in the wide expanses of the cinema.

An audience's expectations are probably less when watching a television series. Characters become accepted and known over weeks or months of viewing, so that an episode that falls below the usual standards is soon forgotten.

In the cinema, such indulgence is uncommon because audiences have to make a conscious decision to leave their homes and pay for their cinema seat. This is one reason why the cinema requires stars, the massively charismatic egos of overwhelming personalities, in a way that television does not. The leading performers in *Dad's Army*, Arthur Lowe, John Le Mesurier, John Laurie and the others were exceptionally skilled character actors whose performances in small roles had often lit up indifferent films with an unmistakable flair. But they were not stars.

That, of course, was part of their appeal to film makers, for versions of television series offered the chance to make inexpensive films that audiences would respond to. There were no publicity problems, no need to explain what the films were about.

The titles were enough: *On The Buses* (1971), *Up Pompeii* (1971), *Mutiny on the Buses* (1972), *The Alf Garnet Saga* (1972), *Never Mind the Quality, Feel the Width* (1972), *That's Your Funeral!* (1973), *Love Thy Neighbour* (1973), *Nearest and Dearest* (1973), *Man at the Top* (1973), *Man about the House* (1974), *Are You Being Served?* (1975), *The Likely Lads* (1976), *Porridge* (1979).

The number of such spin-offs has declined recently, now that television series, particularly those imported from America, owe their origins to films, so that a successful movie becomes, in effect, a try out for television. Whether that is due to the failure of television to produce popular series, or of film producers' desire to be original, it is difficult to know. Certainly the films were mere shadows of the television originals.

Only two of all the adaptations could stand on their own merits as cinema. They were both thrillers: *Callan* (1974), directed by Don Sharp and starring Edward Woodward as a tough, individualistic secret agent, and *Sweeney!* (1976), directed by David Wickes, a familiar variation on the standard cops-and-robbers theme. Neither was outstanding, but both were at least efficiently made.

There was a narrowness and chauvinism about the majority of British movies of the period. They were not so much indigenous films, reflecting a nation's culture, as blinkered responses to the past, exemplified by such period remakes as *The Thirty-Nine Steps* (1978), directed by Don Sharp and a little truer to the original than Hitchcock, but otherwise no more than a slight improvement on the Betty Box–Ralph Thomas version made in 1960. There was certainly no pressing reason to film Buchan's thriller again, any more than there was to remake Hitchcock's thriller of 1938, *The Lady Vanishes*, in 1980, directed by Anthony Page, which once again served to demonstrate Hitchcock's superiority over later British film makers.

Erskine Childer's *The Riddle of the Sands*, with British Edwardian amateurism triumphing over German efficiency, was a subject that somehow escaped Hitchcock, but Tony Maylam's version, made in 1978, had a period air about it, with some stiff upper lip acting from Michael York, and not only because it was set in 1901, anticipating the First World War. The dialogue was of the Little Britain variety, delivered with no trace of parody: 'People don't behave like that, not even Germans'. It was, of course, in keeping with its theme, but the question was why, in the late '70s, such a theme should have been thought commercial enough for an expenditure of just under £1 million, a modest sum for a two hour film, but still nearly £1 million.

The Riddle Of The Sands, as much as *Percy* was symptomatic of the British film industry of the period: low-budget, unambitious, decently average and deliberately avoiding any contact with present day realities or, for that matter, past ones.

Ronald Neame had been right long ago. British cinema needed to be daring, to make fresh and different films. But where was the impetus to come from?

7 ... And The New

Loach, Platts-Mills, Brownlow, Hemmings, Sinclair, Medak, Petit, Losey, Hodges, Frears, Yates, Attenborough, Forsyth

'The "documentary" tradition (which does not, of course, necessarily express itself through documentary) is still the one that British cinema must look back to.'

Penelope Houston, 1975

It seemed as if the prevailing British tradition of documentary realism, the meticulous and socially accurate examination of life as it is lived, was both being ignored and had lost its former power. A critical commonplace is that the strength of British films lies in the style established by John Grierson and the film makers of the 1930s and that the best feature films are those that are part of this tradition.

The New Wave directors, and the proponents of Free Cinema in the 1950s, were certainly a vigorous part of the tradition. The power and attraction of their films came from their focus on the detail of mainly working-class lives. Free Cinema's 1956 manifesto spoke of films which should share a belief in 'the significance of the everyday'.

The British cinema of the 70s might look back to that tradition; but was it one to which it should also look forward? Talented directors, who might well have seen themselves as part of the continuum, nevertheless seemed to find it difficult to work within the system and, even if they eventually succeeded in making their movies, failed to achieve the sort of commercial gain that would have given them power to improve the situation.

In America, in contrast, the unexpected appeal of Peter Fonda and Dennis Hopper's *Easy Rider* (1969) had Hollywood executives (until they learned from experience) signing up every tyro who claimed to be able to direct, in the hopes of making a similar fortune from a cheaply-made movie appealing to the young.

In Britain, it was much harder for people to make the films they wanted, even when working within low budgets. Ken Loach and Tony Garnett, who had worked together in television, spent more than three years trying to film *Kes,* which was finally made in 1969. They had approached every possible source of finance and had been turned down after their original backers – an American conglomerate, the National General Company – had withdrawn at the last moment. That it was made at all, at a cost of just under £160,000, was due to the enthusiasm of another British producer and director, Tony Richardson, who had persuaded United Artists to change its mind and back it. Even after *Kes* was made, the struggle continued. Rank, who usually distributed UA's pictures, disliked it and did their best to pretend it did not exist. *Kes* was finally given a release by ABC, although it took three months before it reached London audiences after opening in the North of England.

Loach, one of the most individual and talented of British directors, has made few films since, working mainly in television and, in recent years, in documentary television where the rigour of his approach and his steadfast belief in the rights of people to control their own lives, has continued to cause controversy.

He did, though, film *Family Life* (1971) scripted by one of Britain's best writers, David Mercer, from his television play, *In Two Minds,* which Loach himself had directed in 1967, and based on the then fashionable views of psychiatrist R. D. Laing that schizophrenia could be a 'healthy' response to family pressures. It was a bleakly moving film, notable for the acting of Sandy Ratcliff, as the girl who breaks down, and Bill Dean and Grace Cave as her uncomprehending parents.

Loach remains expert at getting unobtrusively good performances out of amateur or little-known actors, a skill that reflects his own attitudes to individual worth. It provided a necessary reality for his least successful film *Black Jack* (1979) based on Leon Garfield's Dickensian historical novel of a boy who becomes involved with a highwayman. But the past is not Loach's country, however universal the themes with which he deals. Once again, he had difficulty in finding the finance to make the film. Backing eventually came from the Gaumont cinema chain in France.

Loach's *Looks and Smiles* (1983), a film made for television and seen briefly in the cinemas, again used unknowns for its near-documentary narrative of two young people coping with unemployment.

It remains true that Loach has done his best work for television, a fact that is, in itself, a sad reflection on the British film industry.

Tony Garnett, Loach's producer for many years, turned director with *Prostitute* (1980), a semi-documentary that surfaced briefly in the cinemas, before he decided to move to America to work.

There he made *Handgun* (1983) for Thorn-EMI, another film that failed to find favour with audiences, although it was a skilled and enjoyable work. Ostensibly another reworking of the favourite contemporary theme of an individual taking personal revenge on a wrong-doer rather than relying on police or the judiciary, it managed to make subtle fun of the genre. It concerned a nervous, sensitive woman surviving in the relentlessly masculine gung-ho, gun-toting ambience of Texas, which was observed with great perception so that its masculine rituals, from buying a gun to watching cheer leaders, became absurdly comic. Garnett's heroine, raped and humiliated by an unthinking young man, learns to be better with a gun than he is and humiliates him in a shoot-out. But, instead of the sort of killing that audiences cheered in *Death Wish* and its many imitators, she shoots him with an anaesthetic dart. This witty refusal to meet an audience's expectations seemed to ruin the movie's commercial potential. But it is an excellent small film, of the sort only an outsider could make, and augurs well for Garnett's future as a director away from Britain.

Another young director, Barney Platts-Mills (born 1944), who had left his public school at 15 to train as a film editor, has taken a similar, if less doctrinaire, approach in his few films. Platts-Mills made *Bronco Bullfrog* (1970), set in the East End of London, for under £20,000. His actors were local children who had participated in workshops at the Theatre Royal, Stratford-atte-Bow, where Joan Littlewood's Theatre Workshop, if past its best, was still providing a creative stimulus.

Based on the boys' own experiences and with much of its dialogue improvised, the film was a critical and, in a small way, a commercial success. Yet, a year later, Platts-Mills said that it had 'yet to make a penny of its cost back for the production company, all its earnings having been swallowed up by distributors' expenses'.

He followed it with *Private Road* (1971), using professional actors: Bruce Robinson, Susan Penhaligon and Michael Feast. The film concentrated on the relationship between Robinson, a writer, and Penhaligon, a secretary, both stumbling vaguely through life. The characters and narrative were as deliberately unresolved as in his first film. This time, it was not offered to a big distributor, but handled by the makers themselves. It was to be Platts-Mills' last completed project for twelve years, until he made the dour Gaelic *Hero* (1983) for television.

Kevin Brownlow, a film editor, and Andrew Mollo, an historical consultant to film companies, spent seven years in raising the money to make a film about Gerrard Winstanley, an early social revolutionary who established his commune of Diggers in 1649. Brownlow and Mollo began filming in 1972, with a grant from the British Film Institute. Previously, they had made *It Happened Here*, about a Nazi takeover of Britain, in 1965 for £7,000. This new film, *Comrade Jacob*, based on a book by David Caute, was budgeted at a modest £72,000, and even at that price was rejected by the companies they approached.

Brownlow, writing about the experience in the film quarterly, *Sight and Sound,* quoted a Californian producer who wrote, 'My current contract is one that would make them anxious to waste dollars in the millions rather than the hundreds of thousands required by a project like this.'

When their option on the book ran out, another director, Jack Gold, tried to film it with a script by John McGrath. He, too, found it impossible to raise finance.

Brownlow and Mollo spent another three years shooting the film. They made few concessions to an audience's ignorance of the period so that the resulting movie, fascinating in its historical accuracy and the timeliness of its theme, was seen briefly in only a few cinemas.

Peter Watkins (born 1937), a director whose first feature films, grounded in documentary style, had an almost visceral impact, left Britain in the 70s to work in more sympathetic countries.

The BBC have never shown *The War Game* (1966), his dramatised documentary on the aftermath of a nuclear holocaust in Britain. And film companies and distributors disliked his *Punishment Park* (1971), backed by American finance, and an invigoratingly paranoid and passionate vision of the future as a concentration camp cum obstacle course for the young.

There were abortive attempts to improve a dire situation. In the early 1970s the producer Dimitri de Grunwald and the theatre director Peter Hall set up a company intended to involve some notable talents: playwrights Robert Bolt and John Hopkins and directors Anthony Harvey and Christopher Miles. The plan was to help in developing scripts and packaging films and so escape the artist's usual problem of waiting for other people to offer work. It came to nothing, although Miles later directed a lacklustre comedy, *That Lucky Touch* (1975), starring Roger Moore and Susannah York, which de Grunwald produced for Rank.

Hall himself took several years to find the money to film *Akenfield* (1974), a lyrical but sometimes lifeless version of Ronald Blythe's account of existence in a small Suffolk village. Hall, who used amateur actors, was able to make it for £60,000 because those involved invested their salaries in the production in return for a share of the profits. Some money came from London Weekend Television in return for the TV rights.

It is not only within the sometimes narrow confines of movies and television, of course, that many talented people feel unable to work. There were novelists who have stopped writing and exceptional playwrights, such as John Arden and Peter Barnes, who found themselves isolated from and ignored by conventional theatre. Peter Brook, perhaps the most talented of British theatre directors, chose to work in France with his multi-national company and also has remained outside the mainstream of British cinema. Since his film of William Golding's *Lord of the Flies* in 1962, he directed only a savage and bleakly powerful *King Lear* (1970), with Paul Scofield glowering in the title role, and the more esoteric *Meetings With Remarkable Men* (1979).

The opportunities for young directors were few in the 1970s and continued to be difficult. David Hemmings (born 1941) combined acting with producing and directing from the early 1970s with some initial success. Although he has continued to be involved in the business of film making, his career as a director has faltered. His first film, *Running Scared* (1972), was a downbeat story of a student suicide. He followed it with *The Fourteen* (1973), a cheerfully sentimental film of a family of orphans. Both demonstrated that Hemmings was skilled behind the camera and, as to be expected, capable of coaxing excellent performances from his cast. He regretted directing *The Fourteen*, but was flattered to have been asked. 'Although it was commercially a disaster, *Running Scared* was an infinitely better film than *The Fourteen*', he once told me. '*Running Scared* was very well reviewed and didn't make any money. *The Fourteen* was badly reviewed and commercially successful. My first film, a project I generated myself, was an artistic success, in my opinion.

'So where, as a director, do you then go? Do you try to make commercially successful pictures, which is, of course, what guarantees your future as a director? Or do you try to generate your own projects, which are perhaps less commercial but give one greater satisfaction? I don't know the answer. But any actor who has an interest in the other side of the camera must, if he wants to remain working in England, generate his own product.

'When I come across a picture that I'd really like to direct, it generally is of a quality that prevents me from doing so. It's the sort of picture that needs a major star, not a low life film which can come out of the blue and surprise everybody. My commercial responsibilities are to make sure that the pictures are effective, and my directing them could be to their detriment in generating the further cash for the projects.'

Hemmings the businessman has, to an extent, taken precedence over the actor, although he is still capable of excellent performances, particularly as the lower middle-class spy double-crossing his snobbish superiors in *Charlie Muffin* (1979).

'I think one of the reasons that I gave so many awful performances in the late 1960s was that I was trying to do so many other things as well,' he said. 'I don't consider films at any level on an artistic or aesthetic basis at all. Films are designed by, and designed for, commercial reward and for no other reason. If, along the way, they happen to turn out artistically successful and beautiful to look at, that is totally incidental to their absolute direction, which is to make money and nothing else. To view them as anything else is spurious. The original motives that create films are totally commercial.'

Hemmings has since directed a curious film in West Germany, *Just A Gigolo* (1977), with a cast that included David Bowie, Marlene Dietrich and Kim Novak, and *The Survivor* (1980), a murkily shot horror film, made in Australia, about a dead pilot seeking revenge on those responsible for the crash in which he was killed. It was released in Britain only on video cassette.

Another whose career went awry was Andrew Sinclair (born 1935), one of the better young novelists of the time, who turned director to film his book about a naive soldier, *The Breaking of Bumbo* (1969). The result gathered dust on its distributor's shelves. Sinclair followed it with *Under Milk Wood* (1971), made on location in Fishguard and starring Richard Burton (and Elizabeth Taylor).

That was released, but turned out to be filmed radio, a flat visualisation of Dylan Thomas's aural masterpiece. Sinclair then directed *Blue Blood* (1973), set in a stately home and based on a story by Alexander Thynne, an eccentric aristocrat and son of the Marquis of Bath. It starred Thynne's wife, Anna Gael, and despite the presence of Oliver Reed and Derek Jacobi, looked like a superior home movie.

Peter Medak, who arrived in Britain as a refugee from Hungary, made two excellent films at the beginning of the 1970s. *A Day in the Death of Joe Egg* was a faithful adaptation of Peter Nichols's painfully funny stage play about the relationship between a husband and wife and their vegetable of a child and was more successful than most adaptations of Nichols's work, which often uses music-hall techniques that translate badly to the screen.

Medak's *The Ruling Class* (1972) was also a version of an intensely theatrical work, Peter Barnes's astonishing play in which a mad aristocrat who believes he is God gains social respectability only when he renounces his past and is transformed into Jack the Ripper. Aided by a bravura performance from Peter O'Toole, the film, although often heavy-handed, was bracingly savage in its humour. But it was to be Medak's last British feature film.

The story of neglected talent remains depressingly familiar. The costs of making films are so high that directors need more than artistic sensibilities to survive; they must have commercial successes.

Chris Petit, one of the few British film critics to make the transition to director in the European manner, made *Radio On* (1980) not only heavily under the influence of the German director Wim Wenders, but with his financial assistance as well as that of the British Film Institute. A self-conscious 'road movie', of a rootless factory worker and part time disc jockey driving to Bristol following the death of his brother, it was a minor art house hit.

His next, *An Unsuitable Job for a Woman* (1982), was based on a novel by a highly regarded thriller writer, P. D. James, had a cast of excellent actors that included Pippa Guard and Billie Whitelaw, was backed by two British production companies, Goldcrest and Boyds Co., and was presumably intended as a more commercial work. But Petit showed little interest in the traditional aspects of the whodunnit, preferring to explore the personality of the central character, a woman who takes over an investigation from her dead boss, and the gloomy nature (here, anyway) of English country life.

The film was slow-paced and, although admired, not popular with many audiences. His *Flight to Berlin* (1984) was even more determinedly minimalist in its intentions, concentrating on the tiny happenings of life and refusing to offer any explanation of his characters' actions or motives.

Better, more conventional thrillers were *Get Carter* (1971) and *Gumshoe* (1971). The former, directed by Mike Hodges (born 1932), starred Michael Caine as a cool killer hunting down the criminals who murdered his brother. The director made excellent use of bleak Northern landscapes and people leading bleaker lives among the urban desolation of Newcastle. Caine brought a jaunty integrity to an increasingly unsympathetic role that culminated in his death, at the gun of another professional killer. Hodges' polished direction did not hinder the film's pace. Its regional setting, too, added a gritty reality to the familiar melodrama.

In partnership with Caine and the film's producer, Michael Klinger, Hodges went on to make *Pulp* (1972), which suffered from the influence of John Huston's chaotic *Beat The Devil*, a comic thriller of twenty years earlier. Caine played a writer of cheap detective fiction who became involved with actual criminals. Set in Malta, and filmed with an eye to spurious glamour, it was as confused as Huston's burlesque, but not as entertaining.

Subsequently, Hodges has put his inventive direction at the service of two American movies, *The Terminal Man* (1973), where it almost triumphed over the performance of George Segal as an eye-rolling killer in a blonde wig, and the exuberantly camp *Flash Gordon* (1980), where it had to contend with Sam Jones as the hero. Jones, a former football player, was similarly afflicted with a strange blond hairstyle and further handicapped by possessing as much muscle above the neck as below.

Gumshoe (1971), the feature film debut of Stephen Frears (born 1931), was an assured comedy that played with the theme of the way people can live their lives through the clichés of cinema. Albert Finney starred as a Liverpudlian Bingo caller so caught up with imaging himself as Humphrey Bogart that he becomes involved with petty villains. Excellent acting from Finney and Fulton Mackay, a witty script by Neville Smith and effective music by Andrew Lloyd Webber combined to make it one of the most enjoyable films of the year. Yet it was to be thirteen years before Frears, who has continued to work in television, made another cinema film.

Some of the most exciting British movies of the period were made by Americans. Some of the least exciting, too.

Sherlock Holmes in particular was an obstacle over which many tripped. Paul Morrissey and Gene Wilder each attempted comedies on the subject, but the *Hound of the Baskervilles* (1979), in which Morrissey, the director of some of Andy Warhol's films, was content to allow a collection of British comedians to mug aimlessly, was silly and Wilder's *The Adventures of Sherlock Holmes's Smarter Brother* (1975) was hardly more sensible.

Even the great Billy Wilder (no relation) was unable to contain the famous detective in his sardonic *The Private Life of Sherlock Holmes* (1970) and savagely edited the long film after disappointing previews without, seemingly, improving it.

Perhaps not a failure, but certainly not a film that seemed comfortable set in rural Cornwall (Texas might have been a better choice), was Sam Peckinpah's *Straw Dogs* (1971), in which Dustin Hoffman gains his masculine self-respect through violence.

Yet British cinema would have been the poorer without Joseph Losey's immaculate *The Go-Between* (1971), David Lynch's *The Elephant Man* (1981) and John Landis's *An American Werewolf in London* (1981), all by American directors.

With its clipped script by Harold Pinter matching the well-trimmed speech patterns of its upper-class characters, *The Go-Between* managed not only to dissect attitudes to class but to shift with no perceptible jolt from the past to the present, to suggest lives twisted and thwarted by events of long ago. It was a deft balancing act, a double-focus, that Pinter tried again later, with less success, in *The French Lieutenant's Woman*.

Losey's other movies of the period included *Figures in a Landscape* (1970), a chase film in which everyone seemed to be running after its meaning, and *The Romantic Englishwoman* (1975), one of his forays into romantic melodrama. It was to be his last film with an English theme for ten years, for he left London to move to France where the taxation was kinder to American expatriates.

The Elephant Man provided John Hurt with an opportunity for submerged virtuosity, acting under a sack or buried beneath elaborate make-up, as John Merrick, a hideously deformed gentle man who became a Victorian celebrity.

Like Alec Guinness before him, Hurt is the antithesis of the conventional screen actor who puts his personality on display in the service of whatever role he happens to be acting. Hurt disappears, withdrawing into the role. His performance was an affecting one.

Lynch, a young American whose only previous film had been the low-budget shocker *Eraserhead*, which showed an electrifying energy, was an unconventional choice as director, owing the job to the fact that the film, although financed by EMI, was set up by the production company run by actor-director Mel Brooks.

A bold choice, not approved by all involved, was to make the film in black-and-white, partly to lessen the horror of Merrick's grotesque appearance but also to increase its period atmosphere. Aided by the photography of Freddie Francis, the film had something of the Dickensian feel of David Lean's early work as well as a commendable restraint in its treatment of a freak. The script lacked the complexity of Bernard Pomerance's stage play on the same theme, which had explored the ambiguous nature of the Victorian establishment's response to Merrick, but the movie was still among the best of recent years.

John Landis's *An American Werewolf in London* was a more full-blooded horror movie and the only one to marry successful shock and comedy. The film, a brilliant exercise in the Gothic manner, managed to mock the excesses of the genre while still allowing the horror of lycanthropy, captured in excellent special effects. Its sequence of rotting corpses meeting in the unattended spaces of a London cinema showing soft-core pornography was wonderfully apt.

If Britain gained from the efforts of the American directors, the return to film in London of Peter Yates (born 1929) was a reminder of how much the British industry has lost by failing to provide enough, or enough remunerative, work for its best talents.

Yates came back to film first an expensive fantasy *Krull* (1983), an other-worldly version of Beauty and The Beast which suffered from its anti-climactic ending, and then the very English *The Dresser* (1984). The latter was, in many ways, a traditionally British film. It was based on a successful play by Ronald Harwood, it concerned the sort of lovable eccentricity that an Ealing director would have recognised, and the emphasis was squarely on its star performances by Albert Finney as an old theatrical lion roaring his last, and Tom Courtenay as his limp-wristed dresser, the Fool to the old man's Lear. Yates, who was directing plays when still in his 'teens, responded with affection to the theme, allowing his stars to create two flamboyant and appropriately theatrical performances.

His strength as a director has been the exploration of character, despite the reputation as a director of action sequences that he gained from his first American film, *Bullitt* (1968), with its renowned car chase. Such US films as the low-life *The Friends of Eddie Coyle* (1973), with Robert Mitchum giving his best performance as a small-time loser, and *Breaking Away* (1979), a touching and funny film of an adolescent's search for identity and the resulting generation gap, are also in the best humanistic tradition of British films. That they are American is Britain's loss.

But there are skilled and ambitious directors remaining in Britain. If anyone is to inherit David Lean's role as an epic film maker, the likeliest contender is Richard Attenborough (born 1923). He began his career as an actor typecast in cowardly roles. He is now a knight and a highly successful businessman with interests in commercial radio, television and theatre. His greatest achievement so far is, of course, *Gandhi* (1983), though the film is less a glory of British cinema than an indication of what is wrong with it, since Attenborough spent 20 years trying to raise the finance to make it.

He began by approaching Rank, where he was told that the subject had no appeal whatsoever. Nevertheless, Rank advanced him £5,000 so that he could continue the project by having a script written. Their interest never went further, although they were approached again at a time when they claimed to want to make films. Barry Spikings, the production head of EMI, also turned it down as uncommercial.

At one point, Attenborough lost control of the project and Lean planned to film it with a script by Robert Bolt, who had written Lean's epic films from *Lawrence of Arabia* (1962) onwards. When the project returned to Attenborough and it seemed as if the film finally would be made, he approached Spikings again, seeking a modicum of backing from EMI so that the film should have some connection with Britain. But Spikings again refused, still convinced that it would be unprofitable. Attenborough discovered that the executives in charge of distribution had not even read the script. Backing finally came from Goldcrest Films, then a newly established company investing in film and television.

It may be that the time taken to make *Gandhi* improved it, especially as there was a moment when it seemed as if Anthony Hopkins would play the title role. In the end, the part went to

Ben Kingsley, an actor who showed himself best fitted to play it.

Attenborough's faith in the project and in himself was overwhelmingly justified, though the film might not have had the sweep and grandeur it does, had it not been for the experience he gained in directing other movies.

His first, *Oh! What A Lovely War* (1969) was a brilliantly assured debut and an entirely successful transfer to the screen of the very theatrical revue originally staged by Joan Littlewood. In *Young Winston* (1972), Attenborough demonstrated not only an expected talent for drawing good performances from actors but also a flair for action on a large scale. Attenborough's organisational abilities, his skill at switching from intimate scenes to those of elaborate wide-ranging excitement, were displayed in *A Bridge Too Far* (1977). A $25 million dollar recreation of the Battle of Arnhem, it was sometimes top-heavy with stars, but an impressively vigorous movie.

The discoveries he had made in directing were put to excellent use in *Gandhi*. The crowd scenes were superbly photographed, full of action: long lines of miserable refugees suddenly erupting into desperate battle and the massacre at Amritsar, with the camera swirling through the panic-stricken multitudes. But Attenborough, while taking advantage of the wide-screen beauties of India, also managed to avoid empty spectacle and made a film that may be epic in its scope, but is also very intimate, concentrating, in loving close-up, on its central charismatic character.

For all the excitements of its big set pieces, it never loses a sense of human scale. It is a genuinely provocative movie, in that it forces those watching it to see not only Gandhi's philosophy in action, but to examine their own lives and how they choose to lead them. Films that can achieve that, however imperfectly, are rare enough to treasure.

If Attenborough seemed heir apparent to the grand style exemplified by David Lean, then Bill Forsyth (born 1948) was in a direct line of descent from the directors of Ealing comedies who were on the side of the individual against institutions. Forsyth learned his trade as a maker of documentary films and, in his first two splendid comedies, remained true to that tradition, using amateur actors for the most part.

His first, *That Sinking Feeling* (1979), about a gang of boys on the scrounge in Glasgow was sharply observed and full of wry amusement at the odd ways of humanity. His second, too, used some of the same actors further to explore adolescent behaviour: it was *Gregory's Girl* (1981) that established him as a director and writer of unusual talent. There are no villains in Forsyth's world. It is a sunny, life-affirming place inhabited by people of varying degrees of eccentricity. Manipulating two narratives of equal weight, of a girl who wants to play football for the school and the shy boy who has a mild passion for her, Forsyth still finds time to wander down by-ways to take in scenes that interest or amuse him.

After a slow start, *Gregory's Girl* was not only a success in Britain, but also in the United States so that, with David Puttnam producing, he was able to move into a bigger-budget film with a star actor, Burt Lancaster, to assure continuing American interest.

The resulting film, *Local Hero*, emphasised Forsyth's links with an earlier Scottish director, Alexander Mackendrick, educated at the School of Art in Glasgow, whose films for Ealing Studios included two Scottish comedies of triumphant individuality, *Whisky Galore* and *The Maggie*, before he left Britain to work in Hollywood (*Sweet Smell of Success* with Burt Lancaster) and to become dean of the film department of the California Institute of the Arts.

Here again in *Local Hero*, were familiar figures from the Ealing films: city businessmen being outsmarted by locals, and stubborn eccentrics defeating conglomerates, filmed with a delight in the diversity of humanity. From the capitalist Soviet ship's captain with a wife in the Scottish port and an account in a Swiss bank to Burt Lancaster's oil tycoon with a passion for astronomy, the film is peopled with quiet obsessives. It veers towards whimsy, with Fulton Mackay's herring-barrel philosopher of a beachcomber and a lad in love with a mermaid-like marine biologist, but is sharp enough to avoid sentimentality.

The film showed that Forsyth could handle the complexities of a bigger-budget film, one that moved away from the studies of the young to more complex and adult matters. It was highly praised and much enjoyed in Britain. Not even the presence of Burt Lancaster, however, could gain it acceptance outside America's more sophisticated cities.

Forsyth has the strength and the sense to remain true to his roots. His most recent film, *Comfort and Joy* (1984), re-united him with Clive Parsons and Davina Belling, the producers of *Gregory's Girl*, in a wry comedy about a Glaswegian disc-jockey. Forsyth's success showed that small-scale indigenous films could still find an audience, if they were well enough made and written.

Nevertheless, in the last 20 years, there has been a change in the expectations of cinema audiences. They demand excitement and sensation. They wish to be overwhelmed by films, dazzled, delighted, shocked and surprised by what they see. In part, perhaps, this is due to the increasing drabness of many people's lives during a period of depression and unemployment. The heyday of glamorous musicals was during a similar economic low point in the 1930s.

Popular entertainment, too, has always depended upon spectacle, from the elaborate masques of the seventeenth century to the Drury Lane stage spectaculars of the nineteenth with their shipwrecks, train crashes and earthquakes, to Cecil B. De Mille's Biblical epics with their casts of thousands and the Rolling Stones' rock concerts in football stadiums.

But the great alteration has been in the growth of television viewing. Today, the documentary tradition is alive and well on television. The medium is an ideal one for the painstaking realism of documentary film makers.

It is no coincidence that Ken Loach's most effective work has been for the small screen. Many fine directors commute between television and the cinema, remaining true to the documentary style. They include Michael Apted, Jack Gold, Brian Gibson, John Irvin, Richard Marquand, Mike Newell, Michael Tuchner and Franc Roddam.

The documentary tradition has been reinforced by the success of Channel Four in commissioning feature films to be seen on television and in the cinema. It is nevertheless true that cinema audiences want to see the sort of films that are too big to be properly enjoyed on television, space operas such as *Star Wars* and *Superman* and the technological thrills of *James Bond*.

There were also British directors who preferred a more exuberant style than the documentary one, who trusted images rather than words. And who, perhaps, were helping to create a less restrained style of film making . . .

8 Fools and Visionaries

Monty Python, Alan Parker, Ridley Scott, John Boorman

'Ordinary decent good honest behaviour is utterly foreign to the despicable group of people who masquerade under the cowardly pseudonym of Monty Python.'

Col. 'Muriel' Volestrangler, 1978

Thorn-EMI's video catalogue for 1983/84 includes a few enthusiastic lines about *Monty Python's Life of Brian*. It is, according to the blurb writer, 'a brilliantly funny and daring satire, not on the Church itself, but on people's attitudes to it'.

Then, EMI had not been swallowed by Thorn. EMI's production executives had agreed to finance the film, which was budgeted at $4 million. But Lord Delfont asked to read the script (which was later published as a book without frightening anyone else). And he withdrew EMI's backing. The only losers were EMI, although they still profited from the picture after it was made, because it was shown in EMI's cinemas. And then they bought video rights.

The rise and rise of Monty Python is one of the most gratifying successes of the past decade. The group's progress also mirrors the path taken by British films. Their first movie, *And Now For Something Completely Different*, in 1973 was a spin-off from a television series that seemed to cause the BBC as much embarrassment as pleasure. The film was only a moderate success. And moderation has never seemed part of Python's appeal. Their last film, however, *The Meaning of Life*, released in 1983, was an international hit backed by American money. The path they have trod, from a little local success to part of the US entertainment industry, is one that has been worn smooth by the rush of other English directors, producers, actors and writers.

There has never been a group of comedians – or, rather, writer-performers – quite like Monty Python. Together, they are more than the sum of their parts. Apart, they are among the most talented individuals in comedy. Not only have they created the funniest television series yet seen; they have, seemingly effortlessly, annexed other media, producing best-selling books and records and filling large concert halls with their live performances.

Their individual talents are no less striking. If there is a TV series to challenge *Monty Python's Flying Circus*, it is John Cleese and Connie Booth's *Fawlty Towers*, in which Cleese, as the cringing hotelier Basil Fawlty, created the definitive whimpering bully, a performance refined from earlier impersonations. Michael Palin is creating a gentler, nostalgic comedy as a writer and actor on television, with the Boy's Own earnestness of *Ripping Yarns*, and in the cinema, with *The Missionary* (1983). Eric Idle's *The Rutles* was an affectionate satire of the rock business. Graham Chapman has written a startling book – *A Liar's Autobiography*, in which he came out of several closets at the same time – as well as a variety of television and film scripts. Terry Jones has emerged as a talented director and writer; he collaborated with Palin on the scripts of *Ripping Yarns*, and has written two notable children's books. And Terry Gilliam, too, has developed into possibly the most original director working in British cinema, combining a quirky eye for significant detail with a boisterous relish for the earthiness of life, its guts and gusto.

Python came together haphazardly in 1969. Cleese and Chapman had been at Cambridge University together, where they were members of what seems, in retrospect, to have been a glittering *Footlights*. Michael Palin and Terry Jones were both at Oxford in the mid-1960s, where they worked together on undergraduate revues.

All four were among the university wits recruited to join a team of experienced showbusiness writers by David Frost for his *Frost Report*, which began broadcasting on BBC-1 in March 1966, mixing topicality, old jokes and a few fresh ones. Idle, who arrived at Cambridge University and joined Footlights just as Cleese and Chapman were leaving, was also one of the writers Frost hired.

It was Cleese who was responsible for creation of Python by suggesting that the two teams – he and Chapman, and Palin and Jones – should work together. Palin agreed; he was just recovering from the poor public response he and Jones had received for a London Weekend Television series, *The Complete and Utter History of Britain*. Palin proposed that Idle should join them; Idle, in turn, suggested Gilliam, who was a friend of Cleese. An American who had worked for humorous magazines, Gilliam had come to Britain in pursuit of a love affair and decided to stay.

The six, with producer and writer Barry Took acting as go-between, approached the BBC and they were offered a series of 13 programmes, *Monty Python's Flying Circus* was born on 5 October, 1969. They quickly acquired a cult reputation, something the BBC appeared to discourage by broadcasting the show at different times each week.

And Now For Something Completely Different, a title derived from a catch-phrase used to link sketches, was financed in part by Victor

Lownes, an American who ran the immensely profitable British end of *Playboy*, with its Park Lane club and casino, and tried to live his life in the manner appropriate to that magazine. Lownes thought it would find an audience in America comparable to the one it had in Britain, among college students.

The film was no more than a collection of their television sketches, provided with a slight framing device of an obsequious cinema manager, whose main film turns out to last five minutes. This was a parody of a government information film and Python at its cruellest. Individuals hiding in bushes are asked to stand up to identify themselves, whereupon they are immediately shot. The violence increases, as John Cleese's helpful bureaucratic commentary begins to take on manic tones, and ends in nuclear holocaust. Directed by Ian McNaughton, who performed the same task on television, *And Now For Something Completely Different* is not as funny as the best of the television series. The problem is entirely one of timing (which also bedevils Python's most recent film, *The Meaning of Life*). There comes a point when the attention flags, when you notice that although the sketch is funny, it is not as funny as the one ten minutes before. It proved to be reasonably popular in Britain. In America, to Lownes's chagrin, it flopped.

It was inevitable that the group would move into films proper. In 1969, Cleese and Chapman had been among the writers who turned out scripts for *The Magic Christian*, based on Terry Southern's short satiric novel and starring Peter Sellers. It is curious that these two, tough witty writers and excellent performers, should have been associated with some of the direst film comedies of the past fifteen years. They were also among the scriptwriters of *The Rise and Rise of Michael Rimmer* (1969), which charted with farcical overkill the progress to the top of an ambitious young politician. David Frost, then an ambitious young entrepreneur, had commissioned the script as part of a planned move into films, although he rapidly lost interest in movie-making. The writers, as a sort of private joke, gave some of Frost's characteristics to the character of Rimmer.

Frost also commissioned Cleese and Chapman to write *Rentadick*, a film often, if understandably, overlooked in any discussion of their career. By the time the script was finished, Frost had little interest in producing it and was anxious only to offload its cost on to someone else. That person was Ned Sherrin, the urbanely witty BBC producer who in a sense had created Frost through *That Was The Week That Was*. In the late 60s, Sherrin had tired of producing late-night comedy for the BBC and joined Columbia Pictures, leaving after two years in which he failed to produce anything. At Carl Foreman's instigation, he worked as producer on *The Virgin Soldiers*, based on Leslie Thomas's novel and marking John Dexter's debut as a film director.

It was among the most successful films of the year in Britain, although it flopped when belatedly released in America. Sherrin's next film, a dreary comedy, *Every Home Should Have One*, also found a market at home. Had the budget been lower as it should have been, he has said, the film would have made an immediate profit.

Sherrin was attracted by the script of *Rentadick*, since Cleese and Chapman had written it for themselves and Tim Brooke-Taylor and Marty Feldman among others. In his autobiography, Chapman blames Frost and Sherrin for the fiasco. Their original script had been called *Renta-sleuth* and they had worked on it with Charles Crichton, the director of such Ealing comedies as *The Lavender Hill Mob*.

In *his* autobiography, Sherrin wrote that he only discovered after purchase that Cleese and Chapman were no longer interested in appearing in it. Indeed, Cleese and Chapman had their name removed from the credits of the film, whose only reference to a script is a line 'additional dialogue by John Wells and John Fortune'. Nevertheless, Sherrin persuaded Rank to back it and Jim Clark, a former film editor who had directed *Every Home Should Have One*, tried to impose a sense of style on a heterogeneous group of actors, including Donald Sinden, Richard Briers and James Booth.

There are moments that have an authentic Python ring about them – 'He had such splendid references, one from King Haakon of Norway, the tallest monarch in Europe in his day', bewails Ronald Fraser at one point. But the cast, playing determinedly stupid characters – bogus majors; bent, thuggish detectives; lunatic businessmen – lack the ferocity Cleese and Chapman would have brought to such parts. They rely instead on extensive mugging and the exaggerated technique of farce, which has never been the Python's style. The result was total failure, artistic and financial.

Instead, Python's first original film was *Monty Python and The Holy Grail*, which gave Jones and Gilliam, as co-directors, a chance to indulge their medieval obsessions. The movie was backed by Michael White, a theatrical producer who has increasingly dabbled, and to good effect, in film production. White was one of the first to have appreciated the new comic talents, having brought to London the Footlights' revue of 1963 which included Cleese as well as such now-familiar names as Tim Brooke-Taylor, Bill Oddie and Jonathan Lynn. Chapman had joined the cast in 1964 for a tour of New Zealand followed by a few performances on Broadway (it closed after 23).

Monty Python and The Holy Grail was a great improvement on their first movie. Even before the film itself had begun, it had managed assaults on the conventions of cinema advertising – 'Monty Python showing four minutes from this restaurant' was the caption to an advert at the beginning, reversing the usual appeal from the neighbourhood Chinese take-away – and of film credits, which are progressively taken over by someone with an obsession about moose, who is replaced by another hung-up on llamas.

It is this subversive quality, the ability to see the absurdity of attitudes which many take as normal, that raises Monty Python above the level of most of their contemporaries (or predecessors, for that matter). They have deliberately distanced themselves from traditional styles of humour, although not always with success. There is a wooden rabbit joke in *Monty Python and The Holy Grail* which is identical to a wooden horse joke to be found in the more conventionally knockabout *Up Pompeii* starring Frankie Howerd and made five years earlier.

But it was often impossible to take seriously the format of television programmes, from news to quiz shows to documentaries, after watching Python's half-hour shows. Since *Monty Python and The Holy Grail*, it is difficult to see anything but absurdity in Hollywood's attempts at the medieval – or stars such as Errol Flynn buckling their swashes. Certainly the melodrama of John Boorman's *Excalibur,* a later venture into Arthurian myth, was rendered ridiculous by memories of what Python had done with similar material.

One extraordinary aspect of the film was how, on a small budget, the two directors managed to convey the feel and smell of the Middle Ages better than more serious and expensive movies. Jones's interest in chivalry is well-known; he has written a scholarly book on the dastardly character of Chaucer's 'parfit gentil knight'. As his later films, *Jabberwocky* and *Time Bandits* have shown, Gilliam too has a great affinity to medieval life. Indeed, dressed in baggy clothes and unshaven, as he appears in the films, he himself can resemble some rude medieval carving come to boisterous life.

'I'm an adrenalin freak,' Gilliam said, explaining his approach at his studio in Covent Garden. His favourite artists are Brueghel and Bosch. 'Imagination ran riot in the Middle Ages. The grotesque wasn't seen as abnormal. Then people did not seem ashamed of any aspect of life. You can go into magnificent churches and find carvings of people doing really gross things.'

Gilliam is one of the most individual film makers in Britain today, one who revels in the messiness of life. His *Jabberwocky* (1977) responded wholeheartedly to the repressed violence of Lewis Carroll's poem. Never were toves so slithy as in his tale of a dim apprentice who slays the monster and wins the princess. Gilliam was, however, unable to overcome a difficulty that still besets the group's work; it is all lumped together under the banner of Monty Python and audiences expect comedy. It is a problem he also faced with *The Time Bandits* and which accounts in part for the lack of success of *Privates on Parade,* which starred John Cleese.

Preview audiences expected *Jabberwocky* to be a zany comedy and, faced with a more complex film, rejected it as not amusing. Gilliam re-edited it in order to emphasise that it was more than a simple comedy. It has the feel of the Middle Ages, and almost the smell, so vivid is its creation of filth and squalor. To it, Gilliam added a modern and understated humour; it is one of the more underrated films of the period.

His *Time Bandits* was more winning on every level, a funny and bizarre film that romped through history and fantasy. Gilliam's great achievement was to achieve a coherent style that could comfortably contain ogres and Napoleon, Agamemnon and a suburban housewife. In scene after scene, with miraculous economy, he conjured different times and places with a conviction few conventional directors could match.

One of Monty Python's great achievements was a completely accidental one: the establishment in 1977 of HandMade Films, now one of the liveliest and busiest independent producers and distributors in Britain. It was the direct result of Delfont and EMI withdrawing from *Monty Python's Life of Brian*. The Pythons looked elsewhere for the money. But there were few other places to look. Five years after the release of *The Holy Grail,* they were still regarded by many as a cult group without any appeal for a mass audience.

Michael Palin mentioned the problem to George Harrison, who had become the most unobtrusive of the former Beatles. Harrison told his financial advisor, Denis O'Brien, a 38-year-old American who, just as unobtrusively, ran his financial consultancy, Euro-Atlantic, from a house in Chelsea. Harrison was one of O'Brien's two showbusiness clients; the other was Peter Sellers. Otherwise, O'Brien dealt with banks, leasing companies, educational groups and financial institutions. Between them, Harrison and O'Brien set up HandMade Films to back and distribute the film. Harrison mortgaged his house to raise his share. O'Brien still regards the film as something the company is never likely to surpass. 'I think it's superb,' he said.

The film that reached the cinema differs in some respects from the script that was filmed, as a comparison with the published screenplay shows. 'They shot the script that Delfont turned down. The film the public saw was not that screenplay. George's and my influence was through discussion over a good 15 areas of that film,' said O'Brien. 'It was nothing to do with good taste; it had to do with pacing. And I think it's a better film as a result of those changes.

'The brilliance of *Brian* is Monty Python. I think because we were not EMI, because we were friends who had come in and had not disturbed their principal photography in Tunisia, we were able to sit down and discuss it with the six individuals. And that's not an easy thing to do at the best of times. It was good fun and we got on extremely well together. I don't want to knock EMI at all for their decision. Because had that screenplay come out as the film, I think the financial results and the public attitude would have been very different.

'I think we got all the parameters right and I think we got all the values right. The statements that were made were made properly without anybody sticking the knife in or going over that very thin line of judgement.

'Even with *The Missionary*, which was Michael Palin's film, you'd be amazed at public comments on it. The fact that a missionary ended up having an affair was something that certain members of the public couldn't tolerate.'

Although HandMade maintain a relationship with Palin, it is no longer involved with the group. Some members resented O'Brien's attempts to advise them in various business deals. The group is a volatile and often argumentative one. The chances of them continuing to work together grow less likely all the time.

'We pulled out of *The Meaning of Life* before any deal was done with Universal. We had made an offer and the simple problem was that when there are six individuals involved, all of a sudden balances can start getting out of whack,' said O'Brien.

'It became very political. Film is never an easy thing to complete at the best of times. You certainly don't want any arrangement at all if there's a lot of squabbling going on, and there was a lot of squabbling going on. Both George and I decided that it simply wasn't worth it. And we pulled out. I hope they did extremely well with the film.

'When you have six members commenting on how to approach the solution of a problem, you have certain members who are prepared to believe in their product and wait it out – and you have other members who want cash on day one. What that deal tells me is that the people who wanted cash on day one, won out. That's not to say they've made the wrong decision, because I don't know how successful that film is going to be. Maybe they'll be better off with the cash in their pockets now, rather than waiting for the film to produce whatever it produces at the box office. You only know if it's good or not at the end of the day.'

The Meaning Of Life reverted to the group's old revue-style format and again showed how difficult it is to pace a succession of sketches over a two hour period. The film was Monty Python at its most combative, deliberately pushing against the barriers of taste to see how far they could go without losing their audience. There was dirtier talk and more gore, mutilation and vomit than are to be found in many video nasties. Their audiences laughed heartily, but there was not only a cruelty in their humour, but a contempt, too, as if the fun had begun to sour.

Michael Palin once described the sort of characters he enjoys playing as 'decent, upright, hopeless people. The persistence of the simple, logical mind makes me laugh.' Such characters, he explained, 'unintentionally break the elaborate rules by which society lives and makes the rules themselves look slightly absurd'. That is a function of Monty Python, too, except that they point up the absurdities intentionally.

Away from the crowd, Palin has revealed a talent for a gentler humour that not only added some moments of quiet amusement to *The Time Bandits* but provided the nostalgic pleasure of *The Missionary* (1983), directed by Richard Loncraine, in which he played an Edwardian vicar entangled in sexual diversion.

'Someone with a sense of mission who is thwarted as soon as he realises that everyone in the world is different from everyone else,' as he described it. What was evident was Palin's affection for the era. 'There's a lot of pathos in that period,' he said. 'You have characters who epitomise total confidence in their world. Yet, with hindsight, we know it was all doomed. There were some very fine people then, very public-spirited, full of ideals which have gone now. People really believed that if they acted in a certain way, it would affect the world for the better.

'I believe in things like railways and films and cinema,' Palin added. 'I wish we could go back to the days when each town had four or five cinemas to choose from, and some were family owned, showing what they wanted. Now cinema is rather like television, served up with one or two channels to watch.'

Monty Python's significance was that they not only kept control of their own destinies, but also made films that did more than show off their skills as comedians and writers: they revealed their talents as film makers. Their movies were not only good comedy, but good films, full of a visual inventiveness. Theirs were anarchic talents disciplined enough to respond to the rigours of filming.

In *The Meaning of Life,* they included *The Crimson Life Assurance,* a film within the film that was a wickedly accurate parody of the sentimental side of Ealing comedy, with ancient, downtrodden English clerks revolting against a take-over by their new bosses, buttoned-down smart young American executives – and winning. It was a warning that the realists might not have it all their own way in the cinemas of the future.

For a style of film making that owed little to the documentary tradition was evident. Many of the younger directors have either consciously rejected the restraints of the older approach or have little knowledge of it.

Some have come from filming television commercials, where the message is the medium. Others have learned their craft in an even newer area: making promotional videos for rock groups, one of the growth industries of the moment. Their hard-sell techniques have put a greater emphasis upon imagery, as well bringing a sense of dislocation between the image and its meaning. They are often less concerned with capturing reality than in creating fantasy.

Film makers with a powerful visual sense have been rarer in Britain than Europe. John Boorman (born 1933) is an exception, a director who began by making TV documentaries, but never seemed content to remain within it. His vision is not so much decorative as intellectual, even when it led to painting street buildings all one colour in *Leo The Last* (1970) filmed in Notting Hill, which was then London's nearest approach to a black ghetto. It starred Marcello Mastroianni as a rich innocent encouraging a revolution that would destroy him. It was an exuberant allegory in favour of change, which was perhaps the reason that its American distributors, United Artists, showed great reluctance to release it.

Boorman followed it with the even more metaphysical *Zardoz* (1973), which mixed myth and science fiction to create a society of immortals longing for the death which they dispense to others, an effete universe which is destroyed by a brutality they welcome. Sean Connery's masculine presence as the hero, seeking knowledge, gave the film a strong centre, but it was too rich a mixture for most audiences. Nevertheless, amongst the timidity of most English-language movies of the time, it was a welcome extravagance.

The theme was one that Boorman returned to in *Excalibur* (1981) where, perhaps, the myth and magic were more acceptable, since the story was the oft-told one of King Arthur, Merlin and Mordred. It had an eccentric performance from Nicol Williamson as Merlin and never quite managed to create a believable world, falling instead into the sort of excesses mocked in *Monty Python and The Holy Grail*.

Boorman's most successful films remain those with an American setting, notably *Point Blank* (1967) and *Deliverance* (1972).

A welcome lack of restraint also marked *The Rocky Horror Picture Show* (1975), directed by Jim Sharman, an Australian with a liking for circus who had also staged the show when it opened at the Royal Court's attic theatre.

Richard O'Brien's musical, which mocked the horror genre while adding its own twist of polymorphous sexual perversity, had been a durable theatrical hit and, in its movie version, became a midnight cult in the States.

At its centre, on stage and film, was an exuberant performance from Tim Curry, in stockings and suspenders as a 'transsexual transvestite from Transylvania'. A sort of sequel, *Shock Treatment* (1982) was much less successful.

Directors, of course, are often eclectic in the styles they use. Alan Parker (born 1942) is not a man to be pigeon-holed. Irreverent in his attitudes and a director who began with the encouragement of David Puttnam, Parker made his debut with *Bugsy Malone* (1976), a totally original musical in its conception, with children acting the story of rivalry between Chicago gangsters and their molls, although the concept was close to some television commercials of the time. It had high spirits and a sense of the ridiculous: the gangsters fired foam-spurting machine guns and threw custard pies and rode around in pedal cars. There was also a hint of satire, with its mythic figures, creations not only of the era of Prohibition but of popular journalism and film, cut down to kiddie size. With an excellent score and good performances plus fluid camera work and a script that mocked the clichés of the style, the film was an undoubted stylistic success.

Parker followed it with *Midnight Express* (1978), an ugly story of an American thrown into a Turkish jail for a drug offence. It was the epitome of a documentary approach.

His musical, *Fame* (1980), about the young trying to succeed in entertainment, successfully combined reportage of auditions and training with big musical numbers that were fantasies of wish-fulfilment.

In *Shoot The Moon* (1982), focusing on marital problems, Parker's style was once more straightforward. He saved his flamboyance for *Pink Floyd – The Wall* (1982), which took its inspiration from the rock group's best-selling album of songs subverting conventional views and preaching a defiant ignorance. The film was a frantic mix of styles, including animation sequences by the intense and intestinal cartoonist Gerald Scarfe.

It is significant that none of Parker's films, with the possible exception of the last, had much to do with the condition of Britain. Parker's ambition was too big to be confined within the small compass of British films of the period. It is impossible, for instance, to imagine *Fame* set in the Royal Academy of Dramatic Art. After his first film, Parker relied on American backers for the necessary finance.

Ridley Scott (born 1939) was another whose ambitions surpassed making feature versions of television situation comedies or the farces and soft-core pornography that were the staple of British cinema. Scott's films reflect his training at the Royal College of Art and his background as a designer. He seems less interested in actors, in performance, than do the many British directors who tend to see films as plays on celluloid. Scott's interest is captured by shapes and textures, by people as decor, rather than by the revelation of character.

Even in his first film, *The Duellists* (1978), the protagonists hardly change during the film. The two men, one violent, the other trapped by his soldierly code of honour, fight each other endlessly over the years. But they are filmed as if they are momentary distractions in the landscape, no more individual than scurrying insects. Narrative is secondary to style.

In *Alien* (1979), one of the most commercially successful films of the decade, there is no story in the conventional sense nor any development of character. It is an exercise in suspense and of a very familiar kind. Its effectiveness comes not so much from waiting for the killer to strike again, or from wondering who the next victim will be, as from the sense of unease created by the alien images themselves, which are at once strange and familiar. The incomprehensible spaceship, shaped like the organs of the human body, with its brooding, dead giant and the mutating and increasingly ferocious creature half-hidden in the shadows, conjure a nightmare atmosphere.

Scott's *Bladerunner* (1982) also amalgamated the familiar and the strange, with its weary private eye attempting to cope with super-human robots: Philip Marlowe in the twenty-fifth century. The creation of a future world, with its mean and shabby streets and soaring technologial marvels, took precedence over the actual story, which was based on Philip K. Dick's swift-paced novel *Do Androids Dream of Electronic Sheep?*

With the drama to be found as much in the settings as the actors, Scott gave warning that the documentarists were going to need a greater sense of urgency and ambition to maintain their position in the cinema. A style that stresses the primacy of the image runs dangers of its own. If the documentary tradition can degenerate into dreary earnestness, focusing on bleak moments in uninteresting lives, so the visionaries can become no more than purveyors of chic.

Directors of television commercials and pop videos have relied on images for their powers of indirect association. Bread is advertised by an appeal to a nostalgic never-never land, as in Ridley Scott's commercial for Hovis with a delivery boy cycling through cobbled streets. Rolls of toilet paper are sold through pictures of mother-love, and the Rolling Stones sing their complacent rock to film of a war in El Salvador.

Such images are filmed to be glimpsed for a moment only; they lack any narrative thrust. The dangers of relying on style and ignoring content were manifest in *The Hunger* (1983). Its director, Tony Scott, the brother of Ridley, turned a story of vampirism into a commercial for *Vogue*, all soft focus and wind-blown veils, with the stylish posing of its cast, David Bowie and Catherine Deneuve, substituting for acting.

Nevertheless, the two finest British directors to emerge in the 1970s were strong stylists and superb technicians with a remarkable visual flair. Both, ironically, came out of the mainstream of the British documentary tradition.

One had been a successful television director, the other had worked as a much admired cameraman on a wide variety of films. Both were men whose films attracted controversy, often to their surprise. Their names were Ken Russell and Nicholas Roeg.

9 Rogue Talents

Nicholas Roeg and Ken Russell

'Don't get vulgarity mixed up with commercialism. By vulgarity I mean an exuberant over-the-top larger-than-life slightly bad taste red-blooded thing. And if that's not anything to do with Art let's have nothing to do with Art.'

Ken Russell, 1972

A Cockney thug pulls a gun and aims it at the head of a rock star grown reclusive on drugs. The screen fills with a swirling image, a whirlpool of flesh, blood red. A sharp cut to a car, occupied by the thug's thuggish friends, who have come to take him for a ride. His hunched figure peers out of the back window: except that the face is no longer his, but the singer's. Their identities, killer and performer, mirror each other, have merged indistinguishably into one.

Whatever Nicholas Roeg and his co-director and writer Donald Cammell (who invited Roeg to collaborate with him on the film) thought they were making, *Performance* put a hole through the head of the 1960s. The movie, released in 1970, now seems a goodbye, a last wave for a bad trip, to a swinging, hippy, drug-happy era that had promised freedom and delivered soft slavery.

It came appropriately at the end of the decade, just as Roeg's *Eureka* in 1983 seemed to sum up the intervening period of materialistic self-destruction. Both films had a hard time finding an audience. *Performance* was not given a release for more than two years after it was made. *Eureka* disappeared from view soon after being given a brief London run.

Roeg, together with Ken Russell, was the finest British film maker to emerge in the 1970s. Both possessed visual qualities rarely found in directors of any nationality, producing visceral images with the power to shock and startle and so enable audiences, for a moment, to see the world around them anew.

Roeg (born 1928) had come through the industry according to textbook tradition, going from clapper boy to director, gaining a reputation along the way as a brilliant director of photography. He worked on such diverse films as Roger Corman's *The Masque of the*

Red Death, Schlesinger's *Far from the Madding Crowd* and François Truffaut's *Fahrenheit 451*.

There are those who can remember him as a lowly cameraman, grumbling about the jobs he was forced to do to survive. He followed *Performance* with *Walkabout* (1971), in which two white children are stranded in the Australian outback with a young aborigine boy, *Don't Look Now* (1973), a macabre thriller, *The Man Who Fell To Earth* (1976), which exploited David Bowie's fey frailty in a story about an extra-terrestrial trying to go home, and *Bad Timing* (1979), a film of sexual obsession, made with another rock star, Art Garfunkel. All were marked by Roeg's distinctive visual style, which intercut past, present and future in a disturbing surrealist montage.

Roeg is drawn to individuals on the edge of society: a petty hoodlum, a confused aborigine, an alien hiding behind dark glasses, an artist in a hostile environment, a millionaire whose life lost its meaning the moment he struck gold.

He is an oblique director, approaching his subject matter literally and metaphorically from unexpected angles. He will advise actors in unusual ways, preparing them for scenes not merely by discussing it but by giving them, say, *Moby Dick* to read or a chapter from *The Bible*.

He proceeds by indirection and his focus on isolated individuals is a means of presenting a fresh approach to over-familiar themes. His characters are often uncomprehending. The little boy being shot at by his suicidal father in the opening scenes of *Walkabout* does not understand what is happening, any more than does his sister when confronted by the ritual courtship of the aboriginal boy who rescues them from the outback. The aborigine interprets white society according to his code and is doomed for it, dying because the girl cannot comprehend what he is offering her in his dance.

The theme of rejection and loss recurs in Roeg's work. In the disturbing *Don't Look Now* the father loses his life through his obsession with his dead daughter. Roeg's technique here is at its most effective, cross-cutting between images, with the future foreshadowed in the present: a blood-like stain spilling across a transparency just before the death by drowning of the daughter, a moment that also anticipates the climax of the film, when the father lies dying from a knife wound in a damp Venetian street.

The juxtaposition of images in Roeg's films sets up several kinds of tension in the viewer, beginning with the basic level of confusion: is what is being seen reality or fantasy or a visual equivalent of the protagonist's state of mind?

It is an extraordinarily effective means of conveying the simultaneity of events, where one can be aware of many sensations at the same time in a medium that, for all its dreamlike aspects, is too often concerned with maintaining a strictly linear narrative style.

Roeg likes to work closely with his writers on the scripts of the films so that dialogue is often subsidiary to the action or more indicative of emotion than information. In *Walkabout,* for instance, which was scripted by Edward Bond, the father, shooting wildly at his fugitive children before killing himself, says, 'Come out now, we've got to go. I've got to go,' in the tones of an indulgent parent at the end of a picnic.

Roeg's purpose, like Russell's, is to break through an audience's conventional responses. An audience at any event too often knows how it is expected to respond, with easy emotions triggered by familiar signals. Roeg wants to dispense with such conditioned reflexes in order to reach a more genuine response. Shock and surprise, the sudden impact of an unexpected image or quick cutting between two different scenes, are means to this end through a process of dislocation.

At one time, he was to have directed a film about Donald Crowhurst, the lone yachtsman who gave out false information about his position and died after aimless wanderings on the ocean. His protagonists are often lost individuals, trapped in the process of defining themselves. David Bowie's alien in *The Man Who Fell To Earth,* adrift in a society like his own but still hostile, overloaded with sensory input, is the archetypal Roeg hero.

Archetypes are what Roeg deals in, which is perhaps why he has featured the familiar personalities of rock singers, simple images for a complex world, in several of his films.

His use of simultaneity, of past pleasures mingling with present ones, charges Roeg's love scenes with a powerful eroticism, a quality that tends to overbalance into violence and coarseness in *Bad Timing*.

Roeg plays not only with images, but, through them, with the notion of time itself, as past, present and future coalesce. In *The Man Who Fell To Earth,* he does so literally, as the unageing alien remembers not only his previous life elsewhere but also sees past happenings on earth, including a glimpse of pioneer settlers in America. As Roeg once explained, 'Life goes in fits and starts; it just doesn't unravel.'

His subject matter tends to extremity and death, action precipitated by violent events, from the suicide at the beginning of *Walkabout* to the violation of nature in *Eureka,* and its central character's corroding guilt.

Roeg has displayed little interest in exploring British society as such, or, indeed, any social system. He is concerned with moments of intense feeling, sudden explosions, between individuals. There is passion at the heart of his films – between the girl and the aborigine in

Walkabout, between husband and wife in *Don't Look Now* and the lovers of *The Man Who Fell To Earth, Bad Timing* and *Eureka* – and it becomes an emotion which not only uplifts those caught in it, but destroys them as well in their failure to fully comprehend it. Only in *Performance* does Roeg explore a recognisable world and even then he is dealing with isolated and extreme characters.

Roeg was one of the few British directors of the period whose work was backed, more often than not, by British money. British Lion, for instance, financed the making of *The Man Who Fell To Earth,* which cost just under £2 million and was made entirely in America. Roeg went to Hollywood after *Walkabout* to make a thriller *Deadly Honeymoon* for MGM, but, after he had spent six months working on the film, it was cancelled the week before shooting was to start.

Eureka emphasised Roeg's need for a strong narrative to underlie his visual virtuosity, something the film lacked in its final version. The story itself, based on an actual and unsolved murder of a millionaire, was sensational enough, but Roeg's interest was elsewhere so that he had to resort to an unconvincing court-room scene – one of those in which witnesses are permitted to deliver long, emotional and legally irrelevant confessionals – to provide some explanation of the movie's purpose.

The danger of Roeg's approach is that it can collapse into incoherence, losing all narrative sense in a welter of images. At such times, it offers little more than a succession of charming pictures and degenerates into the self-confident flash of television commercials, although it is truer to say that directors of commercials have plundered Roeg's films for effective techniques.

Like Ken Russell, Roeg displays a flamboyant disregard for documentary niceties with a vitality and drive that suggests life is too complex and sensational to be captured and recreated in a straightforward way, thus challenging an audience's assumptions and opening up new possibilities for the cinema.

Russell was more dependent than Roeg on American finance for his career. He emerged from the BBC–TV arts series, *Monitor,* 'the one and only English experimental film school ever', he called it in John Baxter's sympathetic study of his work, *An Appalling Talent.*

He began making feature films in 1963, but the first to display his individual style was *Women In Love* (1969), based on D. H. Lawrence's novel. It was a restrained film compared with what followed. *The Music Lovers* (1970), about Tchaikovsky, was sold to United Artists, who backed it with $1.6m, as 'the story of a homosexual who falls in love with a nymphomaniac'.

Russell's work was a response to the emotional power of music and to the lives of those who created it. He is a composer manqué and talks of his films in musical terms.

'Musicians are trying to do what I'm trying to do: express the inexpressible,' he said. 'No, not express it, but investigate it, discover the undiscoverable, plumb the umplumbable. If you're a musician, you do it in a musical way. If you're a film maker you do it in a filmic way, which is my craft. Musicians come nearest to plumbing this divine mystery.'

Most of his films are voyages of self-discovery, whatever their ostensible subject matter. The exceptions are *The Boy Friend* (1971), an engaging backstage musical in the manner of Busby Berkeley, and *Valentino* (1977), which starred Rudolph Nureyev as the silent film star who became a romantic idol for millions.

The Boy Friend he regarded as a mistake, because his treatment was too static. 'I thought *Valentino* was quite good at the time,' he said. 'When I saw it again in 1979 I liked bits of it but thought that, as a film, it was a failure. There wasn't enough variation in it and the acting left something to be desired. I wasn't able to help Nureyev enough to make the character convincing. He was miscast.'

During the filming of *Tommy* (1975) on location in a Portsmouth junkyard, he told me, 'All my films have the same theme, but I don't tell anyone what it is. It's like Elgar's *Enigma Variations*: he didn't tell what the theme was. People have to see the films and work it out for themselves. All my films are enigma variations.'

Russell had originally gone to the Portsmouth area to shoot some holiday camp scenes on Hayling Island, but something went wrong and he scouted Southsea instead for various locations – a row of beach-huts, a fun-fair, a ballroom – that could form a holiday camp on film.

He tried Southsea pier and found an ideal ballroom, ornate, genteel ('NO JEANS AND THE LIKE' read a sign outside) which, in the light of the evening sun, was filled with a strange yellow light. It excited him. He told his lighting cameraman to try to achieve that light. 'It's a happy accident,' he told me. 'That's what films are about. Some accidents are happy and some are not, but they're all interesting.'

As it happened, this accident had disastrous consequences. During filming, the ballroom caught alight and the pier burned down. It was somehow what you would expect to happen around Russell. He and excess seem inseparable.

'Typical Russell,' grumbled one of his crew during the filming of *Tommy*. 'He's got it, but he'll do another three takes.'

Tommy has withstood the passage of time better than might have been expected. The film was produced by Robert Stigwood, then perfecting the 'crossover' technique, of films that can generate extra revenue from records and other spinoffs and attract a new audience – a technique that resulted in *Grease* and *Saturday Night Fever*.

Part of the finance came from Columbia and the stipulation was that it should include American stars. Hence Ann-Margret as Tommy's mother and Jack Nicholson as a doctor. Russell remembered Ann-Margret only from Elvis Presley movies ('I'm too busy with my own films to see other people's') and had *Carnal Knowledge* screened for him so that he could catch up on her acting and Nicholson's.

Russell took Pete Townshend's songs and through the act of filming, gave them an extra dimension, other meanings. 'We had to devise character development within scenes which seemed to be about something else, which is what I like to do,' he said. 'You're getting two ideas over at the same time.'

Russell had problems with one scene, where Tommy (Roger Daltrey) sees his mother for the first time since he was small. He rehearsed the scene, a duet for the two, and was unhappy; it sounded too sentimental. He needed to convey Tommy's rejection of his mother. The scene was to be shot on a beach. But he could not decide how. Should Tommy be in the water? Daltrey suggested he sing it while helping fishermen haul in their nets. Russell listened to what everyone had to say and then went off on his own.

The next day, he had made up his mind. 'I think it would only work if Tommy suddenly sees his mother and she's dressed in an appalling red dress, covered in jewels, slit up to her fanny and her tits falling out of it, with her fluffy hair and trying to look 20 years younger, which wasn't how he remembered her as a child.

'And I think he would try to destroy that image: he would tear off the jewellery and throw it into the sea and he'd see her red fingernails, five inches long, and he'd grind them into the sand and he'd duck her head under water and he'd bring her back to being a natural person, which is what he tries to bring everyone back to.'

And that was how, a few days later, he filmed it. 'I'd already shot the later scenes in which we made her spiritual. So we had to think how she became spiritual,' he said. 'In films, the interesting thing is that working backwards, you sometimes have a bonus which you wouldn't get if you shot it in order. I like the jigsaw puzzle element of interlocking everything until it works, whatever order you shoot it in.'

Russell makes films instinctively. 'You find a film has a life of its own,' he once told me. 'You have to go along with it. If you fight against it, you're lost; so I let the film take me after a bit.'

He tends to distrust words and regards his *Savage Messiah* (1972), about the life of the sculptor Gaudier-Brzeska, as not cinematic enough. 'It had a very good script from Christopher Logue and I leant too heavily on the dialogue. It could have been a radio play.'

At the time of *Tommy*, Russell had finished a script of a film about George Gershwin, which he thought would be his next project, and he had another six films planned. 'Gershwin has a lot of strange things about him that I want to bring out. I think it will be a bit of a surprise,' said Russell. But it has never been made.

Instead he shot *Lisztomania* (1975) for David Puttnam and Sandy Lieberson's Goodtimes Enterprises. It was his worst film, with Roger Daltry playing the virtuoso composer as a Cockney Liberace. Even more so than his *Mahler* (1974), also for Goodtimes Enterprises, Russell responded not to the composer or his music, but to his own feelings about the music. The result verged on chaos, with an overwhelming reliance on Nazi imagery to convey his horror.

Music has a powerful effect on him. 'I see shapes and feelings – a feeling which is extremely strong and does have a shape – when I listen to music that I can't put into words but which I feel I can use in my work,' he said.

'I remember playing some music by Respighi, *The Roman Festivals*, after returning from my first visit to Greece. Somehow it was very Mediterranean, and I had a vision of the whole history of the Greeks. Almost as one idea, not as a succession of images, although there were images, overlapping. That was very powerful and I was shaking and weeping. I felt I was part of history, living ten thousand years all at once. Sound and images turn into something else. The challenge is to get that sort of feeling on film.'

There was no sense of mystical fervour about the dispiriting *Valentino* (1977), hampered as it was by Nureyev's clumsy portrayal of the slick-haired lover. Russell, once a ballet dancer himself, had long wanted to make a film about Nijinsky with Nureyev, a project that promised much. *Valentino* was a poor substitute. Russell has never been an actors' director, but it has hardly mattered when he has used talented performers. Here, the difference was crucial.

He went to work in Hollywood for the first time to make *Altered States* (1981) for Warner Brothers. His experience reveals not only the haphazard way the film industry often seems to work, but the difficulties any director faces, even one with a distinguished record, in trying to sustain a coherent career.

Critics may view a director's work as a seamless whole, but from close-up it becomes a patchwork of luck and compromise, opportunity and disappointment, dependent upon the wishes and whims of other people who control the money. And these people themselves are often without real power, since studio executives come and go with monotonous regularity.

Russell took over the film after Arthur Penn, its original director, had quit. Penn had quarrelled with the movie's writer, Paddy Chayevsky, who had adapted it from his novel and felt protective towards it. The book dealt with a scientist who experiments with sense deprivation techniques and regresses to ape-man before he begins to disintegrate totally. On the set, Chayevsky kept countermanding Penn's orders and, for once in films, the writer prevailed.

'I wasn't the first choice,' Russell said. 'They thought I could handle the fantastic stuff, but they were less certain about the acting. A lot of the film is just people talking round a table. I'm not too happy doing that, although I was in this case. So they saw *Savage Messiah*, in which they were very impressed with the acting of Dorothy Tutin, although I'm not sure I had anything to do with that. And they saw the one I did for the BBC on Delius.

'My career has always been up and down. That period was one of its down moments. After *Valentino* my name was mud. I'd had various things which I tried to get off the ground or people wanted me to do, but we could never get the money for them. I'd been commissioned to write the script for yet another version of *Dracula*. By the time I finished it, and I thought it was not bad, three *Dracula* films were out, so that was a dead duck.

'They'd tried everyone else when they came to me. I saw it as a challenge. To me, working with actors wasn't the most exciting part of filming. I was happier doing some action thing or a fantastic sequence. I saw that here the acting had to be really good, because they were just talking to each other. They couldn't be running along naked through a forest while they were doing it.

'I thought I could bring something to the fantasy sequences. And I had more money to spend than usual. Most of my fantasy sequences have been done on very low budgets. The film was budgeted at $10m, but they'd already spent half of that, so it ended up at nearly $15m.

'Arthur Penn had had six months to get going. I had six weeks to get the show on the road. By then Columbia were getting cold feet and wanted to pull out before they got in too deeply. Warners had wanted to do a Paddy Chayevsky film; they'd been courting him for a long time and were delighted to take it over.

'I think the producer and Chayevsky were frightened of getting into a situation they'd already had where everyone started taking sides and everything fell apart.

'I'd never worked in America before. I wanted an English assistant director, they said no. I wanted an English associate producer, they said no. The reason I wanted them was that I thought I could be more efficient with them.

'By pure chance, Richard McDonald, one of the best art directors going, who had worked in America for some time was free and wanted to work on the film. We forged a collaboration that got the film made, because the script was so vague about the hallucinations. Most of them were to do with abstract things like black smoke going through the cosmos at a million miles a second. They were battering their heads to work out things which I thought didn't enhance the story at all, were impossible to do and would have bored everyone to death in any case. It was a matter of getting coherence in the fantasies that would also illuminate the character.'

The relationship between Russell and Chayevsky quickly deteriorated. 'What finished it was that he promised never to interfere with the actors. He said to me that he wouldn't interfere, but be around as a benign presence. Someone asked, "How do you spell benign, Paddy?" "W-i-c-k-e-d," he said.'

The first scene Russell shot was a festive meal in an Italian restaurant. Afterwards Chayevsky complained to the actors that they were playing the scene too drunkenly and walked off the set. Russell phoned him in the evening and they quarrelled. A week later, they quarrelled again when Chayevsky complained about how one actor was saying his lines. 'I told him it was a rehearsal when we were trying to get a complicated camera movement right,' said Russell.

'He was much happier when the camera was locked off, like a stage, and shot a long shot and two close-ups. He'd say, if you shoot a scene in one shot, I can't cut it. He didn't seem to understand that if it's a four minute scene you shoot it and direct it in a different way to a two minute scene. If you cut two minutes from a four minute scene, it just doesn't flow. He wasn't used to that, and I wasn't used to talking to writers and had agreed anyway to do his script as it was.'

Chayevsky went back to New York, declaring that he would never see the movie. He had his name taken off the script, although there was still a credit to him as novelist. Instead, the screenplay was credited to Sidney Aaron, which also happened to be Chayevsky's name.

'They toyed with the idea of firing me and letting him direct it, but he didn't want to,' said Russell.

He plundered Revelations (a seven-horned sacrificial ram), Salvador Dali and primitive religion (the image of a mushroom as a sign of power: tree of knowledge and nuclear explosion) for the hallucinations. He also took a sequence from a 1930s film *Dante's Inferno*, tinting the black and white film red, because it was cheaper than shooting the sequence himself.

The film was a cross between an updated *Dr Jekyll and Mr Hyde* and a pop version of *Faust*. Of its kind, it was a superior example, but for Russell it seemed, at the best, no more than marking time. But it was an experience he valued: 'It taught me not to be afraid of static scenes of pure acting instead of the Douglas Fairbanks school of acting which I've always nurtured.'

After *Altered States*, Russell turned down other Hollywood offers, which were to make other, similar science fiction films and planned to make a film for a German company about Beethoven's life. But the finance failed at the last moment.

He also rejected an approach by EMI to film Evelyn Waugh's *Vile Bodies*. 'It seemed so out of key with the times. There's nothing in it to interest me. It's just a museum piece. The people in it are so bizarre; they're like Martians,' he said.

'One thing I got out of Hollywood: the crew and the producers – I don't say they loved film, but it's in their blood, it's like breathing. It is natural. They have to do it, it's a compulsion. If you get a crew who is enthusiastic, they go on working until you get the scene. That couldn't be done over here. In this country, they've never really enjoyed films. The Americans never say, "I have to go, I'm taking the wife to the movie tonight or she's cooking fish and chips," as they do here. Because the Americans know it isn't easy, they automatically want to help. I never found anyone who ever said, it's time we were going home. I can't tell you what a boost that is. That spirit has gone out of here now. I don't see it.

'Films are much more fluid than television now. When I worked for the BBC there'd be six of you and you'd jump into a car and whizz off. When I did two films for Granada on the Lake poets there were more people than on a feature film.

'It was an archaic system that had grown up with the studio system, but on location it didn't seem to make sense. You had one prop man to bring a pencil to the set and another to arrange it on the table and a third to take it away. I used to make films on a shoestring, but you can't do it now. It's killed a lot of enterprise.'

Russell remains a very English film maker, a romantic whose love of the Lake District, where he now lives, is intermingled with his feelings for its many literary associations. He has shot parts of eight films there, including the television documentaries on Wordsworth and Coleridge. 'It's a very spiritual place,' he said. 'I've gradually become aware of the more pantheistic side of things since moving into the country. Until I became a Catholic, I didn't know what to do with my life: at least I knew what I wanted to do, but I didn't seem to be able to do it. Directly I was converted, my life changed instantly, like switching on a light and everything became feasible.

'Seeing death and rebirth in nature, which I'd never seen before, you do get a sense of mystery. If you're living in the midst of it, it's a constant wonder and revelation. It's very enriching.'

His films are emotional rather than intellectual. 'I don't want to shock in my films,' he said. 'I want to move. Generally, I'm dealing with a very much heightened form of reality. Film has got such a dull reputation generally that any time it steps outside being just a representation of a true photograph, everyone gets very upset. They say it must tell the truth, and by that they don't mean the truth behind the picture but the face value of the picture. I'm not very interested in that.'

Recently Russell intended to make the movie for Robert Stigwood of *Evita*, Andrew Lloyd Webber and Tim Rice's surprisingly successful musical of the life of Eva Peron. But those plans also collapsed.

'It used to be that for every ten scripts, you'd do one. Now it's for every twenty,' he said. So he has turned to directing operas, causing as much scandal and controversy there as he has in his films.

Roeg and Russell mark a distinctive break from an older style of British film making, which was more literary, even stage-bound, in its inspiration. It is true that the two have often relied on literary works, novels and plays, as the basis of their movies. But they have used the works as a springboard, something off which their own visual imaginations can leap.

10 Twinkle, Twinkle British Stars

James Fox, Michael Caine, Robert Stephens,
Glenda Jackson, United British Artists

'My ambition is to influence British movies
through my own taste, which means producing. In
a strange way I think I could make quite a big
contribution here.'

Michael Caine, 1967

In 1970, James Fox was on the brink of becoming a star of the first
magnitude. He had charm, good looks and, less essential but still
useful, he was a good actor. If in some of his roles he had seemed effete
in a rather British way, his violent Cockney thug in *Performance*
showed that he also possessed that edge, that sense of danger, which is
a mark of the greatest performers.

Acting in *Performance* had a profound effect on him, as he revealed
in his autobiography, *Comeback*, published in 1983. It made him
reconsider his attitudes, which chimed with the 'liberated' ethos of
the period, and led him to turn away from using drugs and sex as a
means of finding happiness and satisfaction.

He tried, for a short time, acting in provincial theatres. Then, over
a winter breakfast in a Blackpool hotel, he was converted to evangeli-
cal Christianity and soon after began working as a Phonotas salesman
in Sheffield. (Not surprisingly, he became one of their best.)

Fox, who had begun his acting career as a child in 1950, stayed away
for 10 years. Then he was offered one of the most coveted and sought
after roles of the time, the male lead, opposite Meryl Streep, in *The
French Lieutenant's Woman*.

He turned it down. He objected to the use of 'Jesus' and 'Christ' as
conversational expletives, to a scene set in a brothel and the fact that
the two central characters were married people having an affair. After
discussing it with someone who shared his religious convictions, he

decided that it would offend and confuse other Christians if he were to play the part.

Fox concluded that the offer was an indication from God that something even better was planned for him. He was to have returned as Dan Dare, the lantern-jawed heroic space pilot of the *Eagle* comic of the 1950s. At the last moment, the series was abandoned. In the event, he made his comeback as Waldorf Astor in the glossy but ordinary BBC–TV series, *The Astors*. He also starred in a low-budget British film *Runners* (1983). God works in mysterious ways.

At a time when he had come to Britain to prove that he was more than the handsome star of a television soap opera, I once watched the American actor Richard Chamberlain carefully examine, frame by frame, more than a thousand tiny contact prints of photographs of himself. Only six met with his approval. He insisted that the negatives of all the rest be destroyed.

It is not uncommon behaviour by stars, who jealousy protect the image of themselves that they wish the public to have and which they believe can be easily harmed. Raquel Welch, for instance, has it written into her contracts that she has absolute approval of all still photographs taken of her while she is filming. No outsiders are allowed to take photographs while she is on the set. Nor will she trust looking at contact prints, which need to be studied under a magnifying glass. She insists on 8 × 10 inch glossy prints so that she can see precisely what she is rejecting. She regards her attitude as perfectly reasonable and professional.

'It's no big deal,' she told me, when I once asked her why she bothered. 'Everybody does it. Robert Redford, Marlon Brando, they all do it. I'm not here on a free trip, you know. I'm part of selling this movie and it's my business to see that the producers sell it in the best way, for both of us.

'Some of the photos taken are really not very nice. You learn early on that other people don't care. I remember on my first picture, *Fantastic Voyage,* the publicity department wanted a head shot of me to send out to newspapers. They didn't have one, so they took a long shot of me and enlarged the head and sent that out. It was one where I had a bathing cap on and was playing a scene where I was supposed to be near collapse!'

On the other hand I've watched Glenda Jackson, her hair straggling from under a grubby hand, scrubbing away at the make-up of her face while half-a-dozen photographers snapped her in the act. She might have looked better fainting under a bathing cap, but she was unconcerned by their presence or where the resulting pictures might appear.

It may well be that the different attitudes to stardom are not national, that there are American stars who do not wish to control every aspect of their publicity, just as there are British ones ambitious for such power.

Yet there does seem a suspicion of stardom among British actors which, if it makes for better actors, is one reason why so few of them are able to attract an international following. Not many are, to use the industry's highest praise, 'bankable', which means that their presence in a film can raise the money to get it made.

As a result, few British actors have the power to influence the kind of movies they make, as, say, Robert Redford does. Few, of course, want to. Even those who do often change their minds. In 1967, Michael Caine, then 33 and, he said, a dollar millionaire, was interviewed by Jonathan Aitken for his book *The Young Meteors* on the fashionable successes of the time.

'I'm a tremendously patriotic person and I care a great deal about how this country runs,' Caine told him. 'The only resources we've got in this country are the brains of our young people, and what really annoys me is that we're not using our own talent in films. The young talent in British films, writers, directors, actors, producers, all got discovered when the Americans came over here to start using up their frozen dollars.

'That's the only reason anyone ever heard of half the people who are famous in the film industry in this country today. I think we've got to develop our own talent. When I'm a producer, I'll give all the opportunities to British actors and British directors.

'Also, I'm very keen on the new universities, and I'd like to start courses in film directing in places like Sussex. We can't go on muddling through missing good people all the time.'

In 1978, Caine left Britain. He has his own production company, but he has been content to remain a hard-working actor who has now appeared in more than 50 films.

After he left he complained, with some justification, that he saw Charles Bronson in America being offered parts in movies being made by Lord Grade and wondered what he was doing, waiting for the British film industry to come to him.

On the few occasions it does, he seems to make a little extra effort. He gave his best performance in years in Lewis Gilbert's *Educating Rita* (1983), an old-fashioned British film set in Liverpool, but which had to be filmed in Dublin to accommodate the legal requirements of tax exile.

Sean Connery, the once and current James Bond, also lives abroad and his attempts to become involved in local production have not succeeded.

He can influence the casting of a film in which he appears, as he did with *Never Say Never Again* (1983), which marked his return in the role of James Bond. He was also instrumental in Dick Clement and Ian Le Frenais being hired to add some sparkle to the dialogue, although neither received any credit on the screen for their work.

Albert Finney got as far as directing his own film, *Charlie Bubbles*, and forming a production company, Memorial Enterprises, with another actor, Michael Medwin. He, too, has sometimes shared the disdain for stardom that seems as much a British acting tradition as Shakespeare.

Indeed, Shakespeare and the theatre provide a career that many find more satisfying than films. After *Tom Jones*, when he was the hottest young actor in the world, Finney took a long break. More recently, he joined the National Theatre as their leading classical actor, playing such roles as Tamburlaine, Macbeth and Hamlet. Lord Olivier had even hoped that Finney might have taken over from him as an actor-manager running the National Theatre.

An entire generation of British actors of brilliant talent have shown only a passing interest in film, and not much of one in television.

Tom Courtenay did appear in a few of the best films of the 1960s, such as *The Loneliness of the Long Distance Runner* and *Billy Liar*, but he made it evident that he would act only in films he cared about. His absence from the screen for more than a decade was broken by *The Dresser* (1984), in which he played a limp-wristed homosexual, a part which he had originally created on the London stage. By the time the film opened to enthusiastic reviews for his performance, Courtenay had returned to the stage, acting at a provincial theatre.

Robert Stephens, when he was the leading actor at the National Theatre, similarly refused many film roles because the parts were not good enough. 'Once you become a film actor or a film star, you really can't stop,' he said. 'You have to be before the public's eye all the time. I wouldn't care for that. And the material can't be that good all the time, so you have to make mostly films that aren't frightfully good and that wouldn't interest me either.

'If you consider the great film actors, Spencer Tracy, Bogart, Gable, Cooper, Grant, you'll find that only a few films contain their finest work. They made an awful load of rubbish. But that's being a film star.

'Film acting is difficult to do properly. I remember saying to George Cukor that I thought it was as difficult to be Spencer Tracy as Laurence Olivier. He said it was much more difficult to be Spencer Tracy, because you can't tell lies on the screen.

'Ralph Richardson told me he was terribly nervous just before he did one day on *Death on the Nile*. "Walking into a studio for a day's filming is like walking into a pub and a man saying, take this dart and just hit the bull's eye," he said.'

Stephens' biggest film role was playing the great detective in Billy Wilder's *The Private Life of Sherlock Holmes*, made in London in 1970. 'We were 29 weeks filming it and the original version ran for three hours and two minutes. When it was released it ran for two hours and five minutes. It was cut to shreds. The production company said that long films didn't work. Wilder told me the film would make me a big star, that I should be careful what I did next and that he would advise me. But, of course, when a film is a flop, which it was, the actor is blamed a lot for it. So, if I wanted to be a star, I had a chance and missed it.

'I don't regret it. I don't think I would have liked to have been a star. I've met so many of my contemporaries who are, and who talk of going back to the theatre and doing what they really want to. But they never do.

'Once you are a success in films, there are always three more films waiting to be made. Your whole life style changes. You have to buzz around all over the world. Then you have tax problems or you have to go and live in Hollywood. I don't want to go to live there.'

The present day equivalent of Laurence Olivier and John Gielgud as Britain's outstanding classical actors are Alan Howard and Ian McKellen. Neither has shown much interest in appearing in movies. Howard has never made a film and McKellen only a few.

Jeremy Irons, who became internationally known through the TV serial *Brideshead Revisited* and his role in *The French Lieutenant's Woman*, is another who is drawn to what he calls 'good work' rather than stardom. His performance in the film, followed by his acting on Broadway in Tom Stoppard's play *The Real Thing* has made Irons one of the most sought after actors of the day. But he still talks of wanting to play in Shakespeare with the Royal Shakespeare Company and of avoiding becoming trapped within an image that the public might foist upon him.

'I'm fairly irresponsible,' he said. 'I don't care that much if I fall flat on my face, so I hope I won't get frightened and play too safe. There's so much money involved in pictures. When a producer signs you for a part, he wants something specific from you and that's what you have to give him. In theatre, you can experiment. I don't want to surround myself with Hollywood mega-millionaire producers. If I play safe, I will castrate myself as an actor.'

It is an attitude that emerges whenever you talk to a British actor. Edward Fox put it bluntly, 'You forget what it is to act in films.'

Tim Curry, whose career has encompassed films as different as *The Rocky Horror Picture Show* and *The Ploughman's Lunch*, displays an unexpected caution. 'Stardom is a very irrational state,' he said. 'I've enjoyed success but the only choice I want is to go on developing without too much pressure. I'm really more concerned with growing quietly at my own pace.'

For most British actors, theatre provides an excitement that films cannot match. As Diana Rigg once said, 'You get a chance to reach a point of maturation when you're on the stage.' She also values theatre for 'the process of working with other people, very closely, in rehearsal. It's deeply exciting: you don't get that in films.'

'If you're photogenic and can say a line intelligently, you're home and dry in films,' said Donald Sinden, who as a young actor was under contract to Rank. 'I have no great respect for film acting because it really isn't acting at all. It should be called something else. *Behaving*, perhaps.'

Glenda Jackson epitomizes the British attitude towards stardom, regarding it as an irrelevance. A great star, nevertheless, and a great actress on stage and film, she has a forthright view of acting as a job, and a hard one. Her range of performance demonstrates how well she has mastered her art. It has encompassed comedies as frothy as the otherwise forgettable *A Touch of Class* (1972), for which she won one of her two Oscars (the other was for *Women in Love*), and the emotionally powerful *The Music Lovers* (1971), in which her acting was pitched at the level of hysteria. Yet she is more likely to be found making a small film than an expensive spectacular.

In *Stevie* (1978), a chamber work also notable for the acting of Mona Washbourne, she was brilliantly direct as the suburban-dwelling poet Stevie Smith, and she gave an incisive display as a television reporter in *Giro City* (1983), both films that offered small financial rewards. She speaks not of performances to come, but of stopping acting altogether, although not entirely voluntarily.

'You get to a certain age and the parts aren't there,' she said. 'There is no continuous flow of work for an actress. In the cinema, it happens much earlier and quicker than on the stage. They are still hooked on the idea of externals being very important and your face just gets too old. This will happen long before I'm willing to sit at home and garden or polish the furniture. Bearing that in mind I've thought of what I'd do: some sort of social work, probably.

'One marvellous thing about Britain is that you can do your work and go home afterwards with no pressure on you to live off-stage what you represent on it. It's not difficult to be private in England. I don't think the English are particularly concerned with making heroes and heroines out of actors and actresses. That's not an English fantasy. In America, there is a ferocious desire to have a part of a person.

'In England, you don't always have to be hustling for the best work by presenting an image of yourself. In most countries you have to play that particular game, but here you don't. You can get too cut off if you spend your time playing at being a star. You are really only an actor when you are working, and to fritter away your energy by acting at other times is daft.'

When she was playing the part of another great actress, Sarah Bernhardt, in Richard Fleischer's rather dull *The Incredible Sarah* (1978), she talked to me about attitudes to acting, especially hers.

'Either you want to show off: you are immensely stage struck and believe it is some sort of glamorous profession and that what matters is what you do before you get on the stage and once you're off it. Or you believe that it is an immensely difficult job that requires a great deal of hard work to do and the actual life is a pain in the neck and the only reason to be in the theatre at 7.30 at night, when most respectable women are at home resting, is to do the work on stage. That is my attitude. I mean, I cannot think of any reason to be in the theatre than to do the actual work.

'For me, acting stays continually interesting because you can never learn it, you can never do it. The external rewards don't actually touch that continuing struggle, because that never alters. If anything it becomes more difficult because the more you do, the more people expect of you. So it becomes difficult to approach anything without a great weight of other people's expectations.

'It is also very hard for people to accept that you are actually concerned with the work and not with yourself. It's a world where major egos are allowed to clash against each other without any of the normal restraints that most of the other professions exercise over their participants.

'Quite often you can waste an awful amount of time bumping up against other people's egos, which is really very tedious. I don't tolerate fools gladly. I don't like people getting in my way of working and I tend not to be careful of people's egos or tender sentiments.

'Acting is extremely difficult and I don't think one can waste time on gentling people: you must get down to what is important and basic. If people can't cope with that, they should be in some other job. I don't expect allowances to be made for me. If I can't do it, I simply have to sweat at doing it. The confrontation is very clear, direct and simple, and the solution is equally clear, direct and simple. You just have to do it. And if you have to sweat blood to get it, that's what you have to sweat.'

She does not speak with warmth about most film producers. 'They always tell me, "Come to me with anything you want and we'll do it". And I go to them with something. And they say, "Well, they wouldn't understand it in America, but how would you like to do my project?"

And they hand you some tawdry, tatty script, which they can find the finance for very easily.

'It's a myth that power goes with a name. If you want to do the things that you really want to do, then you have to work for no money. And that's fair enough. It's sad and disheartening, but it's fair enough.'

She also distrusts audiences. 'Audiences only really want to love you and for you to love them. They want things to be confirmed, and not to have to think or to question. You cannot afford to trust an audience, because they really want what is easiest for themselves. They are no help in any advancement.'

Yet she has always tried to control her own destiny. It was not surprising to find her name among those who formed United British Artists in 1983, a bold new company that took its cue from the foundation of the original United Artists Corporation, which was an attempt by the stars of the silent era, Charlie Chaplin, Mary Pickford and Douglas Fairbanks with the director D. W. Griffiths, to wrest some of the power and profits from distributors and bankers (who put the situation rather differently, as 'The lunatics have taken over the asylum').

UBA was formed by the actor Richard Johnson and a producer, Peter Shaw, together with Albert Finney, John Hurt, Glenda Jackson, Diana Rigg and Maggie Smith and a director, Peter Wood. Since its formation, Harold Pinter has joined the board. The group will combine work in theatre, film and television. In January 1984, Finney directed and starred in a play, *The Biko Inquest*, at the Riverside Studios in London, which was filmed for later television transmission on Channel Four.

John Arden's great *Serjeant Musgrave's Dance*, which was revived at the Old Vic in May, 1984 with Finney in the title role, and Giles Cooper's bitter comedy *Everything in the Garden*, starring Diana Rigg and Richard Johnson, will also be filmed for television and sold around the world.

Such a conjunction of new and experienced talents is rare and exciting, although their first venture to reach the cinema screens was worthy rather than thrilling. *Champions* (1984), directed by John Irvin, starred John Hurt as the jockey Bob Champion, who managed not only to overcome cancer but also to win the Grand National. Perhaps because it was a true story, concerning recent events, the film was somewhat stilted, despite Hurt's sensitive performance.

Irvin went on to direct *Turtle Summer*, another UBA production with a script by Harold Pinter from Russell Hoban's novel *Turtle Diary* and a cast that included Johnson, Jackson, Ben Kingsley, Michael Gambon and Rosemary Leach.

UBA promises much. Actors such as Jackson, Finney and the rest could, after all, earn their living in an easier way. (Sherry Lansing, who was production head at Twentieth Century Fox in 1980, turned down Alan Parker's *Shoot The Moon* because Finney wanted $1.5 million dollars for his role and Diane Keaton $2 million, which would have had a knock-on effect on the rest of the budget, increasing it from $5 million to $12 million.)

That they should choose to put their talents and energies into British films and television is one of the most encouraging signs that the current vitality of the industry is real and even lasting and not a myth or a momentary phase.

UBA have links with the American company, Embassy Communications, whose overseas interests are run by Lord Grade. It is also involved in co-productions with another new British production company, Britannic Film and Television, which is backed by Fleet Holdings, owners of *The Daily Express* and *The Sunday Express* and many magazines, and the Industrial and Commercial Finance Corporation.

Peter Snell, Britannic's chief executive, plans to concentrate on films for television rather than for the cinema, although these days the distinction between the two is becoming ever more blurred.

11 Building Jerusalem

David Puttnam and Goldcrest

Bring me my bow of burning gold!
Bring me my arrows of desire!
Bring me my spear! O clouds, unfold!
Bring me my chariot of fire!

I will not cease from mental fight,
Nor shall my sword sleep in my hand,
Till we have built Jerusalem
In England's green and pleasant land.

William Blake

If the British film industry is actually born again and manages to survive as an expression of national concerns, not just as a service industry for visiting American producers, then a major part of the credit will belong to David Puttnam, a bearded, slightly rumpled figure who has been a successful producer for 15 years and is now its most significant single creative force. The films he has produced bear the stamp of his own personality and attitudes. They are also specifically British in their approach, even when the subject matter is not.

Puttnam has an eye for talent and has given opportunities to those who have emerged as among the best British directors of the 1970s, Michael Apted, Alan Parker, Ridley Scott among them. That process continues as he is still discovering and encouraging inexperienced directors and writers.

He is the most visible of British producers and the man who has done much to make British films evident internationally. Since the success of *Chariots of Fire* he has become a public figure, the one local producer since Alexander Korda to have gained such recognition. Puttnam, indeed, has become a sort of symbol of the revitalised British industry. He has, in addition to his other talents, great marketing skills, a gift for publicity and manipulation of the media.

One of his heroes is the great entrepreneur-showman of ballet, Diaghilev. Another is Irving Thalberg, Hollywood's golden-boy producer of the 1930s, who provided a model for F. Scott Fitzgerald's *The Last Tycoon*.

Puttnam was obsessed with films as a schoolboy, to the detriment of his studies, he now says. When he left school at 16, he tried to get a job in films. But at the time it was a studio-based business and the difficulties of travel from Puttnam's home in North London were insuperable, even if he had managed to find employment.

'It was a highly nepotistic business,' he said, a remark that echoes the view of Hugh Hudson, director of *Chariots of Fire*, who complained in 1981 that the British film establishment ran on 'snobbery and nepotism'. So Puttnam drifted into advertising, where he worked for ten years and became a successful account executive while still in his 20s. His colleagues included Alan Parker, then a copywriter, and Ridley Scott, who was working as an art director. For a brief period, he toyed with journalism, joining *London Life*, a self-consciously fashionable metropolitan magazine.

He soon quite journalism to work as an agent to many leading photographers before deciding to try to become a film producer by encouraging Parker to write a script. The result was *Melody*, a comedy of two adolescent boys infatuated with the same girl, directed by Waris Hussein to modest success.

Puttnam, brought up to believe in the values of hard work, has maintained a high level of output. He joined Sandy Lieberson in Goodtimes Enterprises. Following *Melody*, in 1970 they produced Jacques Demy's *The Pied Piper* before beginning more interesting explorations of rock adolescence with *That'll Be The Day* (1973) and *Stardust* (1974), which was the first film to be directed by Michael Apted.

That'll Be The Day got back its costs twice over in Britain and *Stardust* was also profitable, although neither was very successful abroad. There followed two of Ken Russell's extravaganzas, *Mahler* (1974) and *Lisztomania* (1975); *Bugsy Malone* (1976), which was Alan Parker's first film as a director; *The Duellists* (1978), which was Ridley Scott's first film and won a special jury prize at Cannes; Parker's *Midnight Express* (1978) and Adrian Lyne's *Foxes* (1980), the last two deriving from the time when Puttnam moved to Hollywood, where he worked as a producer for two years.

After his return to British film making with *Chariots of Fire*, an international hit as well as an Oscar-winner, he followed it by producing a delightful comedy of Scottish–American manners, Bill Forsyth's *Local Hero*.

It was while filming in Los Angeles in 1979, producing *Foxes*, about four girls sharing a flat in the city, that Puttnam realised he did not feel at home, but was adrift in an alien culture.

'It was to do with Sally Kellerman's earrings,' he remembered, sitting by a blazing fire in his office, tucked away in a London mews one winter's afternoon in 1983.

'She was playing a middle-class mother, brought up in the San Fernando Valley. She asked me whether I thought the earrings she was wearing were in character. Instead of answering, I asked the American wardrobe lady what she thought. Would that character wear those kind of earrings? And I suddenly realised the implications of what I'd done. Reduced my own judgement to the level, good, bad, or indifferent, of the wardrobe lady. And I thought, that's crazy. I felt as though I was producing through glass, that I was never able to directly lay hands on, or touch, the subject matter. So I opted to come back to Britain and stay in films on my own terms or clear out.'

Puttnam maintains his American connections. He has a long-standing agreement with Warner Brothers which gives them first refusal on his film projects. For that he receives a percentage payment on his overheads and money that allows him to develop ideas even if Warners show no interest, which is sometimes the case. Indeed, Warners turned down *Chariots of Fire*, *Local Hero* and *The Killing Fields*, although they did pay handsomely to distribute all three movies.

Puttnam also has an agreement with Goldcrest, the British film and television investment company, giving that company first refusal on his TV and cable TV projects. And he is a director of Goldcrest, 'of the holding company, not the management company that decides on investment, so there is no conflict of interest'. In collaboration with Goldcrest he produced a series of television dramas under the title *First Love* for Channel Four.

In 1983, Puttnam was involved with two feature films. *The Killing Fields*, at a budget of $14.4 million, was the most expensive film he had made so far. Dealing with the relationship between two men, one from the West, the other from the East, against the background of war in Cambodia and filmed in Thailand, it was the first feature to be directed by Roland Joffe.

The other was *Cal*, based on Bernard McLaverty's novel of an Irish youth whose love for the widow of a man he helped to murder and his growing guilt leads him to seek, and find, a redemption of sorts. Directed by Pat O'Connor, an Irish-born television director, it was a much less expensive and ambitious movie, costing $3 million.

Such are the vagaries of film production that it was *Cal* which was the bigger risk of the two. 'The sex-appeal of *The Killing Fields* was such that we'd virtually covered the entire cost of the picture before it opened,' said Puttnam. '*Cal* was a denser piece, a more difficult piece in many respects. So the actual risk was greater. We were running *The Killing Fields* as close to the bone at $14.4 million as *Cal* at $3 million because the actual physical requirements were very tight. In both cases, we were very lucky with the weather, in both cases the directors were extremely responsible and the crews worked magnificently. I was rather more neurotic on *The Killing Fields* because it was the largest budget I'd ever dealt in, so I was concerned with my own adequacy. Having done it, I would say the difference is not much.'

The finance for *The Killing Fields* was raised partly from Warner Brothers, who bought the US and Canadian rights for more than a third of the budget. Thorn-EMI put up a large advance for the video cassette rights, and Puttnam had a tax leasing arrangement which covered about a fifth of the budget. As a result, when Joffe started shooting, around $9 million of the budget was covered. A month later, Warners advanced a further $4 million for distribution rights for the rest of the world. In the end, the film was made for less than its estimated cost.

'One way and another, within pennies, the entire budget of the picture was covered by pre-sales,' said Puttnam.

With *Cal*, Warner Brothers bought the English-speaking rights for an amount that covered half its costs. 'But that left Goldcrest with $1 million at risk. If the film is not successful, they could actually go down the Swanee for that sum of money,' said Puttnam, who favours pre-selling the rights to a film if possible. I quite like the idea of syndicating risk. On the other hand, you can sometimes find yourself with a distributor who is not the perfect one for the picture. It's a far better shot than the one Sandy Lieberson and I went through for many years, the awful business of showing a finished film to a post-lunch, drunk distributor, who's falling asleep, not really wanting to be there at all. And knowing he's got you by the balls because you've finished the movie.'

Puttnam's obvious optimism about the future is more than a side-effect of his own success. 'When I began in the film industry it was to all intents and purposes impossible to raise finance,' he said. 'The first film I managed to get financed [*Melody*] was far more luck than judgement. Really, in a well-run world it would never have happened because the way I went about it was so amateurish. I knew nobody and must have been a grotesque embarrassment to the people I approached. By a fluke, the film got financed and was sufficiently successful for the same company to come in for a second film.

'I think the third film, *That'll Be The Day*, was the first time that I had my feet tucked under the desk, as it were, of the film industry and was a film producer and was clearly going to stay.'

His attitude towards films is unashamedly commercial. He spent much of 1983 supervising the making of *The Killing Fields* and planned to spend longer, most of 1984, marketing it.

'If I really had to depict myself in strictly serious terms, I would say I'm a marketing man who happens to produce films rather than a film producer who markets his own films,' he said. 'Marketing is fundamental. I was in advertising from the age of 16. Advertising to me was what a Jesuitical college might have been to some one else, with all the implications that statement carries.

'Film marketing is appalling. When I came into the film industry in 1968, it had taken on board none of the marketing lessons we had learned. So what we had in Britain in the late 60s was a relatively sophisticated advertising and marketing business and an absolutely primitive film marketing business. This was probably best exemplified by the calibre and salaries of the people who ran the advertising and promotional departments of the film companies, who earned a quarter of the money paid to their equivalents in advertising.

'It meant that the film industry was not getting the world's finest talents. It has improved; not as much as it could, and not as much as it will. The film industry has resisted market research. I certainly don't think you can make films using market research. But I think once you've made it, you're pretty daft not to listen to it. And during a process of marketing that film, you're even dafter not to listen to it. The film industry has tended to shun it.'

After Bill Forsyth had finished filming *Local Hero*, Puttnam screened it at various stages of its cut to audiences chosen to be as representative as possible and discovered their reactions to the film. 'It's a little easier to do with a comedy because you have rather more tangible questions to ask and criteria to judge it by,' said Puttnam. 'We changed it quite considerably as a result. We cut the film by a full ten minutes, maybe more. It wasn't how much we cut, but where we cut. The result, without doubt, was a better film.'

When Puttnam hears the word art, he reaches for his Oscar. 'There's a terrible danger of trying to create an analogy between a commercial film maker and a poet or a painter, and the analogy doesn't exist, fundamentally, because the expectation of the audience is quite different. A film maker has to address himself to the expectations of an audience,' he said.

'I don't think cinema is, of itself, an artistic pursuit. I think it has artistic pretensions, but I don't think it's art. I think a film in hindsight can have been a work of art. On odd occasions. Whilst it's being manufactured, and it *is* manufactured, it is a craft. Now I happen to have the highest regard and respect for craft.

'Very few people would attribute the word art to Chippendale's furniture and yet it is every bit as highly skilled as, and in many respects more so than, the very best movies.

'What I've always tried to apply is commonsense, which is a commodity rarely used in reference to the film industry. People get mesmerized by the film industry, by the movies themselves, the people they become involved with, by the sums of money involved. And the first thing that seems to go out of the window, tragically, is commonsense.

'We apply commonsense rigidly to the manufacture of the films, the development of them and the marketing of them. And commonsense doesn't stack up elegantly with anyone's notion of art. Because I believe so sincerely that it's been the core of any success we've had as a little company I can't really allow the illusion of art to creep in and start damaging it. Because my principle grounding was in marketing, I'm not really interested in something that can't find an audience.'

Nevertheless, it is personal satisfaction that Puttnam seeks first, a satisfaction that comes, in part, from knowing that he can affect his audience. 'If I have to spend a year of my life on something that doesn't give me personal satisfaction either in its manufacturing process or in the result, it is an agony beyond description. I'm arrogant enough to assume that my internal personal satisfaction will find an audience, providing the director, writer and myself get it right. That will obviously, one day, prove to be untrue. Either I'll push too hard or I'll have outdated myself or I'll be unlucky.

'I certainly require a degree of commercial success, so that the next film next year and the director directing it and the writer writing it are not jeopardised by my failure.

'I see cinema as a continuum and my own career is a very good example of the way that continuum can operate. A number of directors, about six or seven, have continuously come through for me, and having come through for me have made the career of the next one possible or easier.

'It's not remotely possible that Roland Joffe would be directing *The Killing Fields* without the success of *Chariots of Fire*. *Chariots of Fire* wouldn't have been possible without the success of *Midnight Express*. *Midnight Express* wouldn't have been possible without the success of *Bugsy Malone*. *Bugsy Malone* wouldn't have been possible without the success of *Stardust*. *Stardust* wouldn't have been made without the success of *That'll Be The Day*. Each of those directors' careers relates directly to the success of their predecessors. That's something that, interestingly enough, people don't want to talk about.'

And what would happen if *The Killing Fields* failed to find an audience? 'It's a bit like Snakes and Ladders,' he said. 'We won't slide right back to the bottom of the ladder, but we'll certainly take a thumping. I would say that it would take me back to pre- or post-*Midnight Express*. What will happen is that the curve that we are all on will have a severe dent in it. I can't afford, at $14.4 million, for it to lose $10 million. If it makes $15 dollars, then we're OK. But I'm spending $14.4 of some else's resources and I have an absolute obligation, in a serious manner, to attempt to get that money back.'

Puttnam's early films reflected his own life and attitudes. They can be read as concealed autobiography. *That'll Be The Day* was about growing up in the 1950s, as he did, and *Stardust* was concerned with coming to terms with the end of youthful dreams. As he has grown older, his subject matter has shifted, although it sometimes relates to films that have influenced him.

Local Hero reflected the mood of Ealing comedies and also the populist Hollywood movies of Frank Capra. *The Killing Fields* owes much to Gillo Pontecorvo's masterpiece *The Battle of Algiers*. 'I've spent the last 15 years with it as a dream to aspire to and all of two years physically aiming at that picture,' he said.

His problem these days is to reconcile his own maturer concerns with those of an audience that is largely younger than he is. The resulting movies point up the great difference between the films of the present revival and those of the New Wave of the early 1960s. Then many films, benefiting from the impetus of radical theatre and a young generation of first novelists, dealt with working-class lives. The directors working today are more concerned with the past.

It is a trend that is also reflected in the most successful television series, from *Upstairs, Downstairs,* concentrating on master–servant relationships in Edwardian England, to *The Far Pavilions,* dealing with master–servant relationships in Imperial India, or *The Jewel in the Crown,* concentrating on the last days of the Raj. Indeed, it sometimes seems that Britain has lost an Empire but gained a subject-matter for movies. The underlying impulse can appear to be a search for reassurance, for escapism and nostalgia. Puttnam, though agreeing that today's audience do seek reassurance, regards *Chariots of Fire* as more allegorical than nostalgic.

Television, he insists, has usurped and improved upon cinema's realist role. His own shift, beginning with *The Duellists,* has been to make films dealing with issues rather than experiences. '*The Duellists,* to me, was about mindless violence, the danger and extraordinary quality of mindless violence, which is something I encountered a lot as a kid,' he said. 'I was brought up in a Teddy Boy area where the terror was never from anything you did, it was always from a group of boys under a lamp post outside a pub in the evening.

'*Chariots of Fire* was about a lot of things: yearnings for a Britain I was brought up to believe in, and began to feel didn't exist, the hypocrisy of this country. It dealt with two people, one of whom I thought I was and one I thought I'd like to be.

'Certainly *The Killing Fields* is about gut-emotions in a world of madness, and about the danger of polarising situations. The temptation of politicians is to polarise situations. In polarising them, they create a void, and in that void must come mayhem. It can be bad enough if it's a strike; it's catastrophic when it's a nation, which is what *The Killing Fields* is about. *Cal,* too, is concerned with the same situation.'

Among Puttnam's projects is *Bodyline,* a film on the still controversial tour of Australia in the 1930s by an English eleven that relied on fast bowling that seemed aimed at the batsman as much as the wicket. 'That is absolutely about hypocrisy,' he said. 'If we can't make that statement, we won't make the movie. I'm not interested in a film about cricket. I am interested in a film where hypocrites use a sport that in many respects is the quintessence of gentlemanliness.

'If I wanted to make a film about tragic youth, I'd find it infinitely easier and, I think, more effective, to set it during the First World War and reflect the tragedy and unemployment of the youth then, than to make a film set in Sutton Coldfield now, because you could give it emotional values and production values you wouldn't find in Sutton Coldfield.

'We're going through a period when people are seeking reassurance rather than threat. I would argue that films such as *Kramer v. Kramer* are pale imitations of a dozen similar works I see on British television every year. Knowing I can't compete with television, I look for another avenue to say the same thing.

'I've been trying for five years to make a film out of the story of Tristram and Iseult, because I think it's a wonderful opportunity to say something about the relationship of individuals and the state, and of the effects of guilt on individuals. It's got absolutely everything. Try to do Tristram in modern dress and the richness of the metaphor goes out the window. I don't know why. But I do know it isn't nearly as effective.'

Puttnam is one of four producers under contract to Goldcrest Films and Television, a company backed by the Pearson Longman Group whose interests include the publishing houses of Longman's and Penguin Books, The Financial Times and the Westminster Press, Britain's biggest regional newspaper group. The producers, Puttnam, John Gau, Paul Knight and Barry Hanson, of whom only Puttnam and Hanson make cinema films, give Goldcrest first refusal on their television projects.

Goldcrest's survival, too, is fundamental to the existence of an independent British film industry, for its policy, according to its founder and former chief executive Jake (John D.) Eberts, a Canadian-born expert in packaging and financing movies, was to make films created in Britain, using British technicians. 'In Britain now I detect a definite trend towards making good, serious pictures,' he told *Variety* in January 1981. He was heartened by the British tax system of allowing a 100 per cent write-offs of negative costs, a financial encouragement to film companies that the Chancellor of the Exchequer abolished in the 1984 Budget.

Eberts left Goldcrest in January 1984, eight years after founding it, to become managing director of Embassy Communications International, the European end of the American film and television production company, working for Lord Grade. His departure followed a restructuring of the company and a change in Goldcrest's policy.

In the early days of its existence, Goldcrest, which had links with the New York-based International Film Investors, put a small amount of pre-production investment in such projects as the two animated films of Richard Adams's novels, *Watership Down* and *The Plague Dogs,* as well as *Breaking Glass* and *Chariots of Fire.* The company's first large-scale movie investment was an auspicious one. Eberts backed Richard Attenborough's *Gandhi* and the reward was not only in having the prestige of an Oscar-winning film, but in seeing a return of around £37 million on an investment of £7 million.

It was a deserved bonus. Attenborough has said that it was Eberts and James Lee, chief executive of Pearson Longman, who were responsible for the film finally being made. Putting together the deal was a difficult one, for the promised money never materialised and funds almost ran out several times during the actual filming.

Ebert's preferred policy was to put up only half the finance for a film. He liked to pre-sell the product around the world before the production went ahead. Only the North American rights were kept back so that they could be sold after the film had been completed, in the hope that the competition between distributors would put up the price.

With television productions, he would ensure that most of the cost was recouped before production began. But, even after the success of *Chariots of Fire,* Goldcrest found it difficult to persuade investors to back Puttnam's production of *Local Hero* and in the end put up the necessary £3.75 million themselves.

When Eberts announced he was leaving Goldcrest, he said that the company had grown far faster than he had ever expected and that he wished to cut himself free from the pressure and the many administrative chores to return to closer involvement with individual films.

Goldcrest then had around £25 million capital but Lee planned to raise a further £15 million and thought that the company might go public in 1987. Lee hoped to change the emphasis of Goldcrest from backing and packaging movies brought to them by independent producers to originating their own productions.

In October 1984, Lee and Eberts' successor, Sandy Lieberson, announced a $75 million production programme which included only one film with a British subject: *Absolute Beginners,* a musical based on Colin MacInnes's novel of teenage life, which was to be directed by Julien Temple. The project also involved two other new British production companies, Virgin and Palace. Goldcrest's other productions included two films that had been turned down by American studios: *The Mission,* a historical film set in South America and scripted by Robert Bolt, and *Revolution,* set in the American War of

Independence, which Hugh Hudson was to direct. Marek Kanievska, director of *Another Country*, a commercially successful film about the education of such British traitors as Burgess and Maclean, was to direct *Horror Movie*, about a film that kills its audience. The fifth film, *Mandrake The Magician*, based on an American comic strip, was also a project that had been announced and then abandoned in the past.

At the time Eberts left, Goldcrest's most ambitious project was not a film, but a television series, a six-part serial of *The Far Pavilions*, M. M. Kaye's best-selling novel of colonial India. Goldcrest had sunk around £10 million in it, as a co-production with the American cable company, Home Box Office.

Goldcrest's television side is controlled by Michael Wooller, a former head of documentary programmes for the weekday London ITV station, Thames, whose activities could have an effect on film.

Puttnam, who produced a drama series *First Love* for Channel Four with Goldcrest's backing, used it as a means of testing and building relationships with directors and writers with a view to possible collaboration on future films.

He felt he could afford to take small gambles with his television productions. 'The length of time a film takes to make is a facet of risk,' he said. 'If you're spending £2 million you get asked an awful lot more questions than if you're spending a few hundred thousand. I get questioned very little on how I do or don't make *First Loves*.

'At £400,000 no one's going to get really damaged. They might take a bath on one, but the company will limp a week or two and carry on. Films and TV help us to remain flexible, working on a big budget one day and a small one the next. It's a cash-flow business, so we haven't the awful thing that was happening to film producers for a decade or more when everything was hit or bust.

'Sandy Lieberson and I twice made films because we couldn't have paid the payroll without making them. In at least one case, and probably two, we knew we shouldn't have been making the film at all. But we had to make the payroll.

'The wonderful thing about having a cash-flow is that you can now make proper judgements. The most important thing is that it gives us a kindergarten, if you like. At least three and maybe four directors and at least three writers from the first seven *First Loves* I now feel absolutely confident taking a shot with as directors. I wouldn't have done that without the opportunity of working with them, knowing their strengths and weaknesses. We don't earn money from them, but we pay a nice chunk of the overhead with it; it takes the edge of fear off the monthly wage-bill.'

Goldcrest's increasing financial muscle and Puttnam's commitment to films of quality both augur well for the future. They probably represent the British film industry's last hope of independent survival. If they can establish themselves in an international market, then they can provide some shelter for other, smaller independent producers, no less determined to make good films. Puttnam has planned ahead his next three years, which include a continuing agreement with Warner Brothers for film and Goldcrest for television. In that time, he hopes to make between 20 and 25 films, the majority of them for television, but including at least three large-scale feature films and three or four low-budget movies. Whatever else they may be, they will be as polished examples of film-craft as he can make them.

'The greatest compliment anyone can pay me is to say that my films are really well finished,' he said. 'It dismays me beyond belief to see a film going out on television where all of that little bit of care goes for nothing. I'm just about to ring a writer with eight tiny points on a film, four to do with cuts, four to do with sound. If he agrees with the cuts, it'll make 35 seconds difference. With the sound, I'll guarantee that no one would notice the difference whether we do them or not. If he agrees, it'll be an extra day's dubbing time. But I care, I care very much indeed, because it will be half-a-percent better.'

The films he will make will at least be recognisably British, even if the subject matter is not. 'I never thought in terms of British films early on, because I was just making the films that were available to me,' he said. 'What happened was that when I went to America and worked on *Midnight Express* and *Foxes*, I did come to the conclusion that I wanted to make a cultural impact, some imprint on the work I was doing.

'If I was going to have any real cultural impact, as opposed to earning a living (and there is a distinct difference; there are plenty of people in the film industry who only wish to earn a living), it became very clear to me that the only way I was going to do so was by making what you might term British films or, at least as I've now come to realise, working from a British base and making films from a British point of view. It doesn't mean that the subject matter has to be British. But the perspective has to be British.'

The reward for this effort stands gleaming on a shelf of Puttnam's bookcase: the glinting figure of an Oscar. Puttnam gestured towards it affectionately. 'I would say three-fifths of the income of *Chariots of Fire* came after it won the Oscar,' he said. 'It would have still been a successful film, but you're talking about the difference between $20 million rentals and $50 million. In real money terms that made me a wealthy man. Without it I would have been OK. But the difference between getting by and being comfortably off is that.'

12 Enter the Amateurs

HandMade Films, Virgin Vision

> 'They have learned the ways of the film world.
> They are all tiresomely self-aggrandising . . . They
> are careless in the use of such terms as "deal",
> "meeting", "project" and "lunch sometime".
> They have increased the amount of personal
> jewellery they wear.'
>
> Advertisement for Virgin Vision, 1983

Sean Connery telephoned Denis O'Brien of HandMade Films and came straight to the point. 'It's the most outrageous action I've ever seen in my career in the film industry,' he said. ' . . . And I applaud you for it.'

O'Brien's good deed had been to spend $5.5 million on the prints and advertising for HandMade's movie *Time Bandits* so that it could open in 825 cinemas across America. It was more than twice the $2.6 million that the film had cost to make.

Time Bandits, directed by Terry Gilliam, the artist responsible for the bizarre animation sequences in *Monty Python's Flying Circus,* had only been a moderate success on its British showing, despite the inclusion of fellow Pythons John Cleese and Michael Palin in the cast, as well as Connery as Theseus, Ian Holm as Napoleon and Ralph Richardson as God.

When O'Brien screened it for Americans in the film business, they had told him that it was too British to cross the Atlantic successfully. O'Brien was convinced there was a large audience who would respond to the fantastic comedy of Gilliam, an expatriate American. For HandMade Films, a partnership between the rock guitarist George Harrison, still best known for being one of the Beatles, and O'Brien's company Euro-Atlantic, the decision to spend a fortune on the film's American launch was a daring one.

What it if had flopped? O'Brien sipped tea in his Chelsea offices and considered for a moment. 'We would have been out of business,' he said. 'We wouldn't be sitting in this building. George Harrison would have taken his next step without a hitch. But Euro-Atlantic would have disappeared. And I would be out looking for a job. It was an academic exercise until the last week. Then the reality of it all came down . . . '

O'Brien, tall, bespectacled and quietly-spoken, trained as a lawyer and an accountant. In his double-breasted grey suit, plain shirt and dark tie, he looked the very model of a discreet financial adviser he was and, to an extent, still is. But he had the laugh of a man who had discovered that there are more enjoyable ways of earning a living than manipulating money. If he entered films by accident, through backing *Monty Python's Life of Brian*, he has stayed by design. 'To have dinner with Michael Palin is a complete joy,' he said. 'To work with him on a film is marvellous. There are so many good people around that it really is a nice business experience.'

In six years, HandMade have not produced many films, although their pace is quickening. Four were released in 1983. Five were planned for 1984. But they are beginning to acquire a reputation for making quirky British comedies, even though O'Brien is an American.

The style is due in part to the participation of members of the Monty Python group, but also to O'Brien's and Harrison's liking for the kind of humour that has its roots in the Goon Show and the rough-and-tumble wit of the music-hall. Peter Sellers's early films are also an influence. O'Brien used to laugh at them in 'local art houses' when he was growing up in America. Later, Sellers, along with Harrison, became one of his clients.

'Peter was always being shipped around the world by his financial advisers before we came along,' he said. 'Every time he was shipped to either Switzerland or Ireland he went into deep depression. You can see it in his films; they just fall off. His heart isn't there, the energy isn't there. The first question I put to him was to ask him where he wanted to live. He said, England, and I said, Then move back.'

O'Brien also encouraged the temporary return to Britain from Hollywood of the British writer-director-producer team of Dick Clement and Ian Le Frenais, creators of the witty television comedy series, arguably among the best situation comedies so far, *The Likely Lads*, *Porridge*, and *Auf Wiedersehen Pet* (the latter based on an idea by another British director working in Hollywood, Franc Roddam). 'They've come back to their roots,' he said of *Bullshot*, their first film for him, which was released in October 1983.

HandMade resembles no other film company. It uses its own money to finance its films and does not seek publicity for itself. O'Brien is reclusive compared to his publicity-conscious rivals. He has given only a couple of interviews to the press, and only for the purpose 'of trying to educate the City as to what happens in films'. Harrison, too, has received enough public attention to last him several lifetimes and now avoids it. HandMade pay little attention to the trade papers, never announcing their productions until principal photography is about to begin. In that way, they have more freedom to call off projects at the last moment without publicly bruising the often fragile egos of directors and actors. 'Whatever we do speaks for itself,' said O'Brien. 'If people want to know about HandMade, then all they need to do is see our films.'

The company began in controversy. After backing *Life of Brian*, they also acquired the distribution rights to Lord Grade's *The Long Good Friday*. It was a film that did well in Britain, but has been harder to sell abroad.

'I think it was a satisfactory arrangement for both sides. I think they were happy to get it off their shoulders. And we were very happy to take it on,' said O'Brien. 'We won't be hurt by the film. It's been a wonderful film for us because it came out of the same controversy as *The Life of Brian*. And I thought that was a wonderful way to get into distribution.

'Plus it was a very good film. It deserved to be seen by the public.It was worth everything we put into it. And we put a tremendous amount of effort around the world into getting that film shown, including the United States, where not one single theatre, let alone a distributor, wanted to show it.

'It took six months to position the film and to get reviews to having the first theatre in New York accept it. We carried on from there. We've tended to take decisions about exploitation that may not be, in the first instance, commercially viable. But we haven't been burned yet.'

HandMade began to distribute other independent movies that the two major circuits had ignored, mainly low-budget shockers such as *The Burning* and *Venom*. O'Brien quickly discovered that it was a way to lose money fast. 'They were disasters,' he said. Now the company concentrates on distributing its own films, handling their release round the world, selling ancillary rights, such as video and television, with great care.

'It's the key to what we do, because we control what happens to our films, certainly in the UK, but we also take that forward and go country by country around the world. We even get involved in the physical distribution in America.

'We work with sub-distributors. For both *The Long Good Friday* and *Time Bandits*, the actual deal was renting a distribution facility in America, guaranteeing the prints and advertising budget and literally running that company, making every single decision: how the money was spent, when it was going to be spent, the selection of theatres, the terms with those theatres.

'Cable sales are all being done directly without anyone being involved in America. So all the proper participants profit to a much greater extent. It means Warner Brothers doesn't take its 35 per cent fee; it doesn't take those receipts against prints and advertising, if there's a deficit. And we don't give them foreign rights. That's what comes from financial independence. And that's what comes from walking away from them and not doing their deal. And that's what leads you to guaranteeing prints and advertising because their deal is so unpalatable.

'It's a disgrace to work that hard on a film and have to give up your future. We have tended to try to break walls down, rather than have ours broken. I would never play the horses, greyhounds, or cards. I don't gamble. I don't own shares. I don't believe in a share portfolio. I do believe in betting on what you do in life and having confidence in what you do. If you don't have the confidence, then why is one doing it? To that extent, I will always bet on what we do as a group. Right or wrong.'

His gamble has paid off so far. *Time Bandits* – six dwarfs romping through history – did for HandMade what *Snow White and the Seven Dwarfs* had done for Disney; it established the company as idiosyncratic film makers. So far, it has taken more than $16 million in the States.

Bullshot (1983) is probably nearer to the type of film that Hand-Made plan to make: a gentle comedy with a touch of adventure, intended to appeal to children and adults, although, in the event, it attracted neither.

It had begun life in the early 1970s as a send-up of Bulldog Drummond, performed on the outer reaches of London's fringe theatres, before its creators, Low Moan Spectacular, took it to America and toured in it with great success. Its appeal to O'Brien was that it provided him with an opportunity of working with Clement and Le Frenais. 'If the people are right, then even if the project isn't right on day one, they'll get it right.' he said. On *Bullshot*, his first task was to persuade them to trim the budget – 'they happily did that'.

Perhaps because O'Brien and his colleagues come from the business world – being lawyers and accountants – HandMade keep a very tight control on all aspects of film-making, making sure that costs are kept low and that as much money as possible is clawed back. In filming as elsewhere, time is money.

Directors on HandMade's films are encouraged to work efficiently by the knowledge that they will receive a lower fee if the film goes over its budget. The company is a small one, no more than 30 people, and intends to stay that way. Budgets are unlikely to go above the figure of £2.5 million that *Time Bandits* cost ('plus interest which was high because it took a long time to finish').

Time Bandits happened because O'Brien had seen and liked Terry Gilliam's *Jabberwocky* and wanted to work with him. 'I thought it was a wonderful film and that he had immense talent.' He asked Gilliam to send some treatments. Gilliam, a man of brilliant invention, provided a batch. His first treatment for *Time Bandits* was a three-page outline. O'Brien read it and decided that he wanted to make it.

Also among them was *Brazil*, a film Gilliam is now making for another company on a $16 million dollar budget. O'Brien turned it down. 'It just doesn't make any sense to me. I don't know where you come in on that. I can work out numbers on £2 million. I have great difficulty when it comes to $16 million! It's just another business and I don't know that business. And therefore we won't enter into that business.'

O'Brien tends to keep quiet about what his films cost, since many distributors associate expense with quality. 'When I first showed *Time Bandits* to some American film men, they estimated that it cost $15–20 million, more than twice its actual budget,' he says. HandMade have no intention of ever making films in America. O'Brien doesn't like the way the American industry is structured.

'Their practices are such that a director better get to them in his fee and during principal photography because once the film is delivered, the major takes over and will get back at the director. That's an atmosphere that simply exists. I don't think that exists with us because what we do is completely different from how a film is made in Hollywood. We do everything so that the incentive is to come in on budget. We produce a film that is much cheaper, has all the values on the screen, and therefore has a much better chance of getting out there and making a profit at the end of the day.

'*Bullshot* went into pre-production on February 1, 1983, principal photography was in April, it was released in the UK at the end of October. If you take that time period, and also the fact that one is going to penalise the director if he goes over budget because he loses part of his fee, then no money is wasted.

'We report to people on a monthly basis. Our fees for distribution are unheard of in the film industry. Our attempt is to get the money back to everyone – to the extent that it is there. I think that has created a different attitude in how one approaches a film.'

HandMade has not attempted the Grade method of pre-selling their films to finance them. 'I think you pre-sell your future if you do that. That's not to say that there are not certain deals which are done. Thorn-EMI have the video rights to our films and an advance is involved.'

The films they make, of course, hardly lend themselves to early hype. As O'Brien said of *Bullshot*: 'No star names that would attract an international market, so there is no reason to go out and pre-sell, because everybody is going to respond in a negative way. I'd rather take the film, open it in a few markets, send out a promo reel and let the film sell itself. And work for itself.' He laughed as he added, 'And live or die.'

Bullshot opened in London to rude reviews and half-empty cinemas. Whatever its fate, Clement and Le Frenais went on to make *Water* (1984) for HandMade, a comedy they scripted about a revolution in one of the last outposts of the British Empire, which will star Michael Caine, Leonard Rossiter and Billy Connolly.

'We had such an enjoyable experience working with them. They're such talented people. I think that if you can have fun and on day one you can sit down together and say, this is the film we're going to make, we're going to try to live together for six months or more – if you can actually do that, and shake hands at the end, have a good time – and everybody's had open discussions and listened to editing proposals from all sides – and the film that you see is exactly what you wanted to do, if not better, then that's been a good exercise. If we break even on that, then I'm happy. If we make money, then so much the better,' said O'Brien.

HandMade's films, apart from *Time Bandits* have done only moderately well. Michael Palin's *The Missionary* attracted appreciative audiences when it opened in March 1983, but was available on video cassette six months later, an indication that it had failed to attract sufficient audiences.

HandMade have faith in Palin's gentle, nostalgic humour and also in his abilities as an actor. He starred (with Maggie Smith) as a chiropodist saddled with an ambitious wife in *A Private Function* (1984), scripted by one of Britain's best playwrights, Alan Bennett.

Mai Zetterling's *Scrubbers*, a violent and passionate film set in a girls' Borstal and almost a companion piece to *Scum*, found only a small audience. O'Brien said that there were specific reasons for making it, although he would not say what they were. 'It did all right for what was a very, very low budget film. It won't burn us,' he said. 'I'm glad we made it because I think one is proud of the film and Mai did a wonderful job of directing it. But would we ever make another film similar to that? No. We don't have a feeling for that kind of film and it's a difficult thing to exploit around the world. It'll be non-existent in the United States.'

The great disappointment was *Privates on Parade*, which Peter Nichols adapted from his play for the Royal Shakespeare Company. At the Aldwych Theatre, directed by Michael Blakemore, it had been a rousing success, notable for Denis Quilley's performance as the reigning queen of a wartime ENSA troupe, never happier than when impersonating Marlene Dietrich or Vera Lynn.

Blakemore, an Australian who had made a highly-praised autobiographical film about his relationship with his father, also directed the film. Quilley repeated his role, giving as good a performance on screen as he had on stage. John Cleese was added to the cast to play a somewhat loony commanding officer.

Despite all this, it was a flop. Possibly audiences were misled by Cleese's name into expecting something different from what they saw, a film that mixes comedy and tragedy. 'And yet the role is still a funny role,' said O'Brien 'And Denis Quilley was marvellous . . . The intentions were all wonderful and it didn't work. Very sad. We didn't get it right and the blame will come back to me. No one else.' For its American opening in early 1984, O'Brien had the film cut by 18 minutes – 'that's not to say it's going to work in America at all' – which shifted the attention more to Cleese's role. The release was planned to be a slow one, city by city, in the hope that good reviews and word-of-mouth might be enough to attract an audience.

HandMade's approach does mean that the big stars are unlikely to appear in their productions, although Connery set a precedent by acting in *Time Bandits*, in a deal that gave him a share of the profits. 'His presence was critical for that film because of the launch we wanted to give it,' said O'Brien. An actor such as Connery can command twice as much as the entire budget of *Time Bandits*. He was persuaded to return to the screen as James Bond for $5 million and received $1 million for a week's work in Cannon's recent remake of *Sir Gawain and the Green Knight*.

'We have plans for other stars coming in, but they won't come in on the normal basis,' said O'Brien. What sort of bait would be used to attract them? 'That's where I have to beat down some of these agents, to give them a new point of view,' he said – and laughed.

'Film making in Britain is a wonderful human experience. It sounds a bit silly to say that, but it is. In my past lives, one has worked with a lot of large corporations and banks – IBM, Ford, Shell, RTZ and so on. But it's much more fun doing this.'

O'Brien regards HandMade films as 'clearly English'. But the fact remains that they cannot find a big audience in Britain to sustain them. The cause, he believes, is lack of confidence from 'the companies which control the cinemas and which also at times produce the films. What they found at times is that the films weren't working and they started cutting back on budgets across the board. That then impacted the cinemas. Capital improvements have been non-existent, cinema sites have remained the same for 50 years. We're in the entertainment industry and you're supposed to have a good time when you go out. And I don't think that exists. You've got to reverse behavioural patterns and almost re-educate the market.'

HandMade's main market is America, although they claim not to think about what America wants when making a film. 'All I tell the director on day one is to avoid difficult accents. People have to be able to understand what is being said. And it's not just America, it applies to Britain, too. The sound reproduction facilities are not as good as they should be.

'We aren't transatlantic in the films we make and we don't compete with Hollywood. I think that's where you end up as a disaster. As long as you do what your writers understand and your directors can work with – and you do something that's unique – then you have the best chance of having a success anywhere in the world. If you compromise issues, then you miss everybody's mark. And it doesn't work in any country in the world. Every film we've taken to America, they've said it was too British. And I don't think that that's the point.

'Is it a good film? Do people laugh? Do they enjoy the adventure? It doesn't have to do $40 million in the US every time if your budget is £1.9 million. And everybody can still smile and make a profit at the end of the day.'

HandMade are not the only production company to have slipped accidentally into films, rather like Alice falling down the rabbit-hole into Wonderland. It is also true of Virgin Films, part of Virgin Vision which involves film distribution, film and video production, video cassettes and cable television.

On a day in August 1983 Al Clark, production head of Virgin Films, could have been found in his office above the Portobello Road in London's Notting Hill, grasping his telephone like a drowning man clutching at an inadequate piece of driftwood. 'I can't believe what I'm hearing,' he said. It was four days away from the beginning of shooting on Virgin's co-production, *Secret Places*.

At the other end of the telephone was an executive from Rediffusion, explaining why the money they were putting into the film would not yet be available. It was the second such call Clark had received that day. The first was from Rank Films, explaining that they were withholding their share of the finance.

Clark, who had already sunk £90,000 of Virgin's money into pre-production costs, was appalled. 'You're just following each other's cues, instead of looking at this matter sensibly,' he told Rediffusion. 'I just don't know how films ever get made in this country.'

The problem was a simple one. Rank and Rediffusion had agreed to part-finance the film in return for, respectively, the distribution rights and the cable television rights to the film. The National Film Finance Corporation had put up half of the film's £1 million budget. Virgin's involvement had been to pay for development costs, rewrites of the script and so forth, and to raise the rest of the finance for the video rights. All parties had agreed to the contracts. The problem was that they had not been signed. The National Film Finance Corporation's lawyer was away on holiday and nothing could be done until his return.

No signature, no money, said Rank. Mamoun Hassan of the NFFC rang Rank to point out that it was customary for the cash-flow to start before contracts were signed. Clark rang them to echo Hassan's views. He was at a disadvantage because his knowledge of what is customary in movies was limited, something he regards as a strength as much as a weakness.

Rank, a company whose attitude to filming has grown more bureaucratic over the years, stood firm. And Rediffusion stood by Rank. Cash-flow was essential. It took another two days of wheedling and compromising by Virgin before the situation was resolved and filming could begin.

The film's two producers, Simon Relph and Ann Skinner, did not seem too concerned by the situation. On their first film, *Return of the Soldier*, made in 1982, the money had dried up halfway through shooting. Then they had had to ask everyone to forgo their pay for a week until they could raise more money.

The deal on *Secret Places* began with Relph and Skinner, who had set up their own production company, Skreba Films. The third partner in the company was Zelda Barron, a person of vast experience in movies, who had scripted the film from Janice Elliot's novel and was to make her directing debut with the film. The three then approached Virgin.

Virgin Films are among the newest of the British production and distribution companies. The future of the British film industry may depend a great deal on their success, or failure. They have the shrewdness and marketing expertise and, most importantly, the cash to succeed. But their future will be linked to what happens to *Electric Dreams*, a love story involving a boy, a girl and a computer, which they are backing with £4 million of their own money.

Virgin's entry into films was a haphazard one, although probably inevitable, as part of the expansion plans of a company that began as Virgin Records, set up by the ambitious Richard Branson (born 1950).

Virgin's management style owes much to the ethos of the 1960s. Branson, self-styled 'a strange man in a baggy sweater who still lives on a houseboat with his relics and his catarrh', was a hip entrepreneur who saw that more conventional businesses were not able to exploit the commercial possibilities that had been created by young and rebellious audiences, potential consumers with nothing much to consume, apart from drugs and rock music. Virgin has somehow managed to retain that laid-back image, of a small, cool company taking on the big boys without anyone really noticing that it is now one of the dominant companies in British entertainment.

In late 1983 Branson was considering raising money by going public and selling some of his shareholding in the firm. He owns 85 per cent of the company, the remainder being held by Simon Draper, who runs Virgin Records. Branson considered selling eight per cent of the company for £10 million, which puts Virgin's worth at £125 million. Virgin's turnover then was estimated to have reached £100 million a year and it had grown to employ nearly 1,000 people.

Virgin Records' early success was founded on one album, Mike Oldfield's *Tubular Bells*, which has sold some nine million copies around the world. The company became a haven for rock groups that were too difficult (and sometimes too unprofessional) for the bigger record firms belonging to large and often staid corporations. From records, Branson has branched out into other areas of the youth culture: record shops, night clubs and discotheques, cheap transatlantic flights, publishing and computer games.

Films are a natural part of that package, for Virgin are also involved in cable television. The company plan to supply rock music programming to cable television companies and have applied for franchises to run such services in Britain.

The success in the States of cable television – broadcasting promotional video films of rock groups performing their latest releases – has already brought much profit to Virgin. The need for more and more material had meant that videos of many British groups were broadcast, resulting in increased demand for the group's records. The most successful had been Culture Club, featuring the fashionably androgynous presence of Boy George (a throwback to the polymorphous sexuality of rock explored in *Performance*). Culture Club were the first British group since the Beatles to have three Top 10 singles in America from their first album. Culture Club were one of Virgin's groups.

Despite the fact that film complements their cable and musical interests, Virgin's early involvement was sporadic and accidental. In 1976, the Sex Pistols, who were to become one of their best known, indeed notorious, groups had decided to make a movie, a thriller called *Who Killed Bambi?* They hired as director Russ Meyer, an American known in the business as 'The King of The Nudies'.

Meyer had risen above his beginnings as a maker of low-budget softcore pornographic movies without losing his obsession for filming women with abnormally big breasts. He became a cult figure and almost respectable, in Hollywood at least, through his financial success with *The Vixen*, which grossed more than $6 million, around 70 times what it had cost to make. It led him to direct *Beyond The Valley Of The Dolls* and *The Seven Minutes* for Twentieth Century Fox (even though Darryl Zanuck afterwards regretted that Fox had ever got involved. 'We went too far,' he said).

The meeting of such British purveyors of bad taste as Sid Vicious and Johnny Rotten with Russ Meyer was as catastrophic as might have been expected. There was no common ground between the fantasies of the aggressive punks and the mammary man. Meyer went back to the States after filming for three days in Wales. Other directors were tried before Julien Temple, a Cambridge graduate and student at the National Film School, took over in 1979.

Temple turned the film into *The Great Rock 'n' Roll Swindle*, a Machiavellian exercise in which the Sex Pistols' manager, Malcolm McLaren, provided step-by-step instructions in the best means of conning the public and record companies into parting with large sums of money to untalented musicians. It was a funny, violent film. McLaren, filmed in a bathtub, one spindly leg over the side so that his toenails could be clipped by a dwarf called Helen of Troy, boasted 'Forget about music and concentrate on creating generation gaps . . . Terrorise, threaten and insult your own generation.'

Images of decadence, hand-me-down Fellini and Buñuel, were intercut with footage shot by Meyer, animated sequences, concert performances by the group and a collaboration in Rio with the fugitive train robber Ronnie Briggs.

By this time the money had run out and the film was in the hands of the official receiver, whose task it was to try to find a distributor.

Temple's clever montage provided problems: it was the sort of film that tends to end up gathering dust on someone's shelf because no one quite knows what to do with it. Virgin, who were releasing the soundtrack album and had sold in the previous 15 months 100,000 copies of a double-album of the Sex Pistols' songs that were featured in the film, decided they should protect their investment in the film and handle it themselves, since they knew the market at which it was aimed.

So Virgin Films was born as a distributor. The company hired an experienced film booker ('We'd never heard of terms like "barring" before,' said Clark) and opened it in May 1980 at the London Pavilion, one of the city's major cinemas, with the slogan 'See the movie that incriminates its audience'.

Said Clark, 'We wanted to signal that it was a film for a wide public, not an art house movie.' The film was well received. The authoritative American show business newspaper *Variety* called it 'the *Citizen Kane* of rock films' and it has continued to be seen at cinemas around Britain, earning a reasonable return.

After that, Virgin Films went into abeyance. The record business was going through a slump and money became tight. Branson put his energies into launching *Event*, a weekly magazine listing current movies, plays and other happenings, intended to rival *Time Out*, London's most successful entertainment guide. Clark, who had been head of Virgin's publicity, was appointed editor, but he soon quarrelled with Branson over the direction of the magazine and left. *Event* ceased to be one, becoming a pale, directionless copy of *Time Out*. It soon disappeared.

Clark rejoined Virgin a few months later, with the title of creative director, at a time when the company was enjoying renewed success with its records. A hit single or album can generate an enormous amount of revenue and Branson had also realised that cable television could become a licence to print money.

Rock music on cable has the great attraction that the cost of videos are borne by the artists or record companies as a means of promoting their latest records. Many are of a high standard and young directors are using them as a means of perfecting their craft, just as directors in the past gained their experience and skills from making television commercials. An example is Steve Barron (born 1959 and the son of Zelda Barron), who directed *Electric Dreams*.

Clark described the film as a 'paranoid love story about a boy, a girl and a computer'. Its soundtrack featured rock songs, many of them by Virgin's groups, including Culture Club. 'We know it is going to be a success in America,' said Clark in the days before it opened in the States to dismal business. Virgin had been approached by an American producer-screenwriter, Rusty Lemorande, while he was in London as co-producer of Barbra Streisand's film *Yentl* (on which Zelda Barron had also worked).

Although *Electric Dreams* is British-made and mainly filmed at Twickenham studios (apart from some location work in the States), it starred Americans Lenny Von Dohlen and Virginia Madsen as well as British Hollywood exile Maxwell Caulfield, who had made his pouting screen debut in *Grease 2*, Robert Stigwood and Allan Carr's unsuccessful sequel to their musical hit.

Virgin's first venture in film had been to spend £15,000 to top up the NFFC's £40,000 in backing a short film, *A Shocking Accident* by Christine Ostreicher, which went on to win an Oscar. 'I'd never met a film producer before and I'd never been sold something by a film producer before,' said Clark. 'It was a good experience because we gained knowledge of the ways of the film world and our co-financiers were the best introduction a private company could have. They were very straightforward to deal with.'

Clark, who also edits Virgin's annual Film Yearbook and is the author of *Raymond Chandler In Hollywood*, learned quickly, together with his colleagues, Robert Deveraux, who originally joined Virgin to run their publishing company but soon switched to become managing director of Virgin Vision, and David Marlowe, who is in charge of Virgin's video business. Their tone remains that of cheeky outsiders, as their advertisements in the trade press demonstrate.

But their choice of movies to back has been exemplary so far. They put money into Richard Eyre's two exceptional films, *The Plough-*

man's Lunch and *Loose Connections*, which was chosen to close the 1983 London Film Festival.

'We made the decision to back *Loose Connections* at the American Film Market in Los Angeles,' said Clark. 'There was something so dispiriting about the films we were seeing there, such as *Bloodsucking Freaks* and *A Night To Dismember* that made *Loose Connections* terrifically attractive.'

When Virgin was approached, most of the finance for *Loose Connections* had already been raised. The company put up £200,000, a quarter of its budget. In future, Virgin plan to be producers rather than investors. 'It's more interesting and, if we make the right decisions, more profitable,' said Clark. Virgin went on to finance the movie of Orwell's *1984*, budgeted at £4.5 million and directed by Mike Radford. That also represented a considerable gamble, particularly when the project went £1 million over its budget. Despite the worldwide interest in Orwell and the fact that the film contained Richard Burton's last performance, no American producer had shown any interest in acquiring the rights when it opened in London in October, 1984. If the film fails to reach an American audience, its chances of earning back its costs are extremely low.

1984 caused Virgin to postpone its other films although it is planned that the projects will go ahead in 1985. Virgin's advantage, Clark believes, is that the company is small enough to move faster than the major studios, where decisions tend to be referred back along a long chain of command. 'If a company doesn't have the bollocks to take a chance then it only deserves to live in a safe world, which film-making certainly isn't,' said Clark.

13 Producing the Goods

Don Boyd, Michael Relph, Lewis Gilbert, Skreba

> 'There's no point in making movies unless they're seen. If they're seen they will make money. That's been my guiding principle since I was at film school. I'm not going to make films just to show them to my friends.'
>
> Don Boyd, 1979

In the dull days of the mid-1970s, when David Puttnam had gone to work in Hollywood, Don Boyd (born 1948) was the one bright spark of the local industry. A young director, born in Scotland, who had made two indifferent films, *Intimate Reflections* (1975) and *East of Elephant Rock* (1976), he had turned producer and was responsible for seven much more engrossing, idiosyncratic low-budget movies within a couple of years. That activity ceased abruptly when he, too, went to the States, in order to produce *Honky Tonk Freeway* (1981) for EMI, based on his own idea. Making the film turned out to be a long and expensive process and, when the result finally reached the cinemas, it was a $24 million flop.

Boyd's energies had been concentrated on the film, and his company did little more than tick over while he was away. On his return to Britain, he became involved the next year in another financial disaster. A fortnight into shooting *Gossip*, a movie about the world of newspaper columnists, the money failed, the filming was abandoned and lawsuits began. Boyd, receiving as many as forty abusive or threatening phone calls a day from disgruntled participants, considered leaving the film business and going to Oxford University to read history. Six months later, his depression behind him, he was putting the final touches to three separate and ambitious enterprises intended to change the structure of the British film industry.

The most far-reaching, in collaboration with producer–writer–director Bryan Forbes and a merchant bank, was to organise an entertainment company that would have its own studio, production and distribution organisations and cinemas, the system of vertical integration that Rank and EMI had pioneered. He wanted the cinemas to operate in a more imaginative way than at present. His scheme came in two sizes, a large-scale enterprise and a smaller one, depending on how difficult or easy it would be to buy out existing owners of studios and cinemas.

'I expect it will be smaller rather than bigger, but it is something we think we will achieve before the end of 1985,' he said. 'I think that the phenomenon of a community going to a place where they can have a combination of entertainments, including a new film, and a combination of entertainment-related products, is something that has a future. I believe people actually like going somewhere where there are a lot of other people and seeing images on a big screen, beautifully projected in great comfort, cheaply.

'There will be fewer cinemas, but the City will provide money to improve the surviving cinemas because they are always interested in the retail situation. One of the problems with a movie is that you don't get to that retail situation for a long time. With a movie house, it's a concept they understand: people paying to go in and do something. It involves property, which the City appreciates.'

The two other plans were to bring together a formidable array of producing and directing talents.

In the first, Boyd had organised a group of producers to make one production each over a three-year period, backed by what he called 'investor-clients', who would include a major American studio, a British distributor, a television company, and two British film investment organisations. The others involved included some of the most energetic of local producers: Forbes, Jeremy Thomas, Barry Hanson, Clive Parsons and Davina Belling, and Ann Skinner and Simon Relph.

His second plan involved a group of British directors from theatre and television: Trevor Nunn, Simon Langton, Charles Sturridge, Bill Bryden and Franc Roddam. Boyd's role would be to help them develop film projects and raise the necessary finance to make them a reality. He also expected to produce several films of his own, including *Neutron*, set after a nuclear holocaust, which Derek Jarman would direct.

Boyd, an untidy and owlish figure in his round spectacles, dabbled in acting, pop music and publishing before making profitable television commercials and deciding in 1978 that his youth and boundless enthusiasm were assets to be exploited. 'Invest in our future is what I told people. Be in on this young bunch who are going places. People listened to that,' he said.

He acquired for a while as a minority shareholder the brilliant accountant and tax expert Roy Tucker, whose Rossminster group later became a cause of controversy. Just as opponents of the Nazis in America during the early 1930s were condemned as 'premature anti-

Fascists', so Tucker was a premature tax avoider, creating a series of complex schemes for his clients to save money that caused official displeasure, although after a lengthy investigation it was decided he had broken no laws.

For investors in Boyd's films, Tucker devised similar partnership schemes, some of which were later incorporated into legislation giving film production companies certain tax concessions.

It provided Boyd with a source of ready finance, although there was never a great deal of money around. The negative costs of his first five films amounted, in total, to £1.2 million. The most successful was *Scum* (1979), rewritten by Roy Minton from his harsh play about life in a Borstal. Intended for BBC-TV, the play was recorded before the BBC decided not to show it. Boyd took it on after other producers had turned it down. Tucker underwrote its financing and promised to use his own money if he could not raise it from other sources, providing Boyd's company paid any extra if it went over its budget of £250,000. It did, but only by £2,000.

Derek Jarman's version of Shakespeare's *The Tempest*, filmed as if by a punk Fellini, was shot in the fire-gutted ruins of a stately home in Warwickshire for even less: £180,000 (which was big budget by the standard of Jerman's other films, *Sebastiane* having cost £40,000 and *Jubilee* £70,000).

Jarman (born 1942) had worked as a set designer for Ken Russell, beginning with *The Devils* where the brutalist buildings, somehow simultaneously medieval and modern, contributed much to the film's disturbing quality. A painter first, Jarman's excellent visual sense was allied with a sense of humour as subversively frivolous as that of the novelist Ronald Firbank. *Sebastiane*, a swooning and homosexual account of the saint and martyr, had dialogue in Latin. *The Tempest* ended with Elizabeth Welch singing 'Stormy Weather' while sailor boys danced together.

Boyd's projects differed widely, ranging from Jarman's camp originality to the most expensive of the seven films, Claude Whatham's treatment of Beryl Bainbridge's *Sweet William*, a conventional film about a philanderer. There were those who felt that Boyd missed a glorious opportunity to establish himself by his failure to concentrate on such straightforwardly commercial films.

He regrets making none of the movies himself, although he now wishes there had been more time spent on *Hussy* (1979), scripted and directed by Matthew Chapman (born 1951), in which Helen Mirren played a nightclub hostess who becomes involved in murder. 'We should have worked longer on the script,' he said. 'But it's become a cult film in America. Jack Nicholson says it's the best British movie he's ever seen.'

Nevertheless, his real education in filming came when working in

America on *Honky Tonk Freeway*. The project had begun as a film Boyd intended to direct himself from a script written by a young American, Ed Clinton. Barry Spikings at EMI was shown the script and wanted to make it as a big-budget film, which meant that, as a safety measure, it would require a well-known director.

As a consolation, he asked Boyd to produce it. During the long process of filming in America, Boyd was fêted and courted by Hollywood production companies; and two of the biggest, Paramount and Universal, made deals with him to develop ideas. When the movie was previewed and the reactions were poor, the relationships quickly cooled; people began to have second thoughts about further projects. The agreed deals were dropped.

'In Hollywood, you have to make films that make money and are designed to make money,' he said. 'But I have absolutely no regrets about *Honky Tonk Freeway*. I like it; it's a funny movie, very well-directed. It was a shame it cost as much as it did; it was a shame that it didn't hit the imagination of the American public. Time will re-evaluate it; it's a definitive statement about the America of the time, and an entertaining one. I'm not remotely ashamed of it. Critics here reviewed the budget, not the film and criticised EMI for putting up the money.' Making the film had occupied three years of his life.

While he was away, scripts for two inexpensive British films, *Scrubbers*, a feminine version of *Scum*, and *An Unsuitable Job for a Woman* had been developed by his company and were filmed, with other companies financing them before he began work on *Gossip*.

Boyd remains an admirer of Hollywood's professionalism and how some North American directors can work wonders on little money. 'John Carpenter and David Cronenberg go off and make films very cheaply, aimed at a specific cinema market. They make films much more cheaply than the glorified television plays that go out on Channel Four masquerading as proper movies,' he said.

He also expects to see Americans financing more British movies. 'The States is a vital market place,' he said. 'You have to go there to sell and it's quite likely you are also going to go there to finance. I think they're important partners, because then they're more likely to want to assist you at the selling stage.

'If you make a British film, they are going to see it in terms of their primary market and are going to want to influence the editorial content. What is interesting is that the Americans have also had an education in what is possible with an English-language film made here. People have been amazed by the success of a film like *The Draughtsman's Contract*. It's a small art film, admittedly.

'I know Paramount are planning a film about Lady Jane Grey to be filmed in England with an English director. The success of films like *Betrayal* has impressed the Americans, and they know that if they get behind such a movie in the States, they can make as much money out of it as they can out of something else.

'It is still cheaper to make a film here than in the States, especially with the dollar rate as it is. I don't think that the American majors will be trying to package mid-Atlantic films. I'm very optimistic about the future.'

Boyd's offices are situated above the hubbub of Berwick Street market in Soho, not far from Wardour Street, the centre of London's film making activities. Not a rotten tomato's throw away, a similar, if more cautious optimism could be sensed in the tiny first-floor office where Michael Relph sat trying to raise money to film *Big Deal,* a script he wrote with Jonathan Lynn. A comedy about the double standards of international big business and the chicanery involved in competing for a contract to build a railway system in a Third World country, it presented difficulties. The setting and subject meant filming in those parts of the world where the costs of travel and location shooting were extremely expensive; there'll be none of the Peter Rogers approach of shooting *Carry On Up The Khyber Pass* in Wales.

Relph had to find more than the magic million which would be needed to make a film in Britain. The problem was that his treatment, from an English angle, was hardly likely to coax money out of the Americans.

Relph, tall and greyhaired, with the courtly, melancholy manner of a Spanish grandee, considered that he would be lucky to find any backers. 'I do foresee problems,' he said. But he was also in the final planning stages for an independent production consortium, backed, like Goldcrest, with money from the City. 'It will provide substantial new funds for the industry,' he said. He hoped that he would be able to begin making the first films in 1984.

Relph (born 1915) is one of the few survivors still at work from the comparatively golden days of British cinema. On the walls of the cramped office where he was beginning again were reminders of that past: posters of old movies, set designs and announcements of awards for *The Blue Lamp* (1949), which he produced at Ealing Studios, and for *Sapphire* (1959). He prefers not to hark back to his Ealing days, although he remains in favour of what might be called the Balconisation of the industry, that is, the production of definably British films.

He began at Ealing as a set designer and art director, working on such excellent films as the genuinely macabre *Dead of Night* and *Nicholas Nickleby*. In his notably productive association with Basil Dearden, which lasted 20 years, he produced, and sometimes wrote and co-directed films that were among the best to be made in Britain in that period, including two thrillers, *Sapphire* (1959) and *Victim* (1961) which managed to deal, convincingly for the time, with matters of racism and homosexuality. Their collaboration ended with the ghost story, *The Man Who Haunted Himself*, in 1970. Shortly afterwards, Dearden was killed in a car crash.

When Boyd set up his production company, Relph worked for him for several years. The relationship must have been an uneasy one, with the confrontation of experience and innocence, age and youth.

Boyd, too, not only seemed to be a one-man film industry, but sometimes acted as if he preferred it that way. 'I found it a very interesting experience, working with young people and so on,' said Relph. 'Since the advent of cable and video and the expansion of television generally, there's a much more optimistic feeling about markets for films.

'We were making films for what was a dying market, so there was a pessimistic view about the future of the film business. But now, primarily because of cable, but also because of video, it's felt that ultimately there is going to be an insatiable demand for films of one sort and another. The problem is, of course, to get sufficient recoupment from those sources. Although there will be a demand for material, I don't think yet that the recovery of costs from these new media is going to match the expenditure that's needed.

'The television outlet has made it much more viable to make small, indigenous films. Sales to cable in America will obviously often get more money than any other form of distribution. Co-productions with cable stations are quite a promising area. A few years ago, you couldn't have done so, because films had to have an international appeal. Now, with Channel Four and satellite broadcasting, there may well be a market to support films that cost up to £1 million.

'I've always thought it a great mistake to believe that because films have an indigenous element, they are not international. Films that are true to the environment in which they are made are the ones that do appeal internationally. Those are the kind of films I've always liked. As English film makers, we should make films about the background that we know. I'm more drawn to that than these so-called international movies that are not really rooted in the way of life that one knows.

'At the moment, there's a wave of optimism about the industry. I'm not convinced that it will last. It's always been a very cyclic business: periods of exaggerated slump followed by periods of overstated optimism.

'The day will inevitably come when there will be a period of reassessment, when the extent of these new markets is fully realised. I suspect that it will be found that we've expected too much from them. There can be no question that the demand for moving pictures of all sorts is bound to increase. But nobody knows whether the level of audiences in cinemas has bottomed out or will go on deteriorating.

'Distribution in the past hasn't favoured the small films. But distributors have been forced to become more flexible and are recognising that there is a variety of different types of product.'

Most of the big American distributors are now developing 'classics divisions' – what we'd call art house release – which are very suitable for certain kinds of English films.

'One has also to be wary of this development because it's also a means of distributors getting product on the cheap, giving one nothing for it. But it does enable them to release a film in a modest way and then, if it performs well, it can move up to a more general release.'

The production company Relph hopes to run will need to raise half a film's finance from outside sources, either by television or distribution deals. 'The danger is over-hyping things so that you pull off wonderful pre-distribution deals, but the film loses money. That is a self-destructive situation. What we'll really be looking for is partners, who share our enthusiasm for a subject and are willing to come in on the risks with us. I think the time could come when the talent available will not keep pace with the demand. It still isn't easy enough to go back and forth between television and film. The unions are still resisting the movement of people.

'The demand for audio-visual entertainment is going to be almost insatiable. It's a question of sorting out the economics and making sure that the rewards are sufficient to finance new product, and good new product. Our market here will always be a minority one, so in order to be commercially viable, we've got to capture foreign audiences as well. But that's no bad thing.

'What is most important is to preserve the stratum of production that is aimed at getting the majority of its revenue back from this country and can afford to experiment with new people and new ideas. Once you've got that, the big blockbusting films will come along afterwards.'

City money also provided the impetus for another veteran film maker, Lewis Gilbert (born 1920) who founded Acorn Pictures in partnership with a banker, Herbert Oakes. Their first production was *Educating Rita*, one of the British hits of 1983. Gilbert's experience goes back to working as a child actor in silent movies. When he was 16, he was on the production side of Alexander Korda's studios. He was part of the success of the 1960s British cinema with *Alfie* (1966), a film that made Michael Caine into a star. He also directed two of the James Bond films, *You Only Live Twice* (1967) and *The Spy Who Loved Me* (1977). Then, by chance, he met a banker Herbert L. Oakes at a London cocktail party.

Willy Russell's *Educating Rita* had been one of the most popular productions of the Royal Shakespeare Company, transferring to the

West End for a long run. The play was an updating of the Pygmalion theme, about a working-class woman desperate for education and a bored, alcoholic lecturer who watches her grow from unsophisticated intelligence to being bright enough to reject much of what she had been taught.

Small in scope, it provided two excellent parts for actors. On the West End stage, it had been remarkable for the performance of Julie Walters as the girl. She was far from a conventional star: thin, with eyes that at times almost disappeared from sight, and a defiantly regional accent. But she was an actress of great ability, able to appear glamorous through sheer conviction and with a sharp wit that made her double act with the writer-performer Victoria Wood in a television series a delight. She transformed *Educating Rita* into a genuinely touching play.

Gilbert saw the play and knew that he wanted her to appear in the film. After buying the rights, he took the project around every studio. They all turned it down, because it lacked a star name. (One producer was interested, but only if the film were given an American setting, with the busty country singer Dolly Parton as Rita.)

Oakes's banking contacts led him to Prudential Assurance, who were interested in a longer term arrangement, preferring to put up most of the finance for three films, budgeted at a total of $20 million. Around $6 million went on *Educating Rita*. A bankable name was found to play the lecturer: Michael Caine, the star of *Alfie*.

Caine, prodded into acting for the first time in several movies, gave an excellent performance, notable for its generosity. He left plenty of room for the less-experienced Julie Walters to display her abilities. The result was a solid, old-fashioned, slightly sentimental British film, although it lost a certain authenticity by being shot in Dublin.

Gilbert's second film was to be based on another stage play, Paul Kember's *Not Quite Jerusalem*. Originally staged at the Royal Court, it was a more uncomfortable and less popular work than the reassuring *Educating Rita*. It concerned three working-class Britons who spend a holiday in an Israeli kibbutz, where they glory in their ignorance and lethargy. Their inadequacies, their lack of national pride or feeling, their brutal philistinism and coarseness are contrasted with the gentler attitudes of other nationalities.

It is impossible to know how much of the harshness of the original will survive in the movie, which is expected to cost $7 million. Gilbert plans that the third film will be made entirely in America.

Simon Relph, Michael's son, is now the third generation of his family to have worked in films. His grandfather was George Relph, a notable character actor on stage and screen and star of the Ealing Comedy *The Titfield Thunderbolt* (1953). Simon, a bluff extrovert, was Technical

Administrator of the National Theatre during its move from The Old Vic to the South Bank in the mid-1970s.

'My father and Basil were a model of a producing-directing team. They were both producers and directors and switched roles. Their great strength was 25 years of working together, even though they were quite disparate personalities,' he said.

Now one of the busiest of the new generation of British producers, he is one third of Skreba Productions, set up by Ann Skinner in 1982. (Relph is also connected, together with Ann Scott, a former television producer, with Greenpoint Films, which is a partnership of directors, including David Hare and Richard Eyre, formed to make films for Channel Four.) Skinner, Relph and Zelda Barron, the third member of Skreba, have spent many years working in various capacities in movies.

Skreba came into existence, says Ann Skinner, because Richard Attenborough told her she would never do it. At the time, she was responsible for the continuity on Attenborough's *Magic,* which was being filmed in America. 'I'd been paid well to do it and was living on expenses so I had a little nest egg to start me off.'

She began by buying an option on Rebecca West's early novel, *Return Of The Soldier,* about a shell-shocked officer coming back from the First World War having forgotten his marriage and remembering only an earlier love affair. She invited Relph and Zelda Barron to join her so that each could help the others survive. They, too, had been in regular and well-paid employment at the time. Both were working in London on Warren Beatty's epic, *Reds,* in which he was producer, director and star. Relph was first assistant director, Barron in charge of continuity. The production provided work for an unusually long period, more than a year.

'When you begin on your own, there's an awful lot of expenditure required and no money coming in,' said Skinner. 'I thought I'd do continuity work on commercials for two days a week while I learned how to produce a film. Even though I'd been in films since 1955, I didn't know anything about it, not even how to acquire an option. I could never have negotiated all the agreements without Simon's help, except by spending a fortune on legal fees. It also helped to have a man in the partnership. Many men do not like dealing with women in business. They feel uncomfortable about it.'

It was the worst of times to begin trying to produce British films. When *Return of the Soldier* went into the studios in 1982, it was the only local film being made. 'We were three technicians taking on the world at a time when nothing much was happening. Everyone told us we were crazy, especially in trying to make a period English film,' said Relph.

Skinner had managed to put together an impressive package: a good script, by Hugh Whitemore, an excellent stage and television playwright, and a cast that included Alan Bates, Glenda Jackson and Julie Christie. Even with such stars, the budget was a modest £1.2 million. But she could find no one prepared to back it. Everywhere she went, she was told that audiences were not interested in a period film, especially a period English film.

George Walker, of Brent Walker, showed some interest in putting up half the cost. So did Lord Grade, on condition that she could raise the rest from an American production company. So she flew to Los Angeles, carrying introductions to production heads from David Puttnam, and spent six weeks vainly trying to find backers. Some refused to believe she had the cast she claimed. In the end, she carried letters from them to prove it.

'Hollywood is full of people doing what we were doing, ambitious technicians hawking their favourite script,' said Relph. In the end, when they had given up hope, they discovered an unusual source of money, a movie-struck and monied American dentist.

Filming began. After five weeks of the ten week schedule, the dentist stopped further payments. For a week, filming continued with no promise of payment from anyone involved. Then Brent Walker agreed to take over the costs.

It was an over-glamourised, well-acted film that received respectful reviews and opened in London to good business. Elsewhere in Britain, it was less successful.

Relph feels it was partly because the attention of Twentieth Century Fox, who distributed the film, switched to *Local Hero*, which was more important to them. Skinner also blames the current distribution pattern which involves a long delay between a movie's opening in London and its appearance elsewhere in the country. Unless the film is a blockbuster such as *Return of the Jedi*, by the time it reaches the regions the impact of its opening has dissipated. At a local level, film publicity hardly exists.

'The distributors decided not to take a date in Bournemouth, which would have been hot on the success of its London opening, because the cinema only had two weeks free. They decided to delay until the cinema had an open-ended booking,' said Skinner. 'As a result, when it did open there, hardly anyone knew about it. My aunt lives there and was desperate to see it and she missed it. If you don't take a local paper there's no way of knowing.'

According to a recent survey by Thorn-EMI, only 15 per cent of the public is aware of what films are showing at the local cinemas. Cinema owners still tend to behave as if they have a captive audience and few do much to bring their films to the attention of the public.

Ann Skinner recalls, with disappointment, travelling to Brighton to see *Return of the Soldier* in the Odeon there, which is regarded as one of the more important regional venues. It is a modern cinema, stuck in a larger building and approached by way of escalators. When she reached the foyer she was surprised to find no posters indicating what films were showing or at what times. 'There was no one around, not even at the cash desk,' she said. 'I knew when the programme started because I'd checked in the paper. As I stood there, a woman approached me to ask me if I knew when the film began. She said she'd tried to ring the cinema but no one had answered the phone.'

When it did start, she found herself watching a 35 minute short. 'It had not been advertised and it was absolutely appalling'. Worse was to come. Before her film began, there were trailers of coming attractions. 'The last was for *Gandhi*, which is a wide-screen film,' she said. 'Then *Return of the Soldier* began and the screen suddenly shrank. It made it seem like it was a mini-film. I tried to find the manager but couldn't. There was no interest at all. I asked why there were no posters in the foyer and was told that a poster cost an extra £1.50 which comes off their returns.'

Both Skinner and Relph acknowledge that, so far, they would have been financially better off remaining employees rather than employers. Because of the financial problems over *Return Of The Soldier* neither took even a salary from the film. Litigation over the film impeded its release in America for more than a year and made the film harder to sell elsewhere in the world. 'An American sale gives distributors elsewhere a sense of confidence,' said Relph.

By the time their second film, *Secret Places*, began shooting in August 1983, they had spent a period of two-and-a-half years working on the project. For the last six months, it had occupied nearly all their time. During that period their financial return was £1,000 each.

The money to make it was only raised four weeks before filming was scheduled to begin, which was only just in time; the movie, set in a girls' school, had to be made on location in an actual school and so needed to be shot during the school holidays. 'We went through until July not knowing whether we were going to make the film or not,' said Relph. 'If it hadn't been made, then we would have had to start again and we would have gone another six months, running our resources down. It's a phenomenal gamble.'

The reward, he says, is not so much financial as being able to control one's own destiny, to be the person who makes the decisions. The inordinate time it takes to set up a film affects the type of movie that is made. 'You have to live with it for years, so it has got to be good enough to sustain you for that length of time,' said Relph. 'Having found the right project, you are often forced back to a low-budget situation simply because you don't believe the film will be one of those that attracts a broad commercial market. I knew *Ploughman's Lunch* was going to be an art house movie and it's been very successful as that. But it's still got a long way to go before it returns its small investment.'

Relph admits to some astonishment over the way the film industry is organised. In most manufacturing businesses, he points out, you buy the materials, make your goods and sell them to a wholesaler or retailer, who then has the task of selling them to his customers. You fix a price at which to sell your goods that allows you to make a profit. In films, the retailer (the cinema) and the wholesaler (the distributor) take their share first. It is only then that the producer gets his money, if there is any left over.

'If you make a successful film you can expect to get back 10 per cent of what it takes at the box office. If you make an unsuccessful film, you get nothing back. But in the meantime the people who are selling it are still making their living off it. They take their money first, so that they can keep going while the people who actually made the product are having a much tougher time. It's ludicrous. The attitude towards the exhibition of movies is depressing beyond belief. Exhibitors had some very good years and now, when things are not so profitable, they want out. But they don't want to let others in. They seem to want to prove that cinemas are totally unprofitable so that they can turn them into something else.'

Skinner agrees: 'It is the exhibitors who talk endlessly about the death of the film industry, which is just putting nails in its coffin. We had to struggle for years to get *Return of the Soldier* made and to make the film good. It was a battle to keep the costs down. We persuaded the actors to take reasonable salaries and we didn't take any money ourselves. But you know that the minute it gets into the hands of the people selling it there is no question of them going without or of cutting down.'

14 Through a Screen Darkly

Channel Four, independent cinemas, video and the new technology

'If the public considers it desirable for political, cultural or economic reasons that British films should be produced, then it must be prepared for the Government not only to protect the industry indefinitely, but also to aid it financially for as far ahead as can be seen.'

PEP Report on the film industry, 1952

Federico Fellini was once asked why he had not made any films in America, despite offers to do so. 'I don't think I could make use of all the help that producers would want to give me,' he said.

Nevertheless, in Britain, it is clear that the survival of cinema depends upon producers more than directors or actors. Directors and actors can, and do, work anywhere. Producers, for the most part, cannot. But their personal survival is impossible to predict.

In the 1970s, Brent Walker were among the busiest independent producers, for the most part making films of little merit. Their most successful films were those odd combinations of sex and soap opera, *The Stud* (1978) and *The Bitch* (1979), dominated by the hard gloss of Joan Collins's screen presence. In 1980, the company moved more into the mainstream of film making with *Loophole*, a tepid thriller directed by John Quested. Its main film activity now is making versions of Gilbert and Sullivan operettas for television and video cassette release.

The Who invested some of the money garnered from their music in Shepperton Studios and also dabbled in film making. *Quadrophenia*, which used the songs from their album of the same name, caused a revival among the young of the fashion of The Mods, sharply dressed, short-haired youths on scooters, although Franc Roddam's film was an over-emphatic recreation of the recent past. *The Kids Are Alright* was an energetic documentary of The Who's career. And Roger Daltrey, the group's lead singer who had enjoyed the experience of starring as Tommy in Ken Russell's film, made *McVicar* (1980), Tom Clegg's tough film of a criminal life. But since then, the group has grown ever more divisive and seems to have lost its cinematic ambitions.

After the recent failures of British producers to establish themselves as powers in America, most producers have their ambitions under control. They know that their survival depends upon the survival of a local industry. That, of course, is nothing new. What is different is that the existence of a group of intelligent and determined producers has coincided with a moment when films are in greater demand than ever before.

Whether there is an audience for British films is difficult to know. Certainly, the British like watching films, at least on television and video. Indeed, they devote more time to watching films now than they did when the cinemas were flourishing.

One critic, C. A. Lejeune, discussing British cinema just after the end of the Second World War, wrote, 'Its present position is secure. Its past record is proud. Its future is a matter of anxious speculation.' The British films of the time had been popular because they reflected the realities of the time. 'British audiences' affection for their native films is no fortuitous thing, but has been brought about by a ripening social consciousness, and a growing sense of what is real and valid in art and entertainment,' she wrote, warning that 'unless the industry recognised the reality, it would become a parochial echo of Hollywood'.

The warning went unheeded. But the success of more recent British films which are based in a recognisable reality suggests that there are audiences eager to respond to a cinema that reflects, in some way, their own lives. As Ken Loach once put it to me, 'When you see a film, you automatically relate it to what you did before you went to the cinema and to what you are going to do afterwards. It's good to make that experience relevant to the rest of your life, rather than encapsulating two hours that have no cross-reference to anything else you do.'

Ironically, it is television that has come nearest to fulfilling Lejeune's and Loach's criteria, particularly Channel Four with its *Film On Four*.

Even before that innovative series, a number of BBC television serials – *The Glittering Prizes*, with its acidly witty delineation of power and privilege, or Loach's direction of *Days of Hope*, with its concentration on working people trying to gain control over their own lives, or *Tinker, Tailor, Soldier, Spy*, a study in treachery made notable by Alec Guinness's virtuoso acting – all these and more were better written, acted and directed than most British cinema films of the period.

What Channel Four provided in addition, under the guidance of David Rose, a distinguished and experienced producer, was opportunities for independent producers, who were commissioned by

Channel Four, as opposed to the usual system whereby television films are produced by the companies' own staff or a subsidiary.

Channel Four's first year brought an unrepeatable bonanza for the independents: 170 companies were commissioned. That number has since fallen and will go on falling. Eventually, there will a third or less still in business and not all will be making dramatic films. Nevertheless, Channel Four has opened up possibilities for many producers, providing the chance of regular work which, whatever the limitations of budget and subject matter, can only be a valuable stimulus to the local industry.

Some of the productions were no better, and were indeed sometimes worse, than television drama of the past. What was different was the emphasis upon them as films rather than as plays.

Among its first 35 productions were several films of unusual quality. Peter Greenaway's *The Draughtsman's Contract*, for instance, was a deliberately teasing film, set in the 1690s and made with the assistance of the BFI production board. An exercise in style and a witty, if lengthy, elaboration on the theme of murder, it enjoyed an extraordinary critical reception and exposure in a few cinemas. Mike Radford's *Another Time, Another Place* (1983) was a tightly focused story of an Italian prisoner of war's relationship with the young wife of a farmer, living in an isolated Scottish community. And Neil Jordan's *Angel* (1983) set the relationship of a singer and a feckless musician against a murder amid the brutal realities of present-day Belfast.

Two films in particular stood out as exceptional, Richard Eyre's *The Ploughman's Lunch* (1983) and Jerzy Skolimowski's *Moonlighting* (1981).

Skolimowski, indeed, showed what enthusiasm and initiative could achieve. A Polish director, he, like his compatriot Roman Polanski, had spent much time filming elsewhere, coming to Britain in 1970 to make *Deep End*, financed by American and West German producers. It was an obsessional adolescent love-story, of a young boy infatuated by a flirtatious girl, set in a public baths and ending in a violent death. His other British-made movie was *The Shout* (1979), a short and oddly sinister work starring Alan Bates as a man who claims that he can kill with his voice.

Skolimowski had left Poland in 1967 after the authorities had banned his third film, *Hands Up*, which was anti-Stalinist in tone. It was finally shown there in 1982, after he returned to shoot a new ending in which an unidentified army intervened in the running of the country. It was seen once before martial law was imposed.

In 1982, Skolimowski had bought a small, scruffy house in one of London's smarter districts. To help him renovate it, he brought four workmen over from Poland. 'It was very democratic,' he said. 'I worked as a fifth member of the team and showed them London. I paid them in zlotys, more than they would have earned at home, and it was still cheaper for me than using English workmen.' He thought of turning his experiences with his friends into a film. He began by writing the diary that the foreman might have kept. 'In that way I was able to use my pidgin English in a semi-literary way,' he said.

In December that year, when martial law was imposed in Poland, effectively stranding him in London, he felt too upset to work. Two weeks later, he wrote a two-page outline of a film in which four Poles, only one of them understanding English, come to London to renovate a house. He called it *Novak*, the name of the English-speaking foreman who hides from the other workers the news of what is happening in Poland.

Skolimowski, seeking backing, approached Mamoun Hassan at the NFFC, who in turn happened to meet Mark Shivas, an experienced television and film producer, and suggested to him that he might be interested in producing it.

Skolimowski had decided, after watching *Brideshead Revisited* on television that the only person to play the foreman was Jeremy Irons. Irons had spent most of the previous year rejecting scripts as uninteresting, but he agreed to meet the director. 'I liked the treatment he read to me and I liked him,' said Irons. 'But I said to him, I'm starting a film in March and then I go on to another one. He said, before then, you have some time. His enthusiasm and passion made me want to work with him.'

Irons agreed to take the part within ten minutes. 'It was a really wonderful gesture which allowed the picture to be made,' said Skolimowski, who spent the next 11 days writing the script while Shivas tried to raise the necessary £1 million. 'Speed was of the essence,' said Irons.

The NFFC put up £11,500 to fund the script being written, although the money was never used. Shivas got Channel Four to agree to put up half the budget and then approached theatrical producer Michael White.

'It is very difficult to raise money quickly,' said Shivas. 'Big corporations have boards that only meet once a month. It was wonderful discovering Michael White who not only made up his mind at once but handed over a cheque so that we could begin hiring the crew.'

The money was available four days before shooting was due to begin. Finding the right location was no problem. Skolimowski used his own just-renovated house. Workmen moved in to disguise the new floors, dirty the sparkling paintwork and disguise the freshness under false walls of peeling wallpapers. 'I shot in my own home because I wanted the situation to be very real,' said Skolimowski. 'I follow my own experience and I can control it in a way I couldn't if I shot it in any other place. It is very difficult to transform the imagination.'

Seventeen weeks after he had first sat down to write his outline, Skolimowski was showing the completed film at the Cannes Film Festival, where he won a prize for the best script. 'That must be a world record and one that has been very wearing on the nerves,' said Shivas.

Moonlighting, a title settled on after *Blackout* (as well a *Novak*) had been tried and discarded, is a lovely gentle and amusing film, which is as revealing about British life as it is about Polish, illuminating both from the underside.

As topical a story of moral inertia, set against an actual Tory Party conference, was *The Ploughman's Lunch*, directed by Richard Eyre from a script by Ian McEwan. In its depiction of a self-seeking journalist, moving through fashionable literary and political coteries, it was devastatingly accurate.

Both films were given a cinema release before being shown on television, as were several others made for Channel Four.

The Ploughman's Lunch, in particular, received a great deal of praise from the critics. Yet, when it was shown on Channel Four in October 1983, it came no higher than eighth in the weekly ratings for the station, drawing an audience of 1.7 million, 200,000 less than watched American football on the same station that week.

Its failure to find a larger audience was dispiriting. The film was, perhaps, of the kind execrated by John Grierson, as of interest only to those who live and work within a mile or so of London's West End. Its characters – journalists, poets and publishers – were certainly metropolitan, but its concerns, with double-dealing in private and public life set against the Falklands war and the Suez crisis, were wider. An audience nearly three times as big had watched *The Country Girls*, Desmond Davis's film of Edna O'Brien's novel of the sexual education of two naive Irish girls – hardly a less parochial subject.

The only people who did not welcome Channel Four's new initiative were the Cinema Exhibitors Association (CEA), who had always fought hard to prevent films from reaching television, objecting strongly to – yet unable to prevent – the shortening gap between a film's release in the cinemas and its showing on television.

In 1980, Lord Grade, followed by EMI, had sold films to television for showing three years after release instead of the five years that had been customary. Channel Four's problem was that it could not afford too long a delay between a commissioned film's showings on cinema and television. But the CEA prevented a wider release for many of their films, including *Moonlighting*, *The Ploughman's Lunch* and *The Draughtsman's Contract*.

The problem is one that has also affected the simultaneous release of films in the cinema and on video cassette, which is the simplest means of combating those who make illicit copies of cinema films on to cassettes and sell them. Exhibitors tend to regard video cassettes with the same loathing as television, although it might have been more sensible for them to take advantage of the new technology, by selling and hiring video cassettes, in the same way as they have become purveyors of hot dogs and ice cream.

'Exhibitors are the Neanderthal men of the industry. But you can understand it, they've got their backs to the wall,' said David Puttnam, who found a way of circumventing their obstructions with his film, *Forever Young*, intended for showing on Channel Four after its cinema release. He had an understanding that Channel Four would not screen it for 18 months in order that it might play the cinemas first. 'It's going as a circuit picture, not an art house picture,' he said. 'I don't have a contract with Channel Four so the exhibitors can't scream. But the truth of the matter is that if they're not booking it after a year and a half, then it will go on television.'

Channel Four themselves were aware of the way potential buyers of their productions regarded television films as somehow necessarily inferior. After their first year of operation, the station even gave up selling the films under its own name. Instead the sales organisation was renamed Film Four.

If the part the station had played in adding direction to British cinema was a cause for celebration, it was also a source of concern. Television puts greater restrictions on subject matter and its treatment than the cinema. There is also an aesthetic difference in work intended to be seen on a big and on a small screen.

'It's arguable whether they're movies,' said Puttnam. 'My friend Alan Parker insists they're not. I'm not sure. I think he has a great case that they're not really movies. They're a different product. There's no possible way you can compare *The Killing Fields* to *P'tang Yang Kipperbang*. They didn't even set out to attempt to be similar.

'The best possible example was John Schlesinger's *An Englishman Abroad*. That was wonderful television. Its length was right, its scale, its density. An hour is great; I wish I could get more of our people to work to an hour's length. But no way was that a movie.'

It may be that the distinction is one made more by film makers than by audiences. Peter Duffell's *Experience Preferred But Not Essential*, a small film about a young woman taking a job in a hotel during her university vacation, was produced by Puttnam for Channel Four. In New York, it was released in the cinemas and, following an enthusiastic review by Vincent Canby of the *New York Times*, enjoyed some success.

'It's not a film in British terms,' said Puttnam. 'It may be in American terms because American television is genuine pulp 99.9 per cent of the time. British television is only 85 per cent pulp so we do have our weekly television leavened by some rather good stuff Americans just don't see. I think *Angel* was a movie. *Another Time, Another Place* was a film for television. The jury is out for the moment.'

But for Don Boyd, *Another Time, Another Place* signified a step forward for British cinema. 'It reminded me of the sort of films that were being made in Italy after the war, the Neo-realist movies,' he said. It's terrible to think that in 1984 our cinema should have to be compared to Italian cinema of the 1940s. We had periods of great value, the Ealing films, the early 60s, but we've never had a tradition of cinema in the way the Italian and French have. *Another Time, Another Place* is the beginnings of establishing a new cinema tradition in Britain, which is going to be one acceptable throughout the world and with a great advantage on our side: the English language.'

Mamoun Hassan regards them as 'a worrying new category, a hybrid which might work if shown in very small cinemas.'

Few film makers seem concerned about the aesthetic differences between the two media. 'One director told me that the only difference was that the TV image is smaller,' said Hassan. 'If that's the level of thinking, forget it, because we're not going to get anywhere. As Kurosawa said, why should people go to the cinema when, if they do, they see what they see at home?'

Channel Four's token releases for the films did give them a prominence that they would not otherwise have received. Potential viewers were able to read reviews of them before watching them, rather than after the event as is usual with television.

According to Puttnam, who has thought hard about the future of the cinema, it will owe its survival to such marketing strategies, which offer a way of attracting attention to movies which will then earn most of their income from television. He draws an analogy with rock music, where groups undertake tours that lose a great deal of money, which they promptly make back many times over on record sales. Whereas touring was once a source of income, it is now a means of promotion.

Such a use of cinemas might also end the current trend where the price of promoting a film can be twice as much as the cost of actually making it. 'What I hope to see in my lifetime is that people who bother to go to the cinema pay less than people who choose to sit at home, to compensate for the inconvenience. You shouldn't, which is what happens at the moment, penalise them,' he said.

'I'd like to see fewer and better cinemas, of between 450 and 700 seats. Everything is in the ratio between screen size and audience. In some small cinemas the screen is postage stamp size, which is ridiculous. There's no point in providing more choice with triple cinemas and offering an inferior product.

'I guess we'll end up with 800 screens spread across 450 cinemas in the country. I think we should be able to hold the audience at 50–55 million. I'd be jolly sorry if it dropped below that, and there's no reason why it should unless we're making poor films or we outprice the product. There's no reason to outprice because we've got this terrific leverage of ancillary rights. I do believe what I've said over and over again for the last six years. The cinema is the promotional device by which you sell and create interest in the aftersales, be it cable, television or video.

'You can't sell a video cassette. What is it? It's a box with a name on it. If you've never heard of the name, who's going to buy it – unless it says across the top "Most Lurid Scene Ever Shot!" And you can't keep doing that. You can only get away with it a couple of times. So you're selling a product with a reputation. And where are you going to develop the reputation? The aura of the product, its reputation, a sense of excitement about it can only be created in the cinema and nowhere else. The cinema will be as crucial to the development of all the other media as radio has been to the development of popular music.'

If Puttnam is right, then the grandiose epics, of the sort that David Lean has made, will, like dinosaurs, disappear. There will be no room for them on television, although it is possible that they will be replaced by more of the epic's television equivalents, the 'mini-series' such as *Brideshead Revisited* or *The Jewel in the Crown*, which have a length denied to the cinema.

One welcome recent development, in London at least, has been the growth of independent cinemas. Usually run as clubs, in order to avoid paying the Eady Levy, they have flourished by offering better service to customers and showing good films. Enthusiasm has replaced the customary indifference and has been rewarded by appreciative audiences.

There are signs that all exhibitors are trying harder to attract audiences. A small but significant change was the alteration in 1983 which meant that cinemas changed their programmes on a Friday: there was a brief and unsuccessful experiment in which the changeover was made on a Thursday.

'Cinemas have been poor from a British perspective,' said Puttnam. 'It isn't true of Australia, France and the United States. England is a whole different problem and probably explains why we are the single largest declining market in the whole of the film industry. I think the exhibitors can't go on blaming everyone else. The cinemas did opt to stay in city centres but the public opted not to go into city centres. The cinemas did opt not to refurbish themselves; when they did it, they did it too late. I'm sure the exhibitors have to accept a good chunk of the blame. I can't pretend that during the 60s and 70s we were making very good movies in Britain, either.'

The future, anywhere, is here. It arrived in Britain on 29 March 1984 when The Entertainment Network (TEN) began showing feature films to subscribers to Rediffusion in 14 towns.

TEN, backed by Rank, Rediffusion, Plessey and involving MGM, United Artists, Paramount and Universal Pictures, offered only a small taste of what cable television may provide in the future, for it was only available at first to an existing network of some 300,000 viewers. TEN's service, for which subscribers paid an extra £7 a month, showed feature films nine hours a day, every day of the week.

The first night's viewing offered *Gallipoli*, *Rocky II*, *Missing* and *Poltergeist*, with not a British film among them, although *The French Lieutenant's Woman* was scheduled to be shown in the early weeks. TEN's selection of films was repeated at different times on different nights and offered, on average, 40 films a month or approaching 500 a year.

It was forecast that, within four years, the service would be available to five million households.

Although it was the first to begin broadcasting, TEN was not the only such service. There was also Premiere, a combination of Thorn-EMI, Goldcrest and the biggest of the American operators of cable television, Home Box Office, who now finance films in order to meet demand.

The success of such networks will obviously affect cinema-going, if not movie-watching. In the not too distant future there may be other rivals to film.

Microcomputers, ever more ubiquitous in British homes, offer an alternative means of entertainment and are still at a primitive stage. Within five years, it will be possible to link a microcomputer to a video-disc player and play complex interactive games, controlling the actions of figures on the television screen.

The principle is already here. It can be seen in *Valhalla*, a game for the Sinclair Spectrum and Commodore 64 computers which offers a self-contained world of Nordic myth, inhabited by gods, goddesses, dwarfs, dragons, wolves, a raven and a snake.

It is possible to watch the characters move about the television screen, apparently of their own volition, eating, drinking and fighting. Below them, on the screen, is printed a running commentary on their actions rather like the subtitles to a silent film. The player can control one of the characters and, by typing words on the computer keyboard, 'talk' to the others, asking favours or haggling with them over the cost of arms and food. The purpose of the game is to undertake a series of heroic quests for five sacred objects.

The technique of animation has been patented under the name of Movisoft and, in the future, will make use of not cartoon-like animation but actual film footage. Already, in amusement arcades, film and computer graphics are mixed to provide games of astonishing reality, such as driving a racing car around an actual track.

In *Dragon's Lair*, the player can participate in what looks like a Walt Disney cartoon, controlling, by means of a joystick, the movements of Dirk the Daring as he attempts to rescue an imprisoned princess from assorted monsters. *Dragon's Lair* was, in fact, animated by a former Disney artist, Don Bluth, who also directed the animated feature film *The Secret of Nimh*, but has earned more money from the arcades.

Valhalla, no doubt to the envy of many film producers, brought in more than £1 million in revenue in three months.

But the point where it might be possible to plug in a computer, switch on the television and duel with the image of Darth Vader is still several years away. It may complement the movies rather than becoming a rival to them, in much the same way that the toy trade depends upon films to sell many of its products.

British cinema seems healthier now than it has been for many years. An explosion of talent in the cinema has coincided with a voracious demand for films. The British industry still lacks showmen, those entrepreneurs who, by risk and daring and flair, can revitalise an industry on their own. The nearest, in recent times, was Lord Grade.

Jerry Epstein, an American producer who came to Britain to set up a film in 1955, once recalled to me his surprise at meeting Rank's executives. 'They were all in waistcoats,' he said. 'You know, movie people have to be slightly vulgarian. They have to come from the people, the workers. It was all so quiet and peaceful at Rank and the pictures had that same feeling. Everyone was very refined and delicate.'

Fortunately, refinement ain't what it used to be. Monty Python, Ken Russell and others have added a zest to British pictures, and probably a producer with a healthy streak of vulgarity will emerge before long.

But the future does depend upon official recognition of the importance of British films as a source of revenue and influence and as a reflection of national feeling. The attitudes of the present government only hinder, combining an obsessive approach to censorship with an insistence on relying on market forces, despite the fact that there is virtually no market to attract the investment needed. The government will not provide the opportunity and occasion for growth. Indeed, in the budget of March 1984, the Chancellor of the Exchequer cut the film industry's tax concessions that allowed producers to write off certain costs and count the entire cost of the production as capital expenditure. It is a move that can only inhibit film production or result in certain films being made elsewhere.

Realising that they have to help themselves, the film industry has declared 1985 the Year of British Film in an attempt to get audiences back to the cinemas. The task is a difficult one: audiences in the early months of 1983 were more than 600,000 a week down on the year before. But for twelve months from March 1985 there will be the first concerted attempt for years to attract audiences.

The aim is to increase attendances by four per cent. There will be exhibitions, receptions and promotions to push the theme expressed in the slogan, 'Cinema – The Best Place To See A Film'. Most importantly, the three circuits of Thorn-EMI, Rank and Cannon Classics will spend money on renovating their cinemas so that the slogan may even reflect the truth.

Perhaps a symbol for the future is Robin Saunders who, in 1983, built and opened his own cinema in Grantham, a town in Lincolnshire of some 36,000 which had been without a cinema since 1971. Called The Paragon, it seats 300 people and cost £45,000 to build.

It has been successful enough for him to set about building a second, more luxurious cinema in the nearby town of Gainsborough, which also lost its last cinema in the early 1970s.

He believes that there are at least 100 towns in Britain where such cinemas would thrive, where people have been too long denied the simple pleasure of going to the pictures. Small may be beautiful, after all, for British cinema.

APPENDIX
British Films and Directors
1970–1985

This listing of the British-made or directed films of the period ignores some of the sleazier low-budget attempts at titillation as well as many experimental movies and also includes the work of foreign directors who added needed vitality to the local industry. It is arranged, for convenience, under directors. It includes some work made primarily for television viewing, since the distinction between one medium of transmission for film and another is becoming increasingly blurred.

Abbey, Dennis. *Never Too Young To Rock* (1975).

Anderson, Lindsay. Outspoken critic, part of the Free Cinema movement of the 50s, and among the best and toughest talents thrown up by the New Wave of the 1960s. Unlike his contemporaries who have gone on to work in America, he has remained concerned with the state of Britain in all his work. His films remain secondary to his work in the theatre and grow increasingly incoherent in their anger. *O Lucky Man!* (1972); *In Celebration* (1975); *Britannia Hospital* (1982).

Anderson, Michael. Began as an errand boy at Elstree and made his first film in 1949. His best work has been done for Hollywood. His recent work is marked by a glossy vacuity. *Pope Joan* (1972); *Conduct Unbecoming* (1975); *Doc Savage, The Man of Bronze* (1975); *Logan's Run* (1976); *Orca* (1977); *Dominique* (1980).

Annakin, Ken. A former journalist with a talent for comedy-drama. His later films, which are not among his best work, have tended to be international co-productions seemingly aimed at no particular audience. *Call Of The Wild* (1972); *Paper Tiger* (1975); *The Fifth Musketeer* (1982); *The Pirate Movie* (1983).

Annett, Paul. *The Beast Must Die* (1974).

Apted, Michael. An excellent television director who moved very successfully into feature films, where he has shown great sensitivity in dealing with adolescent themes. Nevertheless, his best film so far – *Coal Miner's Daughter* – was made in America, about the life of a country and western singer. *Triple Echo* (1973); *Stardust* (1974); *The Squeeze* (1977); *Agatha* (1979); *Coal Miner's Daughter* (1979); *Continental Divide* (1981); *P'Tang Yang Kipperbang* (1982); *Gorky Park* (1984).

Arden, Jane. Actress-writer working in experimental area. *The Other Side of Underneath* (1972); *Anti-Clock* (co-directed, 1979).

Askey, David. *Take Me High* (1973).

Atkinson, Jim. *Can You Keep It Up For A Week?* (1974).

Attenborough, Richard. Actor turned high-powered businessman and director. Knighted in 1976. Adept at epic subjects and an Oscar-winner for directing *Gandhi*. *Young Winston* (1972); *A Bridge Too Far* (1977); *Magic* (1978); *Gandhi* (1983); *A Chorus Line* (1985?).

Austin, Ray.
Virgin Witch (1971); *Fun and Games* (1972).

Avakian, Aram. American director who came to Britain to make a confused thriller about a jewel robbery.
11 Harrowhouse (1974).

Baker, Graham.
The Final Conflict (1981).

Baker, Roy Ward. Began as a studio tea-boy and directed his first film in 1947. He was in Hollywood soon after and latterly worked as one of Hammer's journeyman directors, continuing the style after the demise of that production company.
The Vampire Lovers (1970); *The Scars of Dracula* (1970); *Dr Jekyll & Sister Hyde* (1971); *Asylum* (1972); *Vault of Horror* (1973); *And Now The Screaming Starts* (1974); *The Legend of the Seven Golden Vampires* (1974); *The Monster Club* (1981).

Balch, Anthony. British distributor who also directs experimental films and one horror movie.
Horror Hospital (1973).

Barron, Steve. Director of promotional videos for rock groups whose first feature film mixed rock and computers and young love. He is the son of director, Zelda Barron.
Electric Dreams (1984).

Barron, Zelda. A writer–producer–director who emerged in the 1980s after many years working her way through the industry, especially in continuity.
Secret Places (1984).

Battersby, Roy.
Winter Flight (1984); *Mr Love* (1985).

Baxter, Ronnie.
For The Love of Ada (1972); *Never Mind The Quality, Feel The Width* (1972).

Beaumont, Gabrielle.
The Godsend (1981).

Bennett, Edward.
Ascendancy (1983).

Becker, Harold.
The Ragman's Daughter (1972).

Beresford, Bruce. One of Australia's talented film makers who began with low comedies of Australians in London.
The Adventures of Barry McKenzie (1972); *Barry McKenzie Holds His Own* (1974); *Breaker Morant* (1980); *The Fringe Dwellers* (1985).

Billington, Kevin. A director who also works in television and the theatre and has done his best work away from the cinema.
The Rise and Rise of Michael Rimmer (1970); *The Light At The Edge Of The World* (1971); *Voices* (1974).

Birkinshaw, Alan.
Confessions of a Sex Maniac (1975).

Blair, Les.
Number One (1984).

Bloom, Jeffrey.
The Stickup (1978).

Boger, Chris.
Cruel Passion (1978).

Bolt, Robert. Playwright and screenwriter for David Lean's later films who directed his then wife, Sarah Miles, in a film he scripted.
Lady Caroline Lamb (1972).

Boorman, John. Began as a television director before making films from the mid-60s and soon moved to work in America. Busy in recent years trying, in vain, to keep the Irish film industry buoyant.
Leo The Last (1970); *Deliverance* (1972); *Zardoz* (1973); *Exorcist II – The Heretic* (1977); *Excalibur* (1981); *The Emerald Forest* (1984).

Booth, Harry.
On The Buses (1971); *Mutiny on the Buses* (1972); *Go For A Take* (1972); *Nearest and Dearest* (1973).

Boulting, Roy. With his twin brother John, one of the driving forces of British cinema from the 1950s to the beginning of the 70s and a polemicist

on its behalf since. His last films were far from his best.
There's a Girl in my Soup (1970); *Soft Beds, Hard Battles* (1973).

Boyd, Don. Independent producer who helped keep the flame of local cinema flickering in the dark days of the late 1970s and occasional director of less interesting films. His most recent effort, *Gossip* (1983), was abandoned halfway through filming.
Intimate Reflections (1975); *East of Elephant Rock* (1976).

Bricken, Jules.
Danny Jones (1972).

Bridges, Alan. A television director who began making movies in the 1960s, never less than interesting and usually marked by excellent performances from the cast.
The Hireling (1973); *Out of Season* (1975); *Brief Encounter* (1975); *Phobia* (1979); *Return of the Soldier* (1982); *The Shooting Party* (1984).

Britten, Lawrence.
Feelings (1976).

Brody, Hugh.
1919 (1984).

Brook, Peter. Brilliant theatrical director who is now based in Paris. His films tend to be less interesting and much less experimental than his stage work.
King Lear (1970); *Meetings With Remarkable Men* (1979).

Brownlow, Kevin. Superb historian of the early days of film, whose career as director has been restricted to an occasional low-budget movie of dogged integrity.
Winstanley (1975 co-directed).

Bryden, Bill. Scottish playwright and an associate director of the National Theatre. Influenced by John Ford, he has written scripts for Hollywood and so far directed one film from his own script.
Ill Fares The Land (1983).

Burbidge, Derek.
Urgh! A Music War (1981).

Burnley, Fred.
Neither The Sea Nor The Sand (1972).

Cammell, Donald. Artist, writer and director who has so far directed two films of unusual interest.
Performance (co-directed, 1970); *The Demon Seed* (1977).

Campbell, Martin.
The Sex Thief (1973); *Eskimo Nell* (1973); *Three For All* (1975).

Cardiff, Jack. Noted director of photography who turned to directing in the late 50s and now works in both capacities.
Penny Gold (1974); *The Mutations* (1974).

Carlino, Lewis John. American scriptwriter turned director who made one film, an unsuccessful melange of melodrama and eroticism, in Britain.
The Sailor Who Fell From Grace With The Sea (1976).

Carreras, Michael. Occasional director of horror films for Hammer, where he worked as production head of the company his father founded.
Blood of the Mummy's Tomb (1971 as co-director); *Shatter* (1977).

Cartwright, Justin.
Rosie Dixon, Night Nurse (1978).

Chaffey, Don. Former art director before he began directing films in 1950 and has since turned out mainly fantasy adventures for children or the childish.
Creatures The World Forgot (1971); *Clinic Xclusive* (1971); *Charley One Eye* (1973); *Persecution* (1974); *Ride A Wild Pony* (1976); *Pete's Dragon* (1977); *Born To Run* (1977); *The Magic of Lassie* (1978); *C.H.O.M.P.S.* (1979).

Chapman, Matthew.
Hussy (1979).

Chapman, Roger. Former art director and Oscar-winner for work on *Alien* and *Star Wars* who switched to directing after studying at the National Film School. His first film, made for the American company, Paramount, has yet to be released in Britain.
The Sender (1983); *2084* (1984).

Clark, Bob.
Breaking Point (1976); *Murder By Decree* (1979).

Clark, Jim. b. Former editor, working in television, who began directing in the late 60s in the prevailing styles of farce and horror.
Every Home Should Have One (1970); *Rentadick* (1972); *Madhouse* (1974).

Clarke, Alan.
Scum (1979).

Clarke, James Kenelm.
Expose (1975); *Hardcore* (1977); *Let's Get Laid* (1978); *Sweet Virgin* (1978); *Fiona* (1979).

Clavell, James. Australian-born novelist who became a screenwriter and director after moving to America in the 1950s.
The Last Valley (1970).

Clayton, Jack. Worked as editor and associate producer before making one of the key British films of the 50s, *Room At The Top*. A painstaking craftsman at his best exploring English character, an area he has neglected in his most recent films.
The Great Gatsby (1974); *Something Wicked This Way Comes* (1983).

Clegg, Tom.
Sweeney 2 (1978); *McVicar* (1980); *The Inside Man* (1984).

Clemens, Brian. A writer, most notably for the *Avengers* television series, who also scripted Hammer horrors and directed one.
Captain Kronos, Vampire Hunter (1973).

Clement, Dick. A writer-director who usually works in collaboration with writer-producer Ian La Frenais. Their great success as makers of television situation comedies has not so far been duplicated on film. He and La Frenais moved to Hollywood in the mid-70s.
A Severed Head (1970); *Catch Me A Spy* (1971); *Keep Your Fingers Crossed* (1971); *Porridge* (1979); *Bullshot* (1983); *Water* (1984).

Cobham, David.
Tarka The Otter (1979).

Cohen, Norman.
Dad's Army (1971); *Adolf Hitler, My Part In His Downfall* (1972); *Confessions Of A Pop Performer* (1975); *Confessions Of A Driving Instructor* (1976); *Stand Up Virgin Soldiers* (1977); *Confessions From A Holiday Camp* (1977).

Collinson, Peter. died 1980. Brash director who specialised in shock-horror techniques.
You Can't Win Them All (1970); *Fright* (1971); *Straight On Till Morning* (1972); *Innocent Bystanders* (1972); *A Man Called Noon* (1974); *Open Season* (1974); *And Then There Were None* (1975); *Spiral Staircase* (1975); *The Sell Out* (1976); *Tomorrow Never Comes* (1978).

Connor, Kevin.
From Beyond The Grave (1973); *The Land That Time Forgot* (1974); *At The Earth's Core* (1976); *Trial By Combat* (1976); *Arabian Adventure* (1979); *Warlords Of Atlantis* (1980).

Cooke, Alan.
The Mind of Mr. Soames (1971).

Cooney, Ray. Actor, writer, producer, director whose forte is theatrical farce.
Not Now, Darling (co-directed, 1972); *Not Now, Comrade* (co-directed, 1974).

Cooper, Stuart.
Little Malcolm And His Struggle Against The Eunuchs (1974); *Overlord* (1975); *The Disappearance* (1977).

Couffer, Jack.
Living Free (1972).

Crane, Peter.
Assassin (1973); *Moments* (1974).

Cramer, Ross.
Riding High (1981).

Cukor, George. Major American directors whose films occasionally encompassed British subject matter, with no great distinction.
Travels With My Aunt (1972); *Love Among The Ruins* (1974); *The Corn Is Green* (1979).

Curran, Peter.
The Cherry Picker (1972); *Penelope
'Pulls It Off'* (1975).

Davenport, Harry Bromley.
Whispers Of Fear (1976); *Xtro* (1982).

Davis, Desmond. Made his way via the
traditional route, beginning as clapper-
boy. Director from the 1960s in films
notably sympathetic to their female
characters.
Clash Of The Titans (1981); *The
Country Girls* (1983); *Ordeal by
Innocence* (1984).

Day, Ernest.
Green Ice (1981).

Dearden, Basil. died 1971. Worked at
Ealing Studios as writer and producer
before beginning directing in the 1940s.
He was equally adept at comedy and
films on topical social subjects.
The Man Who Haunted Himself (1971).

Demy, Jacques. French director with
love of romance and elegance who
made one local film.
The Pied Piper Of Hamelin (1972).

Dexter, John. Director associated with
the work of playwright Arnold Wesker
at the Royal Court, and latterly
working in opera in America. He
scored a hit with his first film, *The
Virgin Soldiers* (1969), but has not done
much since.
Sidelong Glances Of A Pigeon Kicker
(1970); *I Want What I Want* (1972).

Donen, Stanley. American director
who made a dull science-fiction film for
Lord Grade.
Saturn 3 (1980).

Donner, Clive. Editor turned director
from the mid-1950s, whose comic gifts
have been long buried in a series of
undistinguished period films.
Vampires (1975); *Rogue Male* (1976);
The Thief of Baghdad (1979); *Oliver
Twist* (1983); *The Scarlet Pimpernel*
(1983); *To Catch A King* (1984).

Donner, Richard. American director
who worked in Britain on high-cost
glossy fantasy films.
The Omen (1976); *Superman* (1978).

Donovan, Terence. Noted fashion
photographer and commercials director
who sometimes produces films and,
once, directed a confused thriller about
a Chinese detective in London.
Yellow Dog (1973).

Douglas, Bill. Former miner who has
made three intensely personal
autobiographical movies on a minimal
budget and proved that artistry counts
for more than money.
My Childhood (1971); *My Ain Folk*
(1972); *My Way Home* (1979).

Duffell, Peter. Television director
whose talent revealed its skills in the
low-budget horror flick and the action
film and came sharply, and briefly, to
life in 1972 in an engrossing version of
Graham Greene's novel. His most
recent work was directing the television
epic *The Far Pavilions* (1984). *The
House That Dripped Blood* (1971);
England Made Me (1972); *Inside Out*
(1975); *Experience Preferred But Not
Essential* (1983).

Edwards, Blake. American actor
turned writer, producer, director who
is married to actress Julie Andrews.
Created successful series of *Pink
Panther* films starring Peter Sellers as
bumbling French detective.
The Tamarind Seed (1974); *The Return
Of The Pink Panther* (1975); *The Pink
Panther Strikes Again* (1976); *Revenge
Of The Pink Panther* (1978); *S.O.B.*
(1980); *Victor/Victoria* (1982); *Trail Of
The Pink Panther* (1983); *Curse Of The
Pink Panther* (1983).

Enders, Robert. American producer
and director who turned Glenda
Jackson's stage success into an affecting
film.
Stevie (1979).

Endfield, Cy. b. USA, 1914. Expatriate
American working in Britain since early
1950s.
Universal Soldier (1971).

Eyre, Richard. Noted theatre director,
formerly with the Nottingham
Playhouse, most recently working at
the National Theatre. Also a television

director. His first two films are among the best British movies of the period.
Ploughman's Lunch (1983); *Loose Connections* (1984); *Laughterhouse* (1984).

Feldman, Marty. Pop-eyed comedian and scriptwriter who moved to America in the 1970s to appear in Mel Brooks's films and graduated to directing and starring in his own films.
The Last Remake of Beau Geste (1977); *In God We Trust* (1981).

Fisher, Terence. Former editor who began directing in the 1940s and enjoyed his greatest success reviving Dracula and Frankenstein for Hammer films, establishing the opulent and gory house-style for that company.
Frankenstein And The Monster From Hell (1973).

Fleischer, Richard. American director who has frequently worked in Britain, making skilful films of greatly contrasting kinds.
10 Rillington Place (1971); *Blind Terror* (1971); *The Incredible Sarah* (1976).

Forbes, Bryan. Actor, producer, writer who turned more to writing novels after resigning as production head of Elstree studios in 1971.
The Raging Moon (1971); *The Stepford Wives* (1975); *The Slipper and the Rose* (1976); *International Velvet* (1978); *Better Late Than Never* (1984).

Ford, Derek.
Suburban Wives (1971); *Keep It Up Jack* (1974); *Diary of A Space Virgin* (1975); *What's Up Nurse* (1977); *What's Up Superdoc* (1978); *Commuter Husbands* (1978).

Forsyth. Bill. Former documentary film maker whose first feature was made with boys from the Glasgow Youth Theatre. His second film established him as a quirky, gentle humourist and one of the best new talents around. To the surprise of many, his quiet wit enjoyed an international success.
That Sinking Feeling (1979); *Gregory's Girl* (1981); *Local Hero* (1983); *Comfort and Joy* (1984).

Francis, Freddie. Former director of photography on many significant films of the 1950s and 60s whose directing career has remained mired in low-budget horror.
Trog (1970); *Tales From The Crypt* (1971); *The Creeping Flesh* (1972); *Tales That Witness Madness* (1973); *Craze* (1974); *Legend of the Werewolf* (1974); *The Ghoul* (1975).

Francis, Karl.
The Mouse and The Woman (1982); *Giro City* (1983).

Frank, Melvin. American writer, director, producer, noted for comedy, who formed production company in Britain in the 1960s.
A Touch Of Class (1973).

Frears, Stephen. Admired television director who made a dazzling film debut and has since worked mainly in television.
Gumshoe (1971); *Bloody Kids* (1980); *Saigon – Year Of The Cat* (1983); *The Hit* (1984).

Friedmann, Anthony.
Bartelby (1971).

Fuest, Robert, Former art director whose visual flair gave style to his wildly romantic movies.
Wuthering Heights (1970); *And Soon To Darkness* (1970); *The Abominable Dr Phibes* (1971); *Dr Phibes Rises Again* (1972); *The Final Programme* (1973); *The Devil's Rain* (1975).

Garland, Patrick. Writer and stage and television director.
A Doll's House (1973).

Garnett, Tony. Producer who worked in a memorable partnership with Ken Loach and began directing in the 1980s. He now works in America.
Prostitute (1980); *Handgun* (1983).

Gates, Tudor.
Intimate Games (1976).

Gibson, Alan. One of Hammer Film's latter-day regulars, now working in American television.
Goodbye Gemini (1970); *Dracula AD*

1972 (1972); *The Satanic Rites of Dracula* (1973); *Martin's Day* (1984).

Gibson, Brian.
Breaking Glass (1980).

Gilbert, Brian.
Prince (1984).

Gilbert, Lewis. Made his film debut as a child actor and began directing in the 1940s. His first great success was *Alfie* in 1966, after which he made many films for American producers before setting up his own London-based production company.
The Adventurers (1970); *Friends* (1971); *Paul and Michelle* (1974); *Operation Daybreak* (1975); *Seven Nights In Japan* (1976); *The Spy Who Loved Me* (1977); *Moonraker* (1979); *Educating Rita* (1983); *Not Quite Jerusalem* (1984).

Gilliam, Terry. American expatriate artist and animator, part of Monty Python's Flying Circus, who displays an astonishing visual sense, an understanding of the tradition of English nonsense and a relish for less tightly-buttoned ages than our own.
Monty Python and The Holy Grail (1975, co-directed); *Jabberwocky* (1977); *The Time Bandits* (1981); *Brazil* (1984).

Gilliat, Sidney. Began in films in the 1920s as a writer, then became producer and director, usually in partnership with Frank Launder.
Endless Night (1971).

Gladwell, David. Trained at art school and became an experimental and documentary film maker, who made his first feature film in 1981.
Requiem For A Village (1975); *Memoirs Of A Survivor* (1981).

Glen, John.
Octopussy (1983); *A View To A Kill* (1985).

Glenville, Peter.
Hotel Paradiso (1971).

Godard, Jean-Luc. Noted French director who investigated London and The Rolling Stones in a perceptive semi-documentary, semi-dialectical, semiological film.
Sympathy For The Devil (1971).

Goddard, Jim.
A Tale of Two Cities (1982); *Kennedy* (1984); *Bones* (1984).

Gold, Jack. Intelligent director whose best work has been for television.
The National Health (1973); *Who?* (1974); *Catholics* (1974); *Man Friday* (1975); *The Naked Civil Servant* (1975); *Aces High* (1976); *The Medusa Touch* (1978); *The Sailor's Return* (1978); *Little Lord Fauntleroy* (1982); *Red Monarch* (1983); *Sakharov* (1984); *The Chain* (1984).

Gollings, Franklin.
Connecting Rooms (1971).

Graef, Roger.
The Secret Policeman's Ball (1980).

Gregg, Colin.
The Trespasser (1981); *Remembrance* (1982).

Green, Guy. Former director of photography who began making films in the 1950s and worked mainly in Hollywood from the 60s.
A Walk In The Spring Rain (1970); *Once Is Not Enough* (1975); *Luther* (1976).

Greenaway, Peter. Experimental film maker who broke through to a slightly larger audience with *The Draughtsman's Contract*, although that retained his enigmatic approach and superb visual sense.
A Walk Through H (1978); *Vertical Features Remake* (1978); *The Falls* (1981); *The Draughtsman's Contract* (1983).

Guest, Val. Former journalist who began scriptwriting in the 1930s and turned to directing in the 40s, becoming a prolific maker of somewhat forgettable movies.
Tomorrow (1970); *The Persuaders* (1971); *Au Pair Girl* (1972); *Confessions Of A Window Cleaner* (1974); *The*

Diamond Mercenaries (1975); *The Boys In Blue* (1982).

Guillermin, John. Of French descent, he worked first as a scriptwriter and began directing in 1947, working in Hollywood from the 1960s.
El Condor (1970); *Skyjacked* (1972); *Shaft In Africa* (1973); *The Towering Inferno* (1974); *King Kong* (1976); *Death On The Nile* (1978); *Sheena, Queen Of The Jungle* (1984).

Haggard, Piers. Director who works in television and movies without yet revealing much personal style.
Satan's Skin (1970); *Wedding Night* (1972); *Venom* (1982).

Hallam, Paul.
Nighthawks (co-directed, 1981).

Hall, Peter. Director of the National Theatre. Knighted in 1977, he is more successful at drama and opera than films.
Perfect Friday (1970); *The Homecoming* (1973); *Akenfield* (1974).

Hamilton, David. Photographer turned director of soft-focus films featuring naked young girls.
Bilitis (1978); *Laura* (1982); *Cousins In Love* (1983).

Hamilton, Guy. Technically excellent director of glossy epics.
Diamonds Are Forever (1971); *Live And Let Die* (1973); *The Man With The Golden Gun* (1974); *Force 10 From Navarone* (1978); *The Mirror Crack'd* (1982); *Evil Under The Sun* (1982).

Hardy, Joseph.
Great Expectations (1975).

Hardy, Robin.
The Wicker Man (1974).

Hare, David.
Wetherby (1985).

Harris, Richard. Actor who became an international star. He took over the direction of one of his films, after much internal bickering, a mistake he has obviously decided not to repeat.
Bloomfield (1970).

Hartford-Davis, Robert.

Incense For The Damned (1970); *The Fiend* (1972); *Black Gunn* (1972); *The Take* (1974); *Nobody Ordered Love* (1977).

Harvey, Anthony. An actor and then an editor who began directing in the 1960s.
They Might Be Giants (1971); *The Abdication* (1974); *Players* (1979); *Eagle's Wing* (1979); *Richard's Things* (1980).

Hatton, Maurice.
Praise Marx And Pass The Ammunition (1970); *Long Shot* (1980); *Nelly's Version* (1983).

Hayers, Sidney.
Firechasers (1971); *Assault* (1971); *Revenge* (1971); *All Coppers Are . . .* (1972); *Deadly Strangers* (1974); *Diagnosis: Murder* (1975); *What Changed Charley Farthing?* (1975).

Hazan, Jack. Excellent and gently revealing documentary film maker, although his first film, dealing with David Hockney, is better than his second, on the rock group The Clash.
A Bigger Splash (1975); *Rude Boy* (co-directed with David Mingay).

Hemmings, David. A former child actor who managed to reach stardom as an adult and then turned to producing and directing as well in the 1970s.
Running Scared (1972); *The 14* (1973); *Just A Gigolo* (1978); *The Survivor* (1982).

Henson, Jim. American creator of lovable children's puppets The Muppets who was encouraged by Lord Grade to turn them into a successful television series. The film versions were less entertaining feature films, but Henson's most recent film used puppets to create a fantasy world of imaginative force.
The Great Muppet Caper (1981); *The Dark Crystal* (1982).

Herbert, Henry.
Emily (1977).

Hessler, Gordon. Expatriate American active in Britain from the early 60s.

Scream and Scream Again (1970); *Cry Of Banshee* (1970); *Murders In The Rue Morgue* (1971); *Embassy* (1972); *The Golden Voyage of Sinbad* (1973).

Heston, Charlton. American star who so far has directed one film in Britain.
Antony and Cleopatra (1972).

Hickox, Douglas. A successful director of television commercials who turned to film in the 1960s.
Entertaining Mr Sloane (1970); *Sitting Target* (1972); *Theatre of Blood* (1973); *Brannigan* (1975); *Ski Riders* (1976); *The Master of Ballantrae* (1984).

Hill, James. A documentary film maker who also worked in television. His feature films are usually concerned with animals.
An Elephant Called Slowly (1970); *Black Beauty* (1971); *Lion at World's End* (1971); *The Belstone Fox* (1973); *Man From Nowhere* (1976).

Hitchcock, Alfred. One of the British cinema's greatest talents, even if resident in Hollywood from the 1940s. He returned to Britain to make *Frenzy*, his penultimate film, but, alas, it was far from his best.
Frenzy (1972).

Hodges, Mike. Stylish director, who gained his experience in television.
Get Carter (1971); *Pulp* (1972); *The Terminal Man* (1973); *Flash Gordon* (1980); *Squaring The Circle* (1984); *Morons from Outer Space* (1984); *Buried Alive* (1985).

Hodson, Christopher.
The Best Pair Of Legs In The Business (1975).

Hoffman, Michael.
Restless Natives (1984).

Holt, Seth. Died 1971. A former actor turned editor who began directing in the mid-1950s, but due to alcoholism never fulfilled his undoubted potential. He died just before completing a Hammer horror.
Blood From The Mummy's Tomb (1971).

Hooker, Ted.
Crucible Of Terror (1971).

Hough, John. Television director who began making films in 1970 and moved to Hollywood soon after. Latterly making Disney movies.
Eyewitness (1970); *Twins of Evil* (1971); *Treasure Island* (1972); *The Legend of Hell House* (1973); *Dirty Mary, Crazy Larry* (1974); *Escape From Witch Mountain* (1975); *Return To Witch Mountain* (1978); *The Watcher In The Woods* (1982).

Hubley, John. A leading animator with Walt Disney who directed a cartoon version of Richard Adams's epic novel of heroic rabbits.
Watership Down (1976).

Hudson, Hugh. Award-winning director of TV commercials who grabbed the big prize, an Oscar, for his brilliant film debut in 1982.
Chariots of Fire (1982); *Greystoke* (1984); *Revolution* (1985).

Hughes, David.
Emmanuelle In Soho (1981).

Hughes, Ken. He began as a projectionist and sound engineer before becoming a writer-director. Recently, he has been working in America.
Cromwell (1970); *Internecine Project* (1974); *Alfie Darling* (1975); *Sextette* (1978); *Terror Eyes* (1981).

Hunt, Peter. After working as a clapper-boy, he became an editor on many big-budget films and made his directing debut with the Bond film *On Her Majesty's Secret Service* (1969).
Gold (1974); *Shout At The Devil* (1976); *Gulliver's Travels* (1977); *The Last Days Of Pompeii* (1984); *Wild Geese 2* (1985).

Hussein, Waris.
Quackser Fortune Has A Cousin In The Bronx (1970); *Melody* (1971); *Henry VIII And His Six Wives* (1972).

Huston, John. Leading American director, and also actor and writer whose films occasionally reflect British life.
The Mackintosh Man (1973); *The Man Who Would Be King* (1975).

Hutton, Brian G.
Zee and Co (1972); *Nightwatch* (1973).

Hyams, Peter.
Outland (1981).

Irvin, John. A television director who was offered Hollywood assignments after his success directing John Le Carre's *Tinker, Tailor, Soldier, Spy* for the BBC.
Dogs of War (1980); *Ghost Story* (1981); *Champion's Story* (1984); *Turtle Summer* (1985).

Ivory, James. b. USA, 1928. In partnership with producer Ismail Merchant and scriptwriter Ruth Prawer Jhabvala, he has made films touching on expatriate and colonial experience and, particularly, Anglo-Indian attitudes.
Savages (1972); *Helen, Queen Of The Nautch Girls* (1973); *Mahatma And The Mad Boy* (1974); *Autobiography Of A Princess* (1975); *The Wild Party* (1975); *Roseland* (1977); *Hullabaloo Over George And Bonnie's Pictures* (1978); *The Europeans* (1979); *Jane Austen In Manhatten* (1980); *Quartet* (1981); *Heat And Dust* (1983); *The Bostonians* (1984).

Izzard, Bryan.
Holiday On The Buses (1974).

Jaeckin, Just.
Lady Chatterley's Lover (1981).

Jarman, Derek. Former art director who worked on Ken Russell's *The Devils* before demonstrating his own flamboyant, high-camp style in some excellent low-budget features.
Sebastiane (co-directed with Paul Humfress, 1976); *Jubilee* (1978); *The Tempest* (1979).

Jarrot, Charles. An actor and director in the theatre before becoming involved in television, he began working in films from the late 1960s.
Anne Of The Thousand Days (1970); *Mary, Queen of Scots* (1971); *Lost Horizon* (1972); *The Dove* (1974); *Escape From The Dark* (1976); *The Other Side of Midnight* (1977); *Condorman* (1981); *The Amateur* (1982).

Jeffries, Lionel. A character actor and a familiar balding and often apoplectic presence in dozens of films from the 1950s. As a director, his films have been for, or about, children.
The Railway Children (1971); *The Amazing Mr Blunden* (1972); *Baxter* (1972); *Wombling Free* (1978); *The Water Babies* (1979).

Joffe, Roland. A theatre and television director, whose work has often dealt with social issues.
The Killing Fields (1984); *The Mission* (1985).

Jones, David. A television director from 1958, before turning to stage where he became an associate artist of the Royal Shakespeare Company before going to America to try to establish a classical repertory theatre there.
Betrayal (1983).

Jones, James Cellan.
Bequest To The Nation (1973).

Jones, Peter Frezer.
George And Mildred (1980).

Jones, Terry. Writer-performer with Monty Python's Flying Circus before becoming a director of their increasingly successful (at the box-office) films.
Monty Python and The Holy Grail (1975); *The Life of Brian* (1979); *The Meaning of Life* (1983).

Jordan, Neil. Irish novelist and short-story writer who began by making a documentary about John Boorman's *Excalibur* and then raised money from the BFI and Channel 4 to write and direct his first feature film.
Angel (1983); *The Company of Wolves* (1984).

Kanievska, Marek.
Another Country (1984); *Horror Movie* (1985).

Kellett, Bob. Director whose speciality has been making film versions of successful television comedy series or low-budget movies that look as if they might have been TV spinoffs.
Up Pompeii (1971); *Girl Stroke Boy* (1971); *Up The Chastity Belt* (1971); *Up The Front* (1972); *Our Miss Fred* (1972); *The Alf Garnett Saga* (1972);

Don't Just Lie There (1974); *All I Want Is You* (1974); *Spanish Fly* (1975); *Are You Being Served?* (1977).

Kelly, James.
The Beast In The Cellar.

Kubrick, Stanley. Expatriate American who came to live in Britain from the 1960s, since when he has made, with great effort, a few highly regarded movies.
A Clockwork Orange (1971); *Barry Lyndon* (1975); *The Shining* (1979).

Landis, John. American director who has made one highly successful film in Britain.
An American Werewolf In London (1982).

Launder, Frank. Writer, producer, director who joined Sidney Gilliat in a long-lasting partnership.
The Wildcats of St. Trinian's (1980).

Leacock, Philip. A documentary film director who turned to feature films in the 1950s and went to work in America, mainly in television.
Baffled (1972); *Escape Of The Birdman* (1972); *Adam's Woman* (1974).

Lean, David. Another who worked his way up from tea-boy. A superb director of Dickens and romantic drama, who, since the 1960s, has become a notable exponent of wide-screen epics. He was knighted in 1984.
Ryan's Daughter (1970); *A Passage To India* (1984).

Lee Thompson, J. A former actor and playwright who began directing in the 1950s and scored his greatest hit with *The Guns Of Navarone* (1961). Since then he has worked mainly in America, with brutality replacing the energy of his earlier films.
Country Dance (1970); *Conquest Of The Planet Of The Apes* (1972); *Battle For The Planet Of The Apes* (1973); *Huckleberry Finn* (1974); *The Reincarnation of Peter Proud* (1975); *St Ives* (1976); *The White Buffalo* (1977); *The Greek Tycoon* (1978); *The Passage* (1979); *10 To Midnight* (1983); *King Solomon's Mines* (1984).

Leigh, Malcolm.
Games That Lovers Play (1971).

Leigh, Mike. A director who works mainly in the theatre through a painstaking process of improvisations with his actors.
Bleak Moments (1971); *Meantime* (1983).

Lennon, John. died 1980.
Imagine (co-directed with Yoko Ono, 1973).

Lester, Richard. Expatriate American with Goonish sense of humour and great understanding of the British which unfortunately has not been put to use in his later films.
The Three Musketeers (1974); *Juggernaut* (1974); *The Four Musketeers* (1975); *Royal Flash* (1975); *Robin and Marian* (1976); *The Ritz* (1976); *Butch and Sundance, The Early Days* (1979); *Superman II* (1981); *Superman III* (1983).

Lewis, Morton M.
Secrets Of A Superstud (1976).

Lindsay-Hogg, Michael.
Nasty Habits (1977).

Loach, Ken. He first made his name as a television director and still seems more committed to that medium than the cinema, to the latter's loss. His film debut was with the excellent *Kes* (1969) and he has continued to make films, often with amateur actors, that explore the tensions and conflicts within our society.
Family Life (1971); *Black Jack* (1979); *The Gamekeeper* (1980); *Looks and Smiles* (1982).

Loncraine, Richard. A director from television whose films have tended to be competent rather than inspired.
Radio Wonderful (1973); *Flame* (1974); *Full Circle* (1980); *Brimstone and Treacle* (1982); *The Missionary* (1983).

Long, Stanley.
Naughty! (1971); *Sex And The Other Woman* (1973); *On The Game* (1974); *Adventures Of A Taxi Driver* (1976); *Adventures Of A Private Eye* (1977); *It*

Could Happen To You (1976);
Adventures Of A Plumber's Mate (1978).

Losey, Joseph. Expatriate American who came to Britain when blacklisted and unable to work in his own country following the Un-American Activities Committee's investigations in Hollywood. As a director here, he explored the British character and class system in some notable films. Moved to France in protest at British tax laws. Died in 1984.
Figures in A Landscape (1970); *The Go-Between* (1971); *The Assassination of Trotsky* (1972); *A Doll's House* (1973); *Galileo* (1974); *The Romantic Englishwoman* (1975); *M. Klein* (1976); *Les Routes Du Sud* (1977); *Don Giovanni* (1979); *Steaming* (1984).

Lumet, Sidney. American child actor and a stage and television director who began making films in the 1950s. His British films are not among his best work.
The Offence (1973); *Murder On The Orient Express* (1974); *Equus* (1977).

Lynch, David. American director who has made one notably Dickensian British film.
The Elephant Man (1982).

Lyne, Adrian.
Foxes (1980); *Flashdance* (1983).

McGrath, Joseph. A director of offbeat comedies.
Digby (1973); *The Great McGonagall* (1974); *Girls Come First* (1975); *I'm Not Feeling Myself Tonight* (1975).

Mackenzie, John. A television director who moved across to feature films in 1969 to reveal a talent for tough action films.
One Brief Summer (1971); *Unman, Wittering and Zigo* (1971); *Made* (1972); *The Long Good Friday* (1980); *The Honorary Consul* (1984); *A Sense of Freedom* (1984); *The Aura* (1985).

McLagen, Andrew. American director of action films who has directed some gung-ho adventures in Britain.
The Wild Geese (1978); *Northsea Hijack* (1980); *The Sea Wolves* (1980).

McMurray, Mary. Television director working in documentary and drama.
Assam Garden (1984).

MacNaughton, Ian. Television director who reproduced Monty Python's sketches on film.
And Now For Something Completely Different (1971).

Mankiewicz, Joseph. Leading American writer, producer and director since the 1940s, who has occasionally worked in Britain.
Sleuth (1972).

Mann, Delbert. American stage and TV director who became a film director in the 1950s. He has worked in Britain on dull films of classics for TV and cinema release.
David Copperfield (1970); *Jane Eyre* (1970); *Kidnapped* (1971).

Marcell, Terry.
Hawk The Slayer (1980); *There Goes The Bride* (1980).

Marquand, Richard.
The Legacy (1979); *Eye Of The Needle* (1981); *Return Of The Jedi* (1983).

Masters, Quentin.
The Stud (1979).

Maylam, Tony.
Cup Glory (1971); *White Rock* (1976); *The Riddle Of The Sands* (1979).

Medak, Peter. A Hungarian-born director with a slightly heavy-handed humour, but a good choice of subjects. He now works in America.
A Day In The Death Of Joe Egg (1970); *The Ruling Class* (1971); *The Odd Job* (1979); *Zorro, The Gay Blade* (1981).

Merrick, Ian.
The Black Panther (1978).

Miles, Christopher. A careful craftsman whose two best films have concerned themselves with D. H. Lawrence's work and life.
The Virgin And The Gypsy (1970); *A Time For Loving* (1971); *The Maids* (1975); *That Lucky Touch* (1975); *Priest of Love* (1981).

Millar, Gavin.
Dream Child (1984).

Miller, Jonathan. A director who has worked mainly in drama and opera. He is also a writer, performer and pundit.
Take A Girl Like You (1970).

Mills, Reginald.
Tales of Beatrix Potter (1971).

Morrissey, Paul. A member of American artist Andy Warhol's 'factory' and director of admired films for Warhol, he came to Britain to make a dismal spoof of Sherlock Holmes involving many British comic talents.
The Hound Of The Baskervilles (1979).

Mowbray, Malcolm.
A Private Function (1984).

Narizzano, Silvio. A television director in North America and Britain who scored a success with his first film *Georgy Girl* (1966).
Loot (1971); *Redneck* (1975); *The Sky is Falling* (1976); *Why Shoot The Teacher* (1977); *The Class of Miss MacMichael* (1979).

Neame, Ronald. A former director of photography who worked with David Lean and then went on to produce and direct many notable films. His most recent work, expensive productions backed by American money, lacks the interest of his films of the 1950s and 1960s.
Scrooge (1970); *The Poseidon Adventure* (1972); *The Odessa File* (1974); *Meteor* (1978); *First Monday In October* (1982).

Nesbitt, Derren.
The Amorous Milkman (1974).

Nesbitt, Frank.
Dulcima (1971).

Newbrook, Peter.
The Asphyx (1972).

Newell, Mike.
The Man In The Iron Mask (1976); *The Awakening* (1980); *Dance With A Stranger* (1984).

Newley, Anthony. A child actor, singer, composer and writer who began

directing in late 1960s. Now lives in America.
Summertree (1971).

Nunn, Trevor. Artistic director of Royal Shakespeare Company. *Hedda* is a film of his stage production.
Hedda (1975); *Lady Jane* (1985?).

O'Connolly, Jim.
Tower Of Evil (1972); *Mistress Pamela* (1973).

O'Hara, Gerry. He began as a production assistant in the early 1940s and worked his way to director by the 1960s, mainly in television.
Fidelia (1970); *All The Right Noises* (1971); *The Brute* (1976); *Leopard In The Snow* (1977); *The Bitch* (1979).

Olivier, Laurence. Our greatest actor and a director who has directed one film since the 1950s, a record of his stage production.
Three Sisters (1970).

Ove, Horace.
Reggae (1971); *Pressure* (1978).

Owen, Cliff. He has worked in films from the 1930s, began directing in television from the 50s and in films from the 1960s, which were mainly adaptations of television successes.
Steptoe and Son (1972); *Ooh You Are Awful* (1976); *No Sex Please, We're British* (1973); *Get Charlie Tully* (1976); *The Bawdy Adventures Of Tom Jones* (1976).

Page, Anthony. A stage director who makes occasional movies.
Alpha Beta (1973); *The Lady Vanishes* (1980); *Absolution* (1981).

Parker, Alan. Former advertising copywriter and gadfly of local film industry. He has worked mainly in America since his early British successes.
Bugsy Malone (1976); *Midnight Express* (1978); *Fame* (1980); *Shoot The Moon* (1982); *Pink Floyd – The Wall* (1982).

Peck, Ron.
Nighthawks (co-directed, 1979).

Peckinpah, Sam. American writer and

director, mainly of tough, bloody films of action since the 1960s. His one British film featured the same macho philosophy, set improbably in Cornwall.
Straw Dogs (1971).

Perry, Simon. A former journalist for film-trade publications, now working as a producer.
Eclipse (1975).

Petit, Chris. A film critic turned director, who approaches film by way of aesthetic theory. Admirer of the work of the German director Wim Wenders, who helped raise the finance for his first movie, *Radio On*.
Radio On (1980); *An Unsuitable Job For A Woman* (1982); *Flight To Berlin* (1984); *Chinese Boxes* (1984).

Phillips, Robin. An actor and stage director, now working in Canada, who filmed one of his productions.
Miss Julie (co-directed, 1972).

Pinter, Harold. Former actor, leading British playwright and screenwriter who has also directed plays by other writers and filmed one of them.
Butley (1973).

Platts-Mills, Barney. A director of individuality who began auspiciously, but has hardly continued.
Bronco Bullfrog (1970); *Private Road* (1971); *Hero* (1982).

Polanski, Roman. A Polish-born former actor and a director from late 50s, who worked in America until legal problems brought him back to Europe. He has occasionally filmed British subjects.
Macbeth (1971); *Tess* (1982).

Poulson, Gerry.
Under The Doctor (1976).

Powell, Michael. One of the great British producers and directors whose best work was done in the 1940s and 50s. He became a consultant to Francis Ford Coppola's ill-fated Zoetrope Studios in Hollywood in the 1980s.

The Boy Who Turned Yellow (1972); *The Tempest* (1974).

Preminger, Otto. German-born producer and director and once a power in Hollywood. His film of a Graham Greene novel, employing many British actors, ran into financial problems as well as artistic ones.
The Human Factor (1980).

Quested, John.
Loophole (1981).

Rackoff, Alvin.
Say Hello To Yesterday (1970); *Death Ship* (1981).

Radford, Mike.
Another Time, Another Place (1983); *1984* (1984).

Rea, David.
She'll Follow You Anywhere (1971).

Reed, Carol. Died 1976. One of the greatest of British directors, who was at his peak in the 40s and 50s, before he went to work for Hollywood.
The Last Warrior (1970); *Follow Me* (1971).

Reeve, Geoffrey.
Puppet On A Chain (1971 co-directed); *Caravan To Vaccares* (1974).

Reid, Alastair.
Something To Hide (1971).

Reisz, Karel. Born in Czechoslovakia, he came to live in England from an early age. A notable critic who was one of the mainstays of the Free Cinema movement and helped the last revival of British cinema by directing *Saturday Night and Sunday Morning* in 1960 and producing *This Sporting Life* for Lindsay Anderson in 1963. He has worked for American companies in recent years.
The Gambler (1974); *Dog Soldiers* (1978); *The French Lieutenant's Woman* (1981); *Sweet Dreams* (1985).

Richardson, Tony. A director at Royal Court Theatre, where he directed John Osborne's *Look Back In Anger*, he was a leading member of Free Cinema. His great success was Tom Jones.

He now lives and works in America.
Ned Kelly (1970); *Dead Cert* (1974); *A Delicate Balance* (1976); *Joseph Andrews* (1977); *The Border* (1982); *The Hotel New Hampshire* (1984).

Rilla, Wolf. Born in Germany, he came to Britain as a child in the 1930s and worked in television and then in films since the 1950s, making mildly salacious movies.
Secrets Of A Door To Door Salesman (1973); *Bedtime With Rosie* (1974); *Naughty Wives* (1976).

Robbins, Matthew.
Dragonslayer (1982).

Roberts, Steve.
Sir Henry At Rawlinson End (1980).

Robins, John.
That's Your Funeral (1973); *Love Thy Neighbour* (1973); *Nearest and Dearest* (1973); *Man About The House* (1974).

Robinson, Dave. Head of an independent record company who films promotional videos for his groups and decided to make a film featuring the most popular, Madness.
Take It Or Leave It (1981).

Roddam, Franc. A television director who went to Hollywood after the success of his first film based on the music of The Who.
Quadrophenia (1979); *Lords of Discipline* (1982).

Roe, Willy.
The Playbirds (1978); *Queen Of The Blues* (1979); *Confessions From The David Galaxy Affair* (1979).

Roeg, Nicholas. Began as a clapper-boy and became one of Britain's finest directors of photography before emerging as a highly original director in the 1970s.
Performance (1970 co-directed); *Walkabout* (1971); *Don't Look Now* (1973); *The Man Who Fell To Earth* (1976); *Bad Timing* (1979); *Eureka* (1983); *Insignificance* (1984).

Rosen, Martin. American who came to Britain to produce an animated film of *Watership Down* and returned to

America to direct an animated version of another of Richard Adams's animal novels.
The Plague Dogs (1983).

Rosso, Franco.
Babylon (1980).

Russell, Ken. A former ballet dancer and television director whose films have been marked by passion (on his part) and controversy (from some of his audiences and critics). One of the most flamboyantly gifted of British directors, particularly attracted by the lives, personalities and music of great composers.
The Music Lovers (1971); *The Devils* (1971); *The Boy Friend* (1972); *Savage Messiah* (1972); *Mahler* (1974); *Tommy* (1975); *Lisztomania* (1975); *Valentino* (1977); *Altered States* (1981).

Sangster, Jimmy. A writer who scripted many horror films for Hammer and turned to producing and directing them as well. *The Horror of Frankenstein* (1970); *Lust For A Vampire* (1970); *Fear In The Night* (1972).

Sarne, Michael. Actor and writer whose career as a director floundered after his third film, *Myra Breckinridge*, made for Twentieth Century Fox, outraged critics and bored audiences.
Myra Breckinridge (1970).

Sasdy, Peter. Hungarian-born director who worked in television and made horror films to which he brought great style and conviction.
Countess Dracula (1971); *Hands Of The Ripper* (1971); *Doomwatch* (1972); *Nothing But The Night* (1973); *I Don't Want To Be Born* (1975); *Welcome To Blood City* (1977).

Savile, Philip. A notable television director who has made occasional forays into films.
Secrets (1971); *Those Glory Glory Days* (1983); *Shadey* (1985).

Schlesinger, John. A former actor and television director who was an important part of the new wave of the 60s. His success has tended to take him away from further exploring the British character. The expensive failure of *Honky Tonk Freeway* momentarily dimmed his reputation.

Sunday Bloody Sunday (1971); *Day Of The Locust* (1975); *Marathon Man* (1976); *Yanks* (1979); *Honky Tonk Freeway* (1981); *An Englishman Abroad* (1983); *The Falcon And The Snowman* (1984).

Scott, Ridley. He trained as a designer, an influence that is evident in the brooding environments his characters inhabit. He worked as a director of TV commercials before making feature films.

The Duellists (1978); *Alien* 1979); *Blade Runner* (1982); *Legend* (1985).

Scott, Tony. A director of television commercials before turning to feature films. He is the brother of Ridley Scott.

Loving Memory (1970); *The Author Of 'Beltraffio'* (1974); *The Hunger* (1983).

Sealey, John.
The Ups And Downs Of A Handyman (1975).

Sewell, Vernon. A former photographer and art director who began directing in the 1940s.
Burke And Hare (1971).

Shabazz, Menelik.
Burning An Illusion (1982).

Sharman, Jim. Leading light of a talented Australian generation of writers and directors, he was responsible for the original stage production of *The Rocky Horror Show* and turned it into a movie that gained a fanatical cult following.

The Rocky Horror Picture Show (1975); *Shock Treatment* (1982).

Sharp, Don. An Australian who came to Britain in the 1950s to work as a writer before becoming an efficient, if uninspiring director.

Puppet on a Chain (1970 co-directed); *Psychomania* (1972); *Dark Places* (1975); *Callan* (1974); *Hennessey* (1975); *The 39 Steps* (1978); *The Four Feathers* (1978); *Bear Island* (1979).

Sharp, Ian.
Who Dares Wins (1983).

Shonteff, Lindsay.
Permissive (1970); *The Yes Girls* (1971); *The Fast Kill* (1971); *Big Zapper* (1974); *The Swordsman* (1976); *Spy Story* (1976); *No 1 Of The Secret Service* (1979); *Licensed To Love And Kill* (1979).

Siegel, Don.
The Black Windmill (1974).

Simmons, Anthony. Writer and director.
The Optimists Of Nine Elms (1973); *Black Joy* (1977).

Sinclair, Andrew. Novelist who began directing in late 1960s.
Under Milk Wood (1971); *Blue Blood* (1974).

Skolimowski, Jerzy. A Polish-born actor and writer who began directing in 1960s and became one of his country's finest talents. Spent much time working elsewhere in Europe and bought a home in London following the recent military takeover in Poland.

The Adventures of Gerard (1970); *Deep End* (1970); *The Shout* (1978); *Moonlighting* (1983); *Success Is The Best Revenge* (1984).

Sloman, Anthony.
Not Tonight Darling (1971).

Spottiswoode, Roger.
Terror Train (1980); *Under Fire* (1983).

Stark, Graham. A character actor, usually in comic roles, who occasionally directs.
Magnificent Seven Deadly Sins (1971).

Stein, Jeff.
The Kids Are Alright (1979).

Sterling, William.
Alice's Adventures In Wonderland (1972).

Stevenson, Robert. A screenwriter who went to Hollywood in the 1940s and has worked as a director for Disney since the 1950s.
Bedknobs And Broomsticks (1971); *The*

Island At The Top Of The World (1974);
One Of Our Dinosaurs Is Missing
(1975); *The Shaggy DA* (1976).

Stuart, Mark.
Please Sir (1971).

Stewart, William G.
Father, Dear Father (1972).

Strick, Joseph.
Portrait Of The Artist As A Young Man
(1977).

Sturges, John. Director of action films
who made one movie with a British
theme.
The Eagle Has Landed (1976).

Sturridge, Charles.
Runners (1983).

Sykes, Peter.
Demons Of The Mind (1972); *The House
In Nightmare Park* (1973); *Steptoe And
Son Ride Again* (1973); *Venom* (1973);
To The Devil A Daughter (1976).

Temple, Julien. A director who may
prove to be to the 1980s what Ken
Russell was to the 1970s. He has
worked as director in television and for
promotional videos of rock singers and
has been on the point of directing
mainstream feature films.
The Great Rock 'n' Roll Swindle (1980);
The Secret Policeman's Other Ball
(1982).

Thomas, Gerald. In films from the
1940s, first as an editor, then as a
director from the 1950s and specialising
in low-budget local comedies.
Carry On Henry (1970); *Carry On
Loving* (1970); *Carry On At Your
Convenience* (1971); *Carry On Matron*
(1971); *Carry On Abroad* (1972); *Bless
This House* (1973); *Carry On Girls*
(1973); *Carry On Dick* (1974); *Carry
On Behind* (1975); *Carry On England*
(1976); *Carry On Emmanuelle* (1978).

Thomas, Ralph. He worked his way
from clapper-boy to editor and then
became a journalist before returning to
film and directing from the 1950s,
turning out in recent years slightly
sexier comedies than his younger
brother Gerald.

Doctor In Trouble (1970); *Percy* (1971);
The Quest For Love (1971); *The Love
Ban* (1973); *It's A 2' 6" Above The
Ground World* (1974); *Percy's Progress*
(1974); *A Nightingale Sang In Berkeley
Square* (1979).

Till, Eric.
It Shouldn't Happen To A Vet (1976).

Trevelyan, Philip.
The Moon and the Sledgehammer (1972).

Tuchner, Michael.
Villain (1971); *Fear Is The Key* (1972);
Mister Quilp (1974); *The Likely Lads*
(1976); *Trenchcoat* (1983).

Turner, Kenneth.
The Love Pill (1972).

Ustinov, Peter. Actor, writer, stage
director of charm and wit, who
sometimes, almost absent-mindedly,
makes films.
Hammersmith Is Out (1972); *Mehmed the
Hawk* (1984).

Vardy, Mike.
Man At The Top (1973).

Viola, Al.
Mr Forbush And The Penguins (1971).

Walker, Pete. A slick exponent of
cheap thrills, sex and violence.
Cool It Carol (1971); *Die Screaming
Marianne* (1971); *Four Dimensions Of
Greta* (1972); *Flesh And Blood Show*
(1972); *Tiffany Jones* (1973); *House Of
Whipcord* (1974); *Frightmare* (1975);
House Of Mortal Sin (1976); *Schizo*
(1976); *Home Before Midnight* (1979);
House of The Long Shadows (1983).

Wanamaker, Sam. Expatriate
American who came to Britain in the
1950s after being blacklisted in the
States. As an actor, he has played the
archetypal American in local films and
plays and is also active in trying to
re-create Shakespeare's Globe Theatre.
From the late 1960s, he began directing
films.
The Executioner (1970); *Catlow* (1971);
Sinbad & The Eye Of The Tiger (1977);
Charlie Muffin (1979).

Ward, James.
Somebody's Stolen Our Russian Spy
(1967).

Warren, Norman J.
Satan's Slave (1976); *Prey* (1978);
Terror (1979); *Inseminoid* (1981).

Watkins, Peter. Director who uses
documentary techniques to convey his
unease at the society we live in. After
his *The War Game,* on the effects of a
nuclear holocaust, was denied a
television showing in 1966, he has
tended to work away from Britain.
Punishment Park (1971).

Weeks, Stephen.
I, Monster (1970); *Sir Gawain And The
Green Knight* (1973); *Ghost Story*
(1974); *The Sword And The Valley*
(1983).

Whatham, Claude.
That'll Be The Day (1973); *All Creatures
Great And Small* (1974); *Swallows And
Amazons* (1974); *Sweet William* (1979).

Wickes, David.
Sweeney! (1976); *Silver Dream Racer*
(1980).

Wilder, Billy. A writer in Germany
who went to Hollywood in the 1930s
and became one of its leading directors.
His only British-made film is one of his
poorest.
The Private Life Of Sherlock Holmes
(1970).

Wilder, Gene. American actor, usually
in comic roles, who made his directing
debut with a movie set in Britain.
*The Adventures Of Sherlock Holmes's
Smarter Brother* (1975).

Winsor, Terry.
Party Party (1983).

Winner, Michael. A director from the
early 1960s, he has made films that
veer from social comedies to violent
action. He has worked in America,
most notably in movies that use actor
Charles Bronson in the role of an
implacable avenger.
The Games (1970); *Lawman* (1971); *The
Nightcomers* (1972); *Chato's Land*
(1972); *Scorpio* (1972); *The Mechanic*

(1973); *The Stone Killer* (1973); *Death
Wish* (1974); *Won Ton Ton, The Dog
Who Saved Hollywood* (1976); *The
Sentinel* (1977); *The Big Sleep* (1978);
Firepower (1979); *Death Wish II* (1982);
The Wicked Lady (1983); *Scream For
Help* (1984); *Death Wish 3* (1985).

Winter, Donovan.
Some Like It Sexy (1971); *Escort Girls*
(1974); *The Deadly Females* (1975);
Give Us Tomorrow (1979).

Wise, Herbert.
The Lovers (1972).

Wood, Peter.
In Search of Gregory (1971).

Wrede, Caspar. Born in Finland, he
has worked mainly in television,
making an occasional film marked by
seriousness of intent.
*One Day In The Life of Ivan
Denisovitch* (1971); *Ransom* (1975).

Yates, Peter. A director who has
worked in America since his success
with *Bullitt* in 1968. One of the few
able to combine action with, given the
slightest opportunity, loving
exploration of character. *The Dresser*
marked a welcome return to a British
subject and to his own theatrical youth,
in a movie about the last performance
of a barnstorming actor–manager.
Murphy's War (1971); *How To Steal A
Diamond In Four Uneasy Lessons*
(1972); *The Friends Of Eddie Coyle*
(1973); *For Pete's Sake* (1974); *Mother,
Jugs and Speed* (1976); *The Deep*
(1977); *Breaking Away* (1979); *The
Janitor* (1981); *Krull* (1983); *The Dresser*
(1984); *Eleni* (1985).

Young, Robert.
Vampire Circus (1972); *The World Is
Full Of Married Men* (1979).

Young, Terence. A writer who began
directing in the late 1940s and made his
biggest impact with his spectacular
James Bond films.
Cold Sweat (1970); *Red Sun* (1971);
The Valachi Papers (1972); *War Goddess*
(1973); *The Klansmen* (1974); *Jackpot*

(1975); *Bloodline* (1979); *Inchon* (1980); *Where Is Parsifal?* (1985).

Zetterling, Mai. Swedish-born actress, star of British films from the 1940s to 60, who occasionally directs to great effect.

Visions Of Eight (co-directed, 1973); *Scrubbers* (1982).

Zinnemann, Fred. Austrian-born meticulous craftsman who worked in Europe as a cameraman and went to Hollywood in the 1930s.
The Day Of The Jackal (1973).

Index of Film Titles